3

# The Best Police in the World

For Harry

# The Best Police in the World

An Oral History of English Policing from the 1930s to the 1960s

## BARBARA WEINBERGER

SCOLAR PRESS

Published by
SCOLAR PRESS
Gower House
Croft Road
Aldershot
Hants GU11 3HR
England

Ashgate Publishing Company
Old Post Road
Brookfield
Vermont 05036
USA

British Library Cataloguing in Publication Data

Weinberger, Barbara
  Best Police in the World: Oral History of
  English Policing from the 1930s to the 1960s.
  I. Title
  363.20942

Library of Congress Cataloging-in-Publication Data

Weinberger, Barbara.
    The best police in the world: an oral history of English policing from the
  1930s to the 1960s/Barbara Weinberger.
      p. cm.
    Includes bibliographical references and index.
    ISBN 1–85928–223–7 (hardback)
    1. Police—England—History—20th century. 2 Police—England—
  Interviews. I. Title.
  HV7728.A475  1995
  363.2'0941'0904—dc20                                          95–19108
                                                                    CIP

ISBN 1 85928 223 7

Printed in Great Britain
at the University Press, Cambridge

# Contents

# List of Plates

# List of Tables

# Acknowledgements

I am very grateful to the Nuffield Foundation and to the Leverhulme Trust for their financial assistance in support of the pilot study (Nuffield Foundation) and of the main research study (Leverhulme Trust) on which this book is based, and without which the research could not have been undertaken.

I have incurred many debts in the course of writing this book. My overriding debt is to the men and women who so generously invited me into their homes, plied me with cups of tea and shared their memories with me. I have been greatly enriched by the many warm and friendly contacts here with former police officers from all over the country, and am grateful to them all. Needless to say, this book could not have been written without their testimonies. I can only hope they will feel that I have done them justice and that they recognize their former world of work in the picture I have painted. I am also deeply indebted to the archivists of the many police and other record offices used for this study. In particular, I must single out Jeremy Glenn, archivist of the South Wales Police Museum, Maureen Scollan from the Essex Police Museum, and David Cross, from Birmingham's Police Museum, each of whom spared no effort to search out and provide me with documents and information beyond the reach of an index. Here, Jeremy Glenn's marathon effort in extracting the Cardiff police's promotion statistics for the 1930s proved especially valuable. I would also like to thank the Trustees of the Mass Observation Archive at the University of Sussex for permission to quote from this copyright material; and the editors of *Oral History* for permission to reproduce the section on police wives in Chapter 6, which appeared as an article in their journal in vol. 21, no. 2, 1993. My thanks also to Deirdre Hewitt and Pauline Wilson for their great help in the preparation of this manuscript. Lastly, I want to thank colleagues and participants, both at Warwick University's Centre for Social History and at the many other venues where I gave papers based on the material in this book, for their helpful comments and criticism. Thus many people have contributed to its making. The interpretation remains my own.

# Abbreviations

| | |
|---|---|
| ARP | Air Raid Precautions |
| BUF | British Union of Fascists |
| CD | Civil Defence |
| CID | Criminal Investigation Department |
| HC Debs | Parliamentary Debates, House of Commons |
| HL Debs | Parliamentary Debates, House of Lords |
| HMI | Her Majesty's Inspector |
| JLO | Juvenile Liaison Officer |
| Mepo | Metropolitan Police Records |
| MPD | Metropolitan Police District |
| NCCL | National Council for Civil Liberties |
| NCW | National Council of Women |
| NUWW | National Union of Women Workers |
| NUWM | National Unemployed Workers Movement |
| PC | Police Constable |
| PP | Parliamentary Papers |
| PRO | Public Record Office |
| RC | Royal Commission |
| WCRO | Warwick County Record Office |
| WPC | Woman Police Constable |
| WAPC | Women's Auxilliary Police Corps |
| WR | War Reserve |

# Introduction

This book, based on oral history interviews as well as archival and other sources, has two main purposes. The first is to fill a gap in the historiography between policing studies that usually end with the First World War, and the contemporary focus of most criminologists. Although there has been some work on the police in the inter-war period, this has largely concentrated on the policing of strikes and demonstrations. Only T.A. Critchley's history, and Clive Emsley's text on English policing provide something of an overview, while Mike Brogden's book on policing in inter-war Liverpool most nearly parallels the period and themes covered here, but within the confines of one city.[1] This still leaves a need for more knowledge about the work of the police and their relations with the public, and about their self-image and views on their role and occupation in the inter-war and Second World War period. So far, there has been no historical inquiry into this question and its implications for the style and content of police work. The key question addressed in the text therefore concerns the police view of the priorities of the job and the aspects they considered the most important, in order to encapsulate the motivation and the norms and values that guided their behaviour, as well as any changes that may have occurred over the period.

The second purpose of the book is to test the thesis that the years from the 1930s to the early 1960s were a golden period when police and public were generally in accord that the English police were 'the best in the world'. The broad acceptance of this view is perhaps one reason why there has been so little research on the institution at this time, and why policing studies themselves did not get under way until the era of the 1960s with Michael Banton's pioneering study.[2] Even then, Banton's purpose as a sociologist was to study an institution that was *working well*, in order to see if anything could be learned from its success.[3] Critical voices were thus slow to emerge in the literature. It seemed worthwhile now to examine the basis for this taken-for-granted view, and to inquire how far the traditional image of the bobby, as portrayed by *Dixon of Dock Green* in the 1960s television drama

---

1   T.A. Critchley, *A History of Police in England and Wales*, 1967; Clive Emsley, *The English Police: a Political and Social History*, Hemel Hempstead, 1991; Mike Brogden, *On the Mersey Beat: policing Liverpool between the wars*, Oxford 1991.
2   Michael Banton, *The Policeman in the Community*, New York, 1964.
3   Ibid., p.vii.

series, corresponded with the reality. Were policemen as benign as they have been portrayed, or did their discretionary actions, their overall control over what happened on their beat, and a more submissive attitude on the part of the general working class public, conceal a propensity for the direct administration of justice in the streets? How far did the beatman's discretion allow him to take action without recourse to a summons or an arrest? The question opens a broad field of inquiry into the whole nature of the constable's authority in a previous era that lies at the heart of the present study.

The main methodological tool used has been the oral history interview. This seemed the most fruitful way to gain insight and information on what went on at the day to day level from the point of view of those doing the policing, whose voices rarely figured in official accounts. There has been much discussion on the status of such evidence, which will not be rehearsed in detail here. Suffice it to say that a great deal of the evidence used by historians past and present has always been based on oral sources, and that its use – supplemented and checked against archival and other sources – is standard procedure, and one that is followed here. The difference, perhaps, is one of balance: where other texts rely more on official or 'conventional' sources, the present study places much weight on oral testimony. One advantage of the methodology is that it enables researchers directly to elicit responses to the questions that interest them; another is the way in which it alerts one to the way in which memory helps individuals construct an image of their social world and of their place in it, whereby certain attributes, events and relationships are given symbolic resonance in people's lives. Historians are becoming increasingly aware of the importance of these symbolic and mythical aspects of memory within every life story, and of the way in which memories are constantly drawn on to accommodate, reinforce, reassure or renew the individual's preferred self-image. It has become ever clearer that myth and history, memory and social identity are inextricably linked in both oral and written texts, which it is the historian's task to incorporate and interpret, without distorting their integrity and meaning.

Within the last few decades, oral history thus has offered a challenge to more traditional methods, not just because its sources are oral rather than written, but through its open acceptance of narrative and subjectivity as a positive gain, rather than as something to be overcome. The reminiscences recorded in life histories are inevitably *subjective,* and indeed this is one of their strengths, since only in this way can we gain insight into the motivation, feelings and reactions and thought processes that have led to the particular outcomes that are the usual focus of traditional historiography.

Oral history, in contrast, tells us less about events than about their symbolic, cultural and personal meaning. It tells us not just what people did, but what they wanted to do, how they perceived events, how they review the past. It also illuminates new ways of thinking about time and space, since memory does not offer a continuous, even account of either. Spatial and temporal clusterings and ellisions become important clues to the construction of individual and popular myths and stories concerning significant places and events.

How is one to make sense of such psychologically expressive material within the historical enterprise? Since oral history testimonies are not spontaneous narratives but are elicited by researchers with a specific purpose or question in mind, this acts as a link between the testimony and its use as historical evidence. Without this, and without an understanding of the socio-historical processes involved, one would be left with a mass of personal reminiscence whose historical meaning would remain obscure. Historical knowledge and awareness thus is essential if one wants to make use of the life history approach within the discipline. Obviously, every life represents a piece of history. However, this is not just because a life history inevitably reflects changes over time, but because every life is lived within a particular socio-economic, political and cultural setting that draws the parameters for that life, and whose inclusion is essential in historical analysis. But just as oral testimony needs checking against other contemporary records, so oral history evidence itself acts as a check on these other sources. The oral life history approach is a tool, which both implicitly and explicitly requires the application of historical perspective and knowledge in order to make sense of a narrative running backwards through time and space.

As far as oral history interviews in research on the police is concerned, the methodology offers a particular advantage, as an especially useful means of inquiry in bureaucratic and hierarchical organizations where the gap betweeen the officially stated means and purposes, and the reality on the ground is likely to be wide, and where this reality can only be recovered through the voice of those who have been, or remained, in the lower ranks. The need to recover that voice is especially relevant in policing studies since, uniquely, those at the bottom of the police hierarchy have wide discretion, with the result that their actions become some of the most critical in the whole criminal justice process. It is the constable on the beat who decides whether or not to take notice of an offence or misdemeanour, and this initial decision is one that rests in his hands. As far as such decisions taken within living memory are concerned, the process can only be recovered through oral history. This is its major advantage in research on policing. If we want to know how individuals functioned within organizations, and how organizational goals and rules were incorporated and operationalized by them, it is oral history that can best help us to find out 'how it was' on the ground, and to differentiate between the formal, legal model of the police institution and the informal, rule-adapting practice.

There remains the question of representativeness. It is rarely possible retrospectively to construct a totally representative sample: Paul Thompson's ambitious attempt in *The Edwardians* probably comes closest.[4] In the present study, every effort was made, within the means and time available to a single researcher, to cover the range of forces and circumstances that made up the English police. Thus respondents were sought from Metropolitan, County and Borough forces, from the specialisms within them, and from a carefully selected number of forces, since it would not have been possible to cover all hundred and eighty-three that were in existence during the period covered by the research. A balance was kept between urban and rural settings, and between city and borough and county. Seventeen forces were represented: the Metropolitan police and eight other urban forces on the one hand, and eight County forces on the other. These were scattered throughout the country, from Durham in the north, Norfolk in the east, West Sussex in the south and Liverpool in the west. The total respondent sample came to eighty-seven, and included six war reserves, and seven women police officers. Care was also taken to select a representative number of respondents from each rank.[5] Excluding the war reserves, this meant that interviews were conducted with twenty-six former constables, twenty-three former sergeants, and thirty-six who reached the rank of inspector or above. Respondents were contacted through branches of the National Association of Retired Police Officers. They have been given pseudonyms in order to preserve their anonymity, and are referred to by the title of their highest achieved rank.

The book is organized as follows: the first three chapters deal largely with structural features, covering the social background, entrance, training, routines and prospects facing those recruited into the service, as well as the problems confronted by the organization. The next three chapters discuss the various specialisms within the police and the attitudes and work practices of those within them. The war forms something of a watershed in the chronology of policing over the period, and is the subject of Chapter 7. This specifically addresses the question of what difference, if any, the war

---

4    Paul Thompson, *The Edwardians: the Remaking of British Society*, 1975.

5    The problems involved and the variations in achieved rank between forces are discussed in Chapter 3.

made to the service. Chapters 8 and 9 turn to look at the actual work of the police in more detail, by covering the policing of theft, juvenile delinquency and assault; and, under the heading of public order policing, of street betting and prostitution, and street demonstrations and marches. Finally, Chapter 10 considers the changing reputation of the police and its relation with the public through the medium of a number of policing scandals. This is followed by a conclusion.

# CHAPTER ONE

# Origins and Sources

The beginning of the 1930s was the start of a difficult era. A general sense of crisis permeated the atmosphere, from the Cabinet and government downwards. Economic and financial difficulties abounded that no one seemed able to solve, while the unemployment figures climbed inexorably upwards. A minority Labour government saw unemployment more than double over the two years that it was in office, with a budget deficit and consequent flight from sterling adding to the crisis. The government, forced to act against its principles and election pledges, fell in the summer of 1931 over its proposal to cut unemployment benefit. It was left to an all-party National Government to carry out the unpopular economies it decided the situation demanded. The 'equality of sacrifice' called for by the Prime Minister, Ramsey MacDonald, resulted in a government decision to cut unemployment benefit by ten per cent and the salaries of public servants from between ten to twenty per cent.[1]

The police were one of the groups directly affected. The May Committee, appointed by the outgoing Labour government, proposed a cut in police pay of twelve and a half per cent, but by the time the new government came to implement its economy measures, this had been whittled down to five per cent from the end of 1931 with another five per cent to follow later, plus a lower pay scale 'B' for new recruits.

Despite these pay cuts, policing remained a sought-after job. Since the large police pay increase which followed on the recommendations of the Desborough Committee in 1919, policing had been ahead of most working-class occupations as far as earnings were concerned, and a cut of five or even ten per cent still left the police towards the top of the league. According to Critchley's calculations for the inter-war period, a constable's maximum pay scale of £4 15s was fifty-five per cent higher than the average industrial wage, quite apart from the fact that the police had free accommodation or rent, as well as other allowances.[2] Another inestimable advantage was the freedom from the threat of unemployment and the prospect of a pension at the end. So even with the wage cuts, joining the

---

1   See Philip Williamson, (1992) *National Crisis and National Government: British politics, the economy and Empire, 1926–1932*, Cambridge, pp. 365–6.
2   T.A. Critchley, (1967) *A History of Police in England and Wales*, p. 249. Probationers received an average of £3.50 per week.

police in the depression years of the early 1930s seemed like the answer to many a young man's prayer. This is bourne out by the large numbers who applied but failed to get in to the service.

## Joining the Police

Nearly all the men interviewed commented on how lucky they were to get taken on, and spoke of the many who were turned down. The average success rate in the early 1930s seems to have been around ten per cent out of the hundreds who applied. Physical requirements were stringent. One man was turned down because he had acne on his back; another because he had more than the allowed seven teeth missing; others because they were half an inch too short; or, in the case of miners, because of the blue marks on their face and hands. There was a written examination covering the rudiments of English and arithmetic to be got through, over which some candidates sweated, while selection might be further tailored to meet more specific requirements. Thus, motor mechanics and drivers were at a premium at a time when motorisation was beginning in the service and such skills were in short supply. Prowess at football or playing a musical instrument also came in handy when chief constables were on the lookout for candidates for the football team or the police band. But the basic requirement was height and physical fitness, and it was chiefly the Metropolitan police – with its huge requirement for men – which was prepared to lower the height limit somewhat (to 5 feet 8.5 inches).[3] Even so, standards generally were beginning to shift, leading the 1930s generation of recruits to comment on the previous generation of huge bobbies of six foot and over. By the 1930s, 5 feet 10 inches (midgets in the older men's eyes) was becoming more acceptable, as other criteria – especially clerical skills – made up the balance. Nevertheless, entry into the service involved a great deal of effort and desperate resolve. One man who was interviewed, along with 500 others, for thirty vacancies in Liverpool in 1934 recalled:

> ... there were chaps there from Scotland, Ireland, Wales and England, and some very well educated chaps as well. I remember one chappie who sat next to me, a qualified marine engineer and in desperation he came here to join the police force ... There were

---

3   Annual Report of the Metropolitan Commissioner for 1928, PP *1928–29* IX.; the height was further reduced in 1937 to 5 feet 8 inches 'because many desirable men are below the stipulated height'. *PRO: HO 45 17459,* 5 January 1937.

others, one had been to Oxford, others who were well up in languages, French, German ...[4]

It was a heartrending business. A successful recruit remembered the reaction of some who had not been so lucky: 'I saw men sit there and cry, they'd never worked in their lives'.[5]

In such circumstances, the motivation to join the police is not hard to discover. Recession and high unemployment pushed well-educated and respectable young men towards an occupation they might otherwise never have considered, that offered adequate if not ample pay, job security and a pension. The precise balance of supply and demand that made up the equation in the early 1930s was rarely to be so favourable for the police institution. Here, oral testimony bears witness to many a recruit's lost hopes for further training or education, as recession bit hard into family budgets or threw men from their chosen occupations. In an earlier period there had been more stress on size, physical strength and the experience of disciplined service, as nervous police authorities built their defences against possible Bolshevist insurrection and turbulence on the industrial front. But for the recruits, both then and later, the principal motive for joining the police was the wage and security the service offered, for whose sake men were prepared to accept strict discipline and the many hours of extra duty for no pay. Indeed, acceptance of harsh conditions is the key differentiating factor between pre and post-war entrants to the service. 'We knew life wasn't a bed of roses and that we couldn't do what we liked' remarked one pc when describing the tyrannical discipline imposed by his sergeant, 'but we were prepared to put up with it, we knew nothing else'.[6] It was this outlook that enabled the service to provide twenty-four hour coverage without paid overtime, that was to prove increasingly untenable in the post-war era. The pcs of the early 1930s perceived that hard times gave little space to vocational preference or complaints over conditions. Vocational preference thus had little to do with it, and it was chiefly the sons of policemen who said they had always wanted to join the police. Apart from this, wages, security, and the lack of prospects in their chosen occupations (such as motor mechanics) were the reasons given by most applicants, while chance suggestions from policemen they knew or friends who had joined encouraged others. This finding contrasts with that in Robert Reiner's study, in which well over half the men after 1960 joined for what he calls non-instrumental reasons, relating to intrinsic aspects of the work itself, with only eleven per cent stating that they had been motivated solely by

4   Interview with Superintendent Driver, Liverpool City police.
5   Interview with Inspector Cooper, Metropolitan police.
6   Interview with Inspector Archer, Durham County police.

instrumental factors such as pay, status or security. But as Reiner himself notes, this contradicts the findings from other, earlier police studies. As he also points out, this simply emphasizes the historical relativity of the reasons men had for joining the police, with the variation depending largely on the current levels of unemployment.[7] Nevertheless, *either* wage levels *or* job security remained the crucial element, depending on the state of the economy, whatever the other reasons given. In the inter-war period, it was fear of unemployment and the search for job security that dominated job choice, even if an underlying preference for an outdoor life, for variety, and for excitement is discernible among pre-war as among post-war recruits. Nor, it would seem, were these largely working class men unduly troubled by the ambiguous class position that was a by-product of their job choice.

## Social Class Position

The anomolous class position of the police and its consequences has been discussed by a number of police historians and sociologists. Steedman, for the Victorian era, stressed their servile status: as paid servants of their police authorities Victorian policemen, she believes, adopted a stance of neutrality and passivity as a way of dealing with their contradictory situation. On the one hand, this underlined their sense of powerlessness, their *unimportance,* as far as the ratepayers and authorities were concerned, on the other it expressed their essential functionlessness within the working-class community. Not until the Summary Jurisdiction Act of 1879 was there general legal sanction for the disciplining of working class social life by the police.[8] From that time onwards, however, the policeman became a more authoritative and distanced character who aroused fear and hostility as well as deference, compliance and support from his working class peers. A number of elements in addition to the legal were later brought into play here. With the upgrading of police pay and conditions and the establishment of the Police Federation, following on the recommendations of the Desborough Committee in 1919, the police began to lay claim to a professional status that ultimately weakened their links with their peers *and* with their local employers. This enhanced sense of independence from their local police authorities was increasingly (if inadvertently) encouraged by the Home Office in the early inter-war period. By ignoring the local

---

7    Robert Reiner, (1978) *The Blue-Coated Worker: a sociological study of police unionism*, Chapter 9.
8    Carolyn Steedman, (1984) *Policing the Victorian Community: the formation of English provincial police forces, 1856–80*, pp. 6, 159.

authorities, and establishing close links with provincial chief constables to see that Home Office policy was carried out during critical periods, support for the doctrine of constabulary independence was encouraged that had its effect on the self-image of the police.[9]

This image of professional independence allowed policemen to resolve their contradictory class position in favour of a 'classless' solution.[10] Reiner argues that while the police should be categorized as working class in economic terms, the part they play in contributing to the political and ideological domination of capital over labour makes their overall class place a contradictory one. This contradictory position is an uncomfortable one, and while the police, I believe, are not simply the instrument of a dominant ruling class but are caught in the interplay between a number of competing interests and ideologies, they seek to detach themselves from these through the doctrine of constabulary independence. It is this stance which makes them 'classless'. This was acknowledged by the men themselves. 'You were treated like a servant by the upper classes and like a lord by the lower' said one – with the result that policemen felt they were a race apart.[11] While not denying their mainly working-class origins, the majority were hard put to it to decide to which class they now belonged – and most settled for 'no class' or 'a separate group'. This was both cause and consequence of their socially inward-looking private lives. The police mostly socialized with their own – as did policemen's wives, especially in rural areas,[12] partly because of the unsocial hours they kept and partly because of mistrust which knowledge of their occupation aroused in civilians. A mutual suspicion inhibited spontaneity, so that when in civvies and on holiday, many policemen said they would never tell others what they did for a living. Consciousness of the possibility of conflict with sections of the public made many policemen keep aloof. A village policeman put it this way:

> *Do you think you didn't have so many friends because you were a policeman?*

> Oh, yes, absolutely. From two ways. From their point of view they didn't want to be the village policeman's friend, and from our point

9   Barbara Weinberger, (1991) *Keeping the Peace? Policing strikes in Britain 1906–1926,* p. 213.
10  See R. Reiner, (1978) 'The Police in the Class Structure', *British Journal of Law and Society,* 5, 2.
11  Interviews with Sergeant Carver, Durhan County police and Chief Constable Wiseman, Lancashire police.
12  A similar response among rural wives is noted in Maureen Cain, (1973) *Society and the policeman's role,* Chapter 4.

> of view we had to be careful who we made as friends because you
> could be up against the situation where your friends could be doing
> something wrong, and you are the law...[13]

In consequence class relations were 'messy and confused'.[14] The thesis that
working class policemen kept their class identification and used it to
support their own classes' concept of justice and order, and to protect fellow
members of the working class cannot really be sustained. Nevertheless, as
put forward by JoanneMarie Klein, the thesis is important and convincing
on many counts. It is her contention that the majority of policemen came
from the respectable working class, which had its own cultural norms and
values that they applied to their jobs. She seeks to show that they were able
to resist control from above and to transform the police from inside through
their own definition of the meaning of justice. Their working-class
identification was further demonstrated, she believes, by their adherence to
working class marriage patterns.[15] There are several pertinent points here. I
would agree that the value system of most policemen was strongly grounded
in that of the respectable working class and its views on what constituted
fair play, justice and decency, and that this operated in tandem with their
employers' version of these concepts. The obverse, in the form of the
racism, sexism and intolerance of deviance that characterized police
attitudes, had similar roots. Resistance to control from above is also
incontrovertible, as are working-class marriage patterns. Where I would
differ is in interpreting the meaning of these cultural forms. Klein seems to
believe that because policemen were not upwardly mobile and kept to their
class values and behaviour patterns, they therefore retained their class
identification. In my view, however, it is not a question of class values, but
of consciousness, and in this respect, oral evidence may be a better guide
than the defaulters files on which Klein's case is built. The policemen in the
present sample in no way denied, nor abandoned, the cultural values with
which they had grown up. They described their families of origin as
working class (whenever this was the case) and frequently married women
from that class. But when asked about their own position in the class
structure, very few replied unequivocably that they were still members of
the working class. The nature of their occupation had placed them in an
ambiguous and constrained position vis à vis their working class peers,

13  Interview with Inspector Smith, West Sussex police.
14  Brogden, *Mersey Beat*, p. 2.
15  JoanneMarie Klein, (1992) 'Invisible Working-Class Men: Police Constables in
    Manchester, Birmingham and Liverpool 1900–1939' Unpublished PhD Thesis,
    Rice University, Houston, Introduction.

without offering an escape into the class above.[16] The outcome was a sense of alienation from the wider society and encapsulation within the work group. It is in this sense, and for these reasons, that the police – correctly – described themselves as classless.

## Social Origins[17]

What of the police's class of origin? This shows a rather different pattern to the country bumpkin stereotype of the traditional bobby. Of the seventy-seven men and women in the sample (thereby excluding six war reserves and four for whom full biographical information is lacking) only four were the child of farm workers. Similarly, a bias in favour of employing those from a military background is not confirmed, since only two recruits were soldier's sons, and only two pre-war recruits had served as professional soldiers. (Naturally, most post-war men would have seen service in the armed forces). The two single largest groups of recruits were the children of former policemen and of railwaymen, which says something about the sort of background preferred by the authorities. While having a policeman father offered some guarantee of an upbringing along the desired lines, railwaymen also shared certain favoured police characteristics, in that they were uniformed public servants subject to bureaucratic discipline. The same preference applies to the considerable number of recruits who had previously held jobs in the post office. The point of interest is that these backgrounds appear to have received preference to a purely military one. This finding is duplicated in Reiner's post-war study.[18] Although Emsley and Clapson, in their work on police recruitment, stress the large number of former soldiers who joined the police, this above all concerns the decade of the 1920s.[19] In our period, there were notable objections to the recruitment

16 One indicator of the lack of channels for upward mobility among the police is the frequency with which men, especially from the higher ranks, joined the Freemasons, which acted in this case as a sort of surrogate for acceptance into a higher social class.

17 See Appendix for tabulations and commentary on social class origins and educational standards (taking school leaving age as a proxy).

18 Reiner, *Blue-Coated Worker*, p. 153. Reiner discusses the small proportion of recruits who chose military service prior to becoming policemen, and concludes that there was little affinity between the police outlook and the military.

19 Clive Emsley and Mark Clapson, (1994) 'Recruiting the English Policeman c.1840–1940', *Policing and Society*, Table 2: Percentage of recruits with army service. This large scale study, based on a computer analysis of police recruitment and personnel ledgers from 1840–1940 in a number of urban and rural forces, shows a variable but high proportion of ex-servicemen in the police

of too many ex-servicemen in the 1930s, for reasons that will be discussed later.


## Educational Standards

Educational standards, as indicated indirectly by age on leaving school, were higher in the 1930s than in the early post-Second World War years. If we look only at the men who joined before the war, the percentage staying on beyond the school-leaving age of fourteen is just under half, of whom thirty per cent had been to grammar school. This is directly comparable with the Metropolitan Commissioner's figures for 1936, where he states that fifty-four per cent of recruits had secondary education and thirty-three per cent had school leaving certificates.[20] In the context of the period, this would tend to confirm the view of post-Second World War recruiting and training officers that after the immediate post-war years had mopped up ex-service applicants, post-war recruits were neither as bright nor as educationally qualified as those from the 1930s. Some of the reasons for this, at least in the Metropolitan police, were given by Sergeant Martin:

> There was a terrible dearth of recruits ... Entering the police in those days involved not just a medical and an interview but sitting the civil service exam ... The civil service used to supervise and mark the papers, and while I was at Peel House the Metropolitan police asked the civil servants to reduce the pass mark ... the civil service said 'we are not going to do it'. About that period, around 1950-51, the Metropolitan police set up their own recruiting system at Paddington, so not only were we having a job to get recruits, we were getting a much lower quality of recruits from then on because they were taking a much lower qualification.[21]

Inspector Roper, who served in the police all through the war, agreed:

---

throughout the 1920s. However, this generally dropped back considerably in the 1930s.

20  Annual Report of the Metropolitan Commissioner for 1936. *PP XIV 1936–37*. Similarly, the annual report of the chief constable of Cardiff for 1933 noted that out of fifteen recruits selected from 600 applicants, most had had secondary education with matriculation or its equivalent. *Police Review*, 20 October 1933.

21  Interview with Sergeant Martin, Metropolitan police. His observations are confirmed by a Metropolitan police file on recruiting statistics. This states that the pass mark in the educational exams was lowered in June 1947, that every possible exception had been made to give the candidate the benefit of the doubt, and that the quality of candidates (in 1948) was low. *PRO: Mepo 2/8088* 'Recruiting Statistics 1948–1958', December 1948.

a lot of ex-service pcs came out of the police force, because pay and conditions had not improved at all. There was a great upsurge in employment ... and then they started to lower the standard. It was just after the war, and I think it was very short-sighted of the government not to improve the job for the men ...[22]

To sum up, while conclusions based on the statistics (as shown in the Appendix) must remain tentative, the trends charted there do tend to suggest that many of the pre-war cohort were better educated than their early post-war counterparts, and that standards did not begin to rise again until after the Royal Commission recommended and achieved a forty per cent pay rise for constables in the early 1960s.

## Recruitment: Limitations and Achievements

Recruitment was a constant balancing act between supply and demand, between the cry for more police and the reluctance to pay for them, and between the desire for better educated and motivated men and the need to select from what was on offer. It was only on very rare occasions that pay and conditions became   positive inducements, as was the case when the recommendations of the Desborough Committee were speedily accepted following the police strikes of 1918 and 1919. It had needed a crisis during a time of political turbulence to bring about this major improvement. From the vantage point of the 1930s, a career in the police still looked very desirable, and the early 1930s was one of the few periods when most complaints were not over the lack of supply of recruits but over police shortages in consequence of the government's economy drive. Nevertheless, a backlog of discontent *was* simmering under the surface after a two and a half per cent pay cut (introduced as a temporary measure under the Geddes Axe economies in 1922) was made permanent in 1926.[23] This had its effect on the attitude of the older men towards recruits in the 1930s who accepted conditions that they themselves thought unjust. A further consequence of the Geddes cuts, of more concern to chief constables, was the Home Office recommendation that economies should be secured by leaving vacancies unfilled. The result was that by 1930 the strength of the Metropolitan

22  Interview with Inspector Roper, Birmingham City Police.
23  There was sharp dealing by government in this matter, since agreement to the measure, and to a reduction in the polices' rent allowances, had only been accepted by the Police Federation on the undertaking that the measure was a temporary one year matter. But the reduction was renewed annually until made permanent in 1926, when it was presented as 'an allowance in aid of pensions'. The rent allowances were then restored. *HC Debs, 5s* vol. 192, 414–5, 1926.

police, for example, was reduced to 19,371 compared with 20,789 in 1913.[24] The growth of the suburbs since that date naturally meant that police manpower was spread much more thinly. Then, with the passing of the 1930 Road Act and the new duties this imposed on the police, manpower shortages became acute. The start of the 'golden years' thus began with a looming crisis as further economies were threatened in the face of the deep recession. Ironically, what saved the situation was the high level of unemployment which brought in and kept top quality recruits within the service.

What qualities were the authorities looking for in their police? These were rarely spelled out beyond the (variable) physical and educational levels set by each authority, each of which had its own views on what characteristics they preferred. What made for incorruptibility among the police? Were better educated policemen more suited to the job? Would more recruits from the armed services bring a more disciplined attitude to it, or were unsophisticated countrymen to be preferred? These questions were largely answered by rule of thumb and the personal prediliction of the chief constable, while the men – judging from the answers in the oral history survey – unfailingly came down on the side of the 'practical' rather than the educated copper. Commonsense and good humour rather than book learning were the qualities needed, good policemen were not made by going by the book. But when scandals erupted and morale was low, not 'going by the book' signalled danger to the authorities.

**Metropolitan Recruiting Reforms**

This was particularly the case in the Metropolitan police at the start of the period, and here an attempt *was* made to describe the qualities necessary to achieve an efficient force. The 1929 Royal Commission on the police, set up after disquiet over police methods in the Savidge case, and the corruption revealed in the Sergeant Goddard case, concluded that a system which limited higher level appointments to those who had entered the police as constables was inimicable to the public interest. A proposal for a national police college to provide accelerated promotion to police candidates and others drawn from the armed services was put forward by Sir A.L. Dixon from the Home Office, but was received with suspicion by chief constables and local authorities, who saw this as a move towards militarization and the wresting of control from local police committees. In

---

24 *Police Review,* 12 December 1930.

any case, the plan failed on grounds of cost.[25] But soon there were renewed calls for changes in the traditional methods of filling the higher ranks, fuelled by corruption scandals in the Metropolitan police. A separately recruited officer class, it was hoped, would provide leadership and eliminate corruption. The idea proved immensely unpopular within the force, and indeed the current Metropolitan Commissioner, Lord Byng, made no moves to implement it. Worried by the unrest and indiscipline in the Metropolitan police, the Labour Cabinet agreed with Sir John Anderson that another, stronger militarist should replace Byng on his retirement. By the time Lord Trenchard reluctantly took up the appointment on the eve of the five per cent police pay cuts in 1931, the government was seriously worried. There was a strong possibility of another police strike which, Sir Warren Fischer told Trenchard, the nation's economy was too weak to withstand.[26] Trenchard's radical restructuring solution was pushed through parliament by a determined Cabinet and Home Secretary, despite widespread opposition.

Trenchard's reforms, as far as recruiting was concerned, involved two major innovations to achieve his aim of providing a younger and more intelligent force. He found that under the existing system, constables who wanted promotion had to present themselves for examination within ten years of their appointment. About half the force never put themselves forward, so that they had nothing to look forward to but their pensions. In order to replace this large group of ageing men, Trenchard – a founder member of the RAF – proposed a short service scheme which he copied from the RAF, whereby 5000 young men would be signed on to serve for no more than ten years, without pension rights or membership of the Federation, but who would receive a gratuity when they left. This would reduce the average age of the constable grade, while improving the promotion prospects of the rest. As far as the officer class was concerned, Trenchard proposed setting up a police college to train men of a higher intelligence, with higher educational qualifications and of younger average age than existed at present. Admission was to be by competitive selection for candidates from within the force and from the universities. After completing their two years training, they would be appointed to a newly created rank of junior station inspectors, and from there promoted to station inspector and upwards. In addition, there was a need for more senior officer posts, since the number above the rank of superintendent had only risen

---

25  Emsley, (1991) *The English Police*, p. 156 ; Critchley, (1967) *History of Police in England and Wales*, p. 205.

26  Andrew Boyle, (1962) *Trenchard*, p. 591. Sir John Anderson was permanent head of the Home Office, and Sir Warren Fisher was permanent head of the Treasury.

from ten in 1887 to thirteen at the present. Imbued with a sense of crisis, the Home Office duly authorized fifty more, and gave the go ahead for the founding of the Metropolitan police college.

Hendon Police College opened in 1934 to begin training the new officer class, with twenty of the thirty-two places filled by police applicants. Trenchard hoped that within twenty years the Metropolitan police would have become a profession that produced its own leaders.[27] But the college closed finally and for good in 1939, and the short service scheme was also terminated. Neither had been destined for a long life, faced as they were by sustained resistance and practical difficulties. The principle of direct entry to an officer class foundered on the implacable hostility of the majority of serving policemen. It offended against the service's most deeply held article of faith – that its quality depended on that of the constable rather than on his supervisors, for which academic qualification was no substitute. Superintendent Carling gave voice to a typical objection when asked what he thought of the Trenchard boys:

> Well, it depends how much sympathy you've got for people being pitchforked into a job that they didn't know very much about. They wanted a lot of looking after ... its just one of those things, you have to sort of grow up with the job ...[28]

While constables were contemptuous of supervisors who had not gone through the experience of walking the beat, which alone was the making of a copper, the higher ranks resented direct entry as impairing their chance of promotion by seniority, on which the system had largely rested. 'All the station sergeants and inspectors saw the Trenchard boys as somebody stopping them getting the next rank', Inspector Blake recalled.[29] As it was, their chance of promotion was only one in five, and it took on average from twenty to twenty-five years for a constable to reach the rank of superintendent.[30] Any increase in the odds raised hackles. The resistance to change was thus enormous, while the quality of outside applicants also left a lot to be desired, since the entry age of twenty was too high to attract high-fliers. The short-service idea found even less support, both in principle and practice. The theory behind the scheme was that it would rid the force of constables who had grown weary in the job once they had passed the age of promotion, and that the infusion of a number of younger men who had not become deadened by routine would lower the age profile and raise levels of efficiency. But, not surprisingly, short term service proved very

27  Ibid., p. 645.
28  Interview with Superintendent Carling, Metropolitan police.
29  Interview with Inspector Blake, Metropolitan police.
30  Debate on the Metropolitan Police Bill, *HL Debs, 5s,* vol. 28, 600, 1932–33.

unpopular, with recruits either refusing the offer, or accepting and then passing on to other forces who were only too glad to get trained officers at another's expense. It soon became clear that the scheme was a failure, with the Metropolitan police only managing to recruit around half its estimated quota of 500 short-term men a year.[31]

Despite these innovations, the Metropolitan manpower shortfall – exacerbated by the economies imposed at the beginning of the decade which had reduced the authorized establishment – continued inexorably up to the war. A reduction to 200 below establishment called for by the Home Office at the end of 1931, was increased by 300 in 1932, by 350 in 1934, and by 150 in 1935.[32] By 1937 the metropolis had 800 less police than in 1933. In addition, the national standardization of wages penalized Metropolitan officers since the cost of living in the city was considerably higher than in rural areas. Recruitment campaigns were mounted in the provinces and Metropolitan policemen on leave were asked to try to obtain recruits at their holiday centres,[33] but these produced few results. By 1937 resignations were outnumbering intake, partly due to short-service men resigning to move to provincial forces.[34] It became ever clearer that after the economy had begun to pick up in the second half of the 1930s, noticeably fewer suitable candidates were coming forward. Unfortunately, the one fertile source – of ex-servicemen who had served their time – presented problems. Although the Cabinet committee on recruitment for the army was keen to be able to provide promises of employment after army service, the Home Office found that many ex-soldiers had neither the education nor the physique to become policemen, and that if they had served their full time they were too old to earn their police pension.[35] But the major obstacle, with war looming on the horizon, was the number of ex-army men with reserve liability, which had been limited in the Metropolitan police to around five per cent of the total force. In desperation, it was nevertheless decided to increase the percentage of army reservists on the understanding that these would not be called up immediately in the event of war, and to accept as many suitable ex-servicemen without reserve liability as offered

---

31 *Police Review*, 17 April 1936.
32 *PRO: Mepo 2, 7570/280H*, 15 December 1931; /327A 1 September 1934; /331A 30 March 1935.
33 *Police Review*, 30 June 1939. Each policeman was supplied with an application form for any police candidates they might come across.
34 Voluntary resignations from the Metropolitan police were up from 125 in 1935; 178 in 1936; to 263 in 1937. *Police Review*, 29 October 1937; 11 February 1938.
35 *PRO: HO 45 22862/32A*, 20 January 1937.

themselves.[36] In the face of rising wages in industry, nothing could have demonstrated more clearly the contingent nature of police recruitment. No longer was it the case that an ample supply of well-qualified candidates was always available, as in the years of economic depression in the early 1930s. Then, they had experienced 'an embarrassment of riches much beyond their limited needs.'[37] Now, they were facing a problem that was to bedevill the force in increasing measure until well into the post-war period.

## Recruitment in the Provinces

The experience of recruitment in the provinces was more variable, although by the mid-1930s nearly all were finding it difficult to maintain their full establishment. The cities suffered more than the counties (and indeed than the metropolis)[38] but there was general complaint over the small percentage of applicants who proved suitable, an eight per cent acceptance rate being about average for the whole country.[39] The provinces also recruited more ex-servicemen, since they were not so troubled by the latter's reserve liabilities. From the mid-1930s, a third of entrants to the Glamorganshire force and a quarter in Surrey were ex-soldiers; Chester gave preference to ex-soldiers, as did Essex. Leeds, however, was against the recruitment of ex-servicemen, while other forces stated that they considered applications on their merits.[40] It was chiefly London that felt constrained over the appointment of ex-soldiers, since it considered itself in the front line and unable to envisage letting go of any of its police in the event of war. A Cabinet committee of inquiry in 1937 revealed that the counties had the highest percentage of ex-service recruits, at an average of twenty-five per cent, with nineteen per cent in the boroughs and nine per cent in the metropolis. This led the *Daily Herald* to warn that the Home Office was pushing the police throughout the country to appoint ex-soldiers.[41] In fact,

36  *PRO: HO 45 22862/35,* 27 January 1937.
37  'Past Experience and Recent Trends in Recruiting'. Report by Metropolitan Assistant Secretary, Mr Scoley, 12 November 1948. *PRO: Mepo 2 8192.*
38  In 1939 the counties had a two per cent shortfall in their establishment, the metropolis had three per cent and the boroughs, four per cent. See A.L. Dixon, (1966) *The Home Office and the Police between the Two World Wars.* M/S, Police Staff College, Bramshill, Table A: Police Establishments and Strengths.
39  *Police Review,* 24 March 1939.
40  'Cabinet committee on recruiting for the army: sub-committee on local government and local authority employment for ex-regulars' *PRO: HO 45 22862/42,* 23 March 1937.
41  *PRO: HO 45 22862/39,* 23 March 1937.

the Home Office remained ambivalent, and it was the army that was doing the pushing. Its success depended on the fact that other sources were drying up. Concessions had to be made, here as elsewhere, and in the search for untapped sources the service was even forced to give up its cherished restriction on the recruitment of married men.[42] As the chief constable of Luton reported in 1939:

> No doubt the pay and conditions of service are not so great an attraction as some people would have us believe, and the type of young man required to fill the vacancies can usually find satisfactory employment elsewhere.[43]

With the new ease of employment went a change in attitude. 'The police service today has become known for what it is – just a job – and not the special type of employment which only a few extremely fortunate men can enter'[44] is how one police correspondent described it. The years when forces had long waiting lists and queues of men desperate to get taken on were over. In truth, given the harsh nature of police discipline, its intrusion into the private lives of its members, and the steady erosion of pay since the time of the Desborough award, those years had barely outlasted the height of the depression.

## Wartime and After

The war brought its own stresses and strains as far as manpower was concerned, and these are discussed in Chapter 7. Suffice it to say that after the first year, with its large influx of untrained or semi-trained war reserves and special constables, when the service was overwhelmed by the number of volunteers with too little to do, the rest of the war – once the bombing and the call-up of regulars had begun – saw the police working at full stretch. A sixteen hour day became normal, with no time off at all when raids were on. In this way a reduced and ageing force had to deal with ordinary policing duties as well as the numerous additional tasks brought by the war, at a time when no recruitment of regulars or retirement was allowed.

---

42 The general rule had been that only single men could join the police, that probationers were not allowed to marry, and in some cases that marriage was not permitted until the constable had been four years in the service. The rule was abandoned early in 1939.

43 *Police Review*, 24 March 1939.

44 Ibid., 19 August 1938.

When the war ended, the Home Office calculated that 10,000 recruits would be needed.[45] Police regulars in the armed service were quickly sent home on priority release. Superannuated policemen were finally able to retire, some ex-service police returned to their jobs, and new ex-service candidates – often married and hopeful of getting accommodation by joining the police at a time of great housing shortage – entered or re-entered the service.[46] But manpower shortages were soon to become a serious problem. Recruiting reopened at the beginning of 1946, and at first a good number of applicants came forward, but by the end of the year this had slowed down well below the number required to fill vacancies, and resignations – even from long service members – were topping the 2000 mark.[47] Starting pay was therefore raised from £4 10s to £5 5s but this had little effect. From now until the 1960 pay increase, HMI, Commissioner and Home Office reports contain little but a litany of despair at the dearth of recruits, at their poor quality, and at the rate of resignations. The reasons were straightforward and oft repeated: poor pay, lack of police housing, lack of promotion prospects, disciplinary restrictions and high wages in industry. As early as the end of 1946 chief constables were calling for 'another Desborough' to report quickly on pay and conditions.[48] But as so often in policing history the remedies were slow, reluctant and piecemeal.[49] The service ideal of the early 1930s, when well qualified men came forward in large numbers and were prepared to work all hours under strict supervision and with no questions asked, had set a standard, so that it was seen as a bad lookout for the 'deeply ingrained tradition of the British police' if – as it now seemed – the call of duty did not come before personal convenience.[50]

Advertising campaigns, chiefly by the Metropolitan police, did not produce the required results. 'While such publicity may stir into action

---

45 *PRO: HO 45 23198/27*, August 1945.
46 By April 1946, some 9000 of the 13,000 police in the armed forces had returned to police duty. The Police Federation estimated that this still left 15,000 vacancies. By June, over 6000 regulars and 14,000 auxilliaries had left the service, and the Metropolitan police were asking their auxilliaries to stay on until 1947. *Police Review*, 19 April 1946; 21 June 1946.
47 *Police Review*, 25 October 1946.
48 *PRO: HO 45 24155*, 10 November 1946.
49 For example, in response to chief constable concern over poor recruiting and resignations in 1946, the Home Office thought that a minimum rise of £1 per week would be sufficient, subject to review in 1–2 years' time. In the event, only 15s was given. The pay scales recommended by the Oaksey Committee in 1949 were also universally regarded as disappointing and had little effect on recruitment levels.
50 *PRO:HO 4 5 24155*, 7 March 1947.

some men who have been considering a career in the force' the recruiting expert at Scotland Yard noted 'it tends mainly to attract the mere job-seeker who has no real interest and is usually not a very suitable man for the service'.[51]

In desperation, it was decided to try advertisements in the army, but even this was unsuccessful. The army was unsympathetic. It could not afford to lose men to the police, since those the police wished to attract were the same that the armed forces wished to keep.[52] All that was achieved was a promise from the War Office to advertise the police's needs among those national servicemen who had decided not to volunteer or re-engage in the Territorials.[53]

A number of forces began to set up cadet schemes in the 1950s as a way to secure dedicated recruits and to bridge the awkward gap between leaving school and entering the service.[54] Against this was the tradition that a policeman should have experience of other occupations before joining, and although cadet schemes played a continuing part, many forces were reluctant to adopt them – possibly for the reason given by Sir Robert Mark when, as Chief Constable at Leicester, he found a high degree of wastage amongst them, and a lack of any superiority over recruits from other sources.[55] It was therefore not until the Metropolitan police introduced a large scale scheme in 1960 and the Home Office gave general encouragement in 1965[56] that cadets began to form a major source for recruits.

---

51 'Past Experience and Recent Trends in Recruiting', Memo by Mr Scoley *PRO: Mepo 2 8192*, 12 November 1948.

52 *PRO: Mepo 2 7932/45A*, 15 July 1950; */95B*, February 1953.

53 But the War Office warned that everything possible was being done to encourage national servicemen to volunteer for extended service with the territorials during their three and a half years compulsory service liability, with a view to having a hard core of men available for active service immediately an emergency arose. Any that joined the police would be a dead loss to them since after one year's police service, they could not be embodied. *PRO Mepo 2 7932/80A*, 28 March 1952.

54 A small number of forces before the war had begun to recruit 'cadet clerks' who might join the regular police at the age of twenty if they turned out well. By the outbreak of war, eighty forces were together employing around 500 such boy clerks. This expanded after the war to 3,500 cadets by the mid-1960s. See Dixon, (1963) *The Home Office and the Police between the two World Wars*, pp. 200, 203.

55 *Police Review*, 23 June 1961.

56 A Home Office working party in 1965 recommended that ex-cadets should form thirty to forty per cent of recruit intake - a major break with the past. See Critchley, (1967) *History of Police in England and Wales*, p. 322.

The years between 1946 and 1960 remained critical as far as police manpower was concerned. By the mid 1950s the country was at least 10,000 men short of requirements, the situation in London being particularly acute. Here, a murder inquiry revealed that at the relevant station, there was only one constable available to cover six beats on night patrol.[57] The city was 4000 men short, with wastage exceeding intake, so that – in the Commissioner's words – there were not even enough men to take full advantage of the potentialities of team policing.[58] But following the large pay increases in 1960, the situation quickly improved, even in the metropolis, with the national shortfall cut by nearly half. The following table, giving police establishment and strengths in 1939 and 1963, also shows how police/population ratios improved beyond the levels in place just before the war.[59]

Table 1.1: *Police Establishments and Strengths, 1939-1963\**

|  | Metropolitan | | Counties | | Boroughs | |
| --- | --- | --- | --- | --- | --- | --- |
|  | 1939 | 1963 | 1939 | 1963 | 1939 | 1963 |
| Establishment | 19,358 | 20,297 | 21,616 | 36,088 | 21,092 | 25,307 |
| Vacancies | 525 | 2,414 | 460 | 1,424 | 819 | 1,659 |
| Strength | 18,833 | 17,883 | 21,156 | 34,664 | 20,273 | 23,648 |
| Population per pc | 423 | 400 | 828 | 726 | 656 | 500 |

*Source: Sir A.L. Dixon, (1963) *The Home Office and the Police Between the two World Wars*, Appendix 17, Table A.

This chapter has discussed the manpower difficulties which lay at the heart of the police institution's problems from the mid-1930s until the 1960s. It makes clear that only in periods of high unemployment or of high police wages was the calibre, flow and retention of recruits considered satisfactory. In the latter half of the 1930s, but more especially in the post-war period, there was a strong sense of crisis within the institution over manning levels and over the disinclination of young men to join the police on the terms offered. However, this sense of crisis did not spread to the outside world,

---

57  *Police Review*, 25 November 1955.
58  *Police Review*, 9 October 1953.
59  The large rise in the Counties establishment is chiefly due to the absorption of non-county boroughs by the relevant counties under the Police Act 1946, in which 'every non-county borough shall cease to be a separate police area ... and shall be treated as part of the police area of the county in which it is situated'.

nor did it emanate from that world. The police establishment was fixated on a traditional police/population ratio, and on a struggle between keeping down costs and attracting dedicated men. But in the absence of public concern over crime, or law and order, or police behaviour, what was the rationale for the looked for levels of police? Were these largely based on a mythical belief in a standard police/public ratio? How many police did the police institution really need? It seems somewhat ironical that in a period now regarded as the golden age of policing, chronic manpower shortages should have given rise to an extended organizational sense of crisis. It is equally ironic that this found no reflection in society at large. The police manpower shortage does not seem to have mattered much in practice, since society – it would appear – was largely policing itself.

# CHAPTER TWO

# Organizing the Daily Round

**Training**

How did one turn men from widely different backgrounds and occupations into policemen? By the 1930s everyone who joined the police had to undergo some period of formal training before being assigned to a division and station – unlike their nineteenth century counterparts who received most of their training on the job. Nevertheless, the extent and content of the training varied greatly between forces, from structured and wide ranging in the Metropolitan police to the most cursory and basic. Many small forces had difficulty in running their own training schemes, and relied on those offered by larger forces. Thus Chief Inspector Sheen, who joined the Norfolk police in 1933, was posted to Attleborough, issued with a uniform, and sent out on the beat.

> *Did you know where to go, and had anybody shown you the beat?* I didn't. There was nobody. The sergeant, he was a holy being, you had to ask permission to speak to him ... He just discouraged questions, and said 'you'll have to do the same as I did, look in your books'

After six months, Sheen was sent for training to Birmingham,[1] which by then he found 'a piece of cake' since he already had a working knowledge of policing and of the legal definitions which made up the bulk of the rote learning. A more rudimentary training was undergone by a recruit to the West Sussex police in 1933. Here, Inspector Astley recalled:

> We reported to Chichester for training on the Saturday, we didn't do much apart from digging the chief constable's garden and hoeing up his gravel drive, that was our initiation ... Training was in Chichester, very, very basic too, I only had about ten days ... The reason was because Goodwood races was coming up and we were wanted on the streets, so they bunged us out.

At this time, none of the smaller provincial forces had full-time training officers, so many took advantage of co-operative schemes such as the one

---

1    Birmingham ran one of the largest provincial training schools in the country, where recruits from 33 other forces were trained in the 1930s. See Sir A.L. Dixon, *The Home Office and the Police between the two World Wars*, p. 118.

offered by Birmingham. It was not until after the war that a system of regional training schools was set up, as well as a national police college for the inservice training for the higher ranks.[2] Sir A.L. Dixon's earlier attempt to inaugurate a national training centre had foundered, ostensibly on the grounds of expense, but also no doubt because of resistance from provincial chief constables with their traditional stonewalling of most nationalizing moves or suggestions. The Home Office only had direct influence over the Metropolitan police which, perhaps because of the great number of its own recruits, rarely trained men for other forces. Here, there was a formalized twelve week programme consisting of two-thirds legal and practical instruction and one third foot drill, self-defence and first aid. But whereas the extent of the training varied between forces, the aim of 'breaking in' the men was similar. A haircut as close as a convict's (so that recruits in their time off would keep on their hats in order not to get mistaken for old lags) and a ferocious disciplinary routine were designed to erase individuality and instil submissiveness. Learning was by rote. 'Every night you had to learn by heart three definitions, I think there were 180 to get through' Inspector Hay recalled; while Inspector Brierley described how 'for thirteen weeks, our training consisted of standing up and reading aloud from Moriarty'[3]. The first definition went as follows: 'Law, as defined by Blackstone, is a rule of action prescribed by a superior which an inferior is bound to obey'. This, one supposes, will have put many a recruit as well as his public firmly in their place.

While much of the physical training imitated that of the armed forces, its different purpose distinguished it essentially from that of the military. 'The actual training you got was really self-defence, you weren't being trained to go and clobber someone' a former Metropolitan pc recalled. Similarly, in Birmingham, the men were taught during foot drill how to give traffic signals and how to slow march:

> At the time we could see little sense in this because we thought
> normal marching was more spectacular with swinging arms, but a

---

2    These schools were based one in each of the eight chief constables' Conference Districts under a management committee of chief constables, with general oversight of the scheme maintained by a central advisory committee. See Inspectors of Constabulary report for 1946, *PP XIII 1946–47*, pp. 7–8. In 1948 a national police college for the in-service training of the higher ranks was inaugurated. This system, which is still in place, finally put paid to the idea of an officer class recruited from outside the ranks of the police.

3    C.H.H. Moriarty was the Deputy Chief Constable of Birmingham whose manual *Police Law*, first published in 1929, became the standard training guide used to instruct generations of police recruits.

lot of thought had been put into everything we did and this slow march was a boon to us in the future. With this training we were able to saunter quite smartly along the streets of Birmingham, commanding some respect, and implying that everyone move out of our way ... Traffic drill also came under the heading of foot drill and to see a class practising this was a sight for sore eyes. No driver could ever mistake the stop signal. This was a very majestic movement, the arm held up to the full extent with the palm facing the oncoming traffic. This was the only 'Stop' signal that we were allowed to use. The signal to start moving was also one on its own. The right arm, not the left one, was extended from shoulder level towards the traffic in question. Then very slowly and deliberately the hand and forearm were raised from the elbow, keeping the upper arm parallel to the ground, and the movement carried on until the fingers were alongside the right ear. Very impressive, and the motorist certainly knew what he had to do when he saw that signal.[4]

## Becoming Policemen

Having passed through their training period, recruits now faced the task of becoming 'real' policemen, over a two-year probationary period in their first posting. How did they construct their professional persona, and what forms of negotiation with their superiors and the public went on in the process? There was little time for reflection on these matters, as recruits were thrown in at the deep end, but the  reception they received soon provided them with their first object lesson in the norms and values on which police work at the bottom of the hierarchy was based. The rationale behind the initial posting varied from forces where the tallest and strongest were posted to the city centre, to those whose special skills – whether sporting, musical or clerical – led to postings at divisional headquarters. But wherever the posting, the first lesson to be learnt was that new recruits were the lowest of the low and counted for nothing beyond their nuisance value. Recruits were often ignored and often resented by an older and less well educated group of pcs. The reception was coolest in the capital, where the police were being reorganized after a corruption scandal at the end of the 1920s. Here, younger pcs were regarded with a certain amount of suspicion by the older men, who thought they had been brought in to spy on them. In addition, the cut in police pay as part of the government's economy measures in the early 1930s had caused widespread resentment. In consequence, the older men more or less made a pact to ignore newcomers

---

4    Inspector Hay, (1970) *The Saga of a Practical Copper*, M/S autobiography.

coming in at lower rates of pay because they considered that such undercutting diminished their chances of getting the pay cuts restored. The result was made evident to one probationer during his showing round by an older bobby, whose first spoken words were 'we go for breakfast now' after they had been walking the beat in silence for three hours.[5]

Two things were imperative for survival in the force: a quick appraisal and understanding of the way the hierarchy functioned, and the ability to form bonds within one's peer group. Good relations with the sergeant lay at the heart of the recruit's chances of survival and promotion, while the sergeant's elevated status was made clear in all manner of ways. Most recruits were terrified of him, 'it cost half a crown to speak to him' was how one of them put it. Life on the beat was dominated by the fear of being caught out, while inside the station he had his annointed place and woe betide anyone who sat in his chair. Only the sergeant sat near the fire.[6]

If promotion depended on good relations with one's superiors, a tolerable daily existence on the beat depended on bending the rules and outwitting the sergeant and those above him. There was thus a built in conflict between the strategies needed to satisfy both aims. For the latter, cooperation between pcs was essential. Since pcs had to serve several years before they could apply to be made up to sergeant, and even then had to wait for ten or more years before achieving their first promotion, solidarity rather than competitiveness mostly marked social relations at the bottom of the hierarchy. These men passed their leisure time together, especially if they were housed in single men's quarters, and engaged in much horseplay and crude practical jokes. Pcs naturally covered up for one another when questions were asked about absence from one's beat or other transgressions, while injustice against a fellow pc elicited a general response of non-coperation and dumb insolence. The trick was not to get caught. Asked whether he had gained any medals, a respondent replied 'Only the NFA (never found out) medal'.[7]

## On The Beat

Life on the beat created its own its own dynamics, and varied according to whether one was part of an inner city or an outlying or rural division, a problem area or a trouble free one. Problem areas could often be identified

5   Interview with PC Moppett, Metropolitan police.
6   Interviews with Inspector Archer, Durham County police; Inspector Cooper, Metropolitan police.
7   Interview with Inspector Astley, West Sussex police.

by the presence of a divisional police station there that ensured an abundance of police attention. One of the worst off in this regard, where the policing of what was regarded as a rough area amounted to a self-fulfilling prophecy, was Jarrow. Here, the inhabitants had the bad luck to find a police training school in their midst. The consequences were described by Superintendent Hearn:

> Jarrow ... it was a bit rough, it had a reputation ... and I would say the unfortunate point of having a police training school there, before the war it was four hours on the beat and four hours in the school, and policemen were expected to get arrests and offences when they were doing their training, and I think it was hard on the population. It was over-policed, well, that's the wrong expression. Actually it was policed too officiously...it was quite well kept free from violence but some of the population was hounded, I would say.[8]

In the inner city, divisions competed with one another to come top of the statistical league table for summonses and arrests – and this was quite openly acknowledged and passed on to the constable – whereas elsewhere value was placed on being part of a division where there was no trouble: no break-ins, no disorder, no conjestion. There was little the pc could do to prevent break-ins, beyond 'shaking hands with padlocks' in the nightly testing of shop doors and warehouses, marked with bits of whale bone inserted in the door jambs. No one, it would seem, ever caught a burglar this way, but nevertheless this routine provided the framework around which the beat was structured, with the beatman held directly responsible for any break-ins occuring on his patch during his hours of duty.

The control of disorder on the streets involved different tactics, and recruits had quickly to learn who might cause  trouble, who might do them a bit of good. The learning process started immediately after the donning of police uniform, which had a magical effect on the reactions of the public. While many pcs at first felt extremely self-conscious and thought 'every-one was staring at them', it soon became clear that the uniform was a source of power and authority, with members of the public assuming that the wearer was omniscient and an infallible source of knowledge on a wide variety of topics. Recruits soon learned who to pal up with and who to avoid, and the best way of dealing with those who might cause trouble. Drunks were a case in point, and an object lesson in the use of police discretion. Whether to arrest, or caution or chastise a drunk was part of the acquired expertise that went to make a good copper. It was not only the event but the circumstances that had to be taken into account. If a drunk made a nuisance of himself at the end of the constable's shift, he had to

8    Interview with Superintendent Hearn, Durham County police.

weigh up the extra time the arrest would take against the time off he would get next day for appearance in court. In the cities, one could try and push a drunk over the boundary into someone else's division if one wanted to avoid making an arrest. On the other hand, if one went to court after a night arrest, one automatically got four hours time off, however long was actually spent in court. In the metropolitan area, the divisional surgeon received a fee for examining drunks, and in some divisions would offer the bobbies a shilling per drunk as an inducement. As against these advantages, there was the station sergeant to be taken into consideration, who might not want to be bothered with trivial offences that involved him in a lot of paperwork. So it was a question of balancing the choices to be made.

What of the response to the public? Here, the pc developed a clear and simple working model of who constituted a villain and with what matters the police should concern themselves. Villains were usually born and not bred, you knew which social group they belonged to, you knew where to look for them, and that is where you first went when a crime had been committed. Other members of the public might simply be unruly, such as those given to brawling or other offensive public behaviour, and it was up to the police to provide the discipline. Here, the Irish came in for their share of police prejudice, with the Irishman cast in the role of 'the other'. This was especially the case in the Midlands, where a rapid expansion of road building and other developments brought in troups of Irish navvies, who never stayed long in one locality and who tended to be regarded as the source of trouble and to get picked on by the police. If a pc was assaulted, it was important that he dealt with it without bringing a charge. It was alright to have a fight with someone who attacked you, but a charge of assault would earn you a black mark. 'What's the matter with the man, can't he handle himself?' would be the sort of comment made. Otherwise, the beatman expected the public to show him respect. Men who gathered at street corners moved away automatically at the approach of a policeman, and he would be satisfied with this token gesture. A north country pc recalled the situation during the depression years in Jarrow before the war:

> The people in that part of the country, I've never seen so many men, cowed. They used to lie beside the walls in ragged, dishevelled clothing, and when you appeared in your uniform, they all used to step from the wall to the kerbside and stand there like zombies, and when you'd passed, they'd all lie back on the wall again. That was showing their respect for the law, you know.[9]

---

9    Interview with Inspector Archer, Durham County police.

Similarly, in London, pcs would demand demonstrations of respect from barrow boys, who might otherwise be summonsed for obstruction. One pc recalled that

> Barrow boys were a bit of a nuisance causing an obstruction, and that was an offence. But we used to have a working arrangement that if they saw you coming, they would move on, or just lift the handles of their barrows to make a show. I remember one who didn't lift his handles when I came, so I said 'Come on', so he just lifted his handles and I went on my way.[10]

The prime purpose of the uniformed pcs was thus to establish their authority and keep order on their own patch. The comments of a city and a country pc will be cited to show the pc's view of his relations with the public and the underlying values that guided such men in their day to day actions. When asked how the local population regarded the police, the country bobby replied:

> You could almost be thought of as a chief constable up in the valleys. An out-station man there would be a chief constable in his own right ... because he lived among the people, he was their sole advisor. If there was any complaint they had, they would come to the local pc and seek his advice.[11]

Similarly, a city bobby commented that

> One of the greatest differences between today's bobby and our day is, you were the governor. You were conscious when you went on the beat that parliament gave you certain powers, not your sergeant or your superintendent, and you individually had to exercise them and if you exercised them wrongly you bore the brunt ... so what becoming a good policeman meant was learning to use the resources around you. Everybody that lived on that beat, they didn't know it, but they were crime prevention ... You would be posted to your beat for a month, the first week you were a right old tarter, there would be no rubbish or anything like that left on the pavement, and news got around that there was a new bloke on here. Then the second week you didn't have to work, you could just go around and have a cup of tea here and there and it would be very pleasant ... you were tidying up your beat, that was the main thing. And at the end of four weeks, the less crimes recorded in your book, the better ... You were accountable, that was the whole basis of policing in those days, which doesn't apply now.[12]

---

10  Interview with Deputy Commander Blatchley, Metropolitan police.
11  Interview with Chief Inspector Eyre, Glamorganshire police.
12  Interview with Sergeant Martin, Metropolitian police.

Here, in the words of the practioners of the time, were the goals that the police aspired to, and the values on which their work rested. In the idealized picture they painted, this provides the strongest possible contrast to, and basis for their criticism of present day policing. However, the day by day reality involved in pounding the beat offers a rather different perspective.


## Organizing the Beat

The work of probationer constables, whatever their subsequent speciality, centred on walking the beat. The beat was the bedrock of the service, its rationale enshrined in precedent set by the founding fathers. To walk at a steady pace along a prescribed route at all hours and in all weathers was the basic strategy devised to keep the police in the public eye, to preserve the peace and to protect property on the way. Beats were laid out on an unvarying pattern – shorter in conjested areas and longer in outlying ones – and were patrolled in a manner as fixed as the lay-out. The main concern of supervisory officers was to keep the beats fully manned, so that extra duties led to requests for a bigger establishment. In order to provide continuous coverage a conventional number of beat officers and supervisory staff – assessed on the basis of a police/population ratio – were considered necessary. The nineteenth century ratio of 1:1000 police per population in the counties and roughly 1:700 in the boroughs provided the benchmark, which slowly improved and converged towards an average of 1:670 in the inter-war years and of 1:540 by the 1960s.[13] Yet police spokesmen consistently claimed that authorized establishments were out of date. They were rarely reviewed, were based on out of date calculations concerning population growth and distribution, and so masked the true extent of the deficiency in manpower.[14] Thus there was constant police pressure for an increase in establishment. Partly, this was due to the police institution's perennial view that it would be better able to solve its problems if it were given more manpower. Partly, it was due to reductions in establishment at a time of the economy cuts in the 1920s and again in the early 1930s. Chiefly, however, it was due to the assumed need for continuous beat coverage at a time when finite numbers of police were faced with competing and

---

13  This average masks continuing divergences between the conurbations, boroughs and counties. In the metropolis, the ratio was nearer to 1:400. See the *Tables* drawn from the *Annual Abstracts of Statistics* and *Annual Reports of H.M. Inspectors of Constabulary* in J.P.Martin and Gail Wilson, (1969) *The Police: A Study in Manpower*, pp. 47–48; and Dixon, (1966) Appendix 17, Table A.

14  See discussions in *Police Review*, 13 April and 15 June, 1956; 21 March 1958.

escalating demands. In an attempt to curb this expansive pressure, the Home
Office had set up a review of the beat system in the metropolis in the 1920s
which concluded that requests for additional manpower were inflated and
ill-founded.[15] But supposed over-manning was not the only problem. By
1930 the mismatch between beats and the population they covered in the
spreading metropolis was such that the beats inquiry was continued. In
consequence, a new system to cover the move to the suburbs came in at the
start of 1932 that was to make greater use of motor transport, telephones
and wireless. The unvarying system of patrolling the beat was altered, as
was the doubling of night beats and the manning of fixed points. The sub-
division, in charge of an inspector, was made the new administrative unit,
which allowed a reduction in the number of sergeants (although somewhat
offset by an increase in the number of inspectors).[16] These measures were
intended to take account of changed circumstances, such as the greater
incidence of housebreaking by day than of burglary at night in the suburbs,
the need for an element of surprise through a mixture of beats and patrols
working different shift hours, and the use of police boxes throughout the
metropolitan area to reduce the need for sergeant supervision. However, it is
not clear that the changes made a fundamental difference, apart from
enabling beat constables to communicate directly with the police station,
and vice versa. Metropolitan reorganization, which had taken nearly a
decade to bring to fruition, and which was the first alteration to a beat
system that had been in existence since the coming of the new police,
ultimately resulted in little more than bringing in patrols to busy parts of the
city to alternate with normal beat policing, the greater use of police boxes
instead of sergeants to control the beat timetable, and the transfer of more
men to the suburbs. A fixed beat pattern and timetable was still adhered to,
while reorganization – and technical advances, such as the institution of
police boxes – do not seem to have been able to counteract the impact of
falling police numbers. Indeed, given the innate conservatism of the service,

15 Dixon, pp. 195–6. A 'Beats Committee' of senior Metropolitan officers under
   the Deputy Commissioner, aided by the head of the Home Office's 'F' Division
   was set up in 1924 to review levels of manning of beats in the metropolis, and
   its recommendations adopted in 1929. A further review in the early 1930s
   resulted in reorganization in 1932.
16 Annual Report of the Metropolitan Commissioner, *PP XXI*, 1931–32, noting
   that reorganization would require fifty-five more inspectors, but allow for a
   reduction of at least a hundred station sergeants. *PRO: HO 45
   20064/472444/49*, 14 March 1930; *HO 45 20065/472444/66*, 25 March – 15
   December 1931.

it may in some cases even have added to the pressure. Thus, PC Moppett noted that under the fixed points system in his Tottenham division,

> all the local people knew where to find a pc. So when they did away with a lot of these (fixed) points because they weren't necessary, they *still* posted a man there because that's where people expected to find a pc.

Beat work remained rigidly controlled, whether in town or country, and whether by police sergeant or police box. In London street supervision by sergeants continued – even if at a reduced level – in addition to the discipline imposed by the need to ring in at fixed times from police boxes, while most urban beats were still worked according to the old pattern:

> you had to walk round right handed ... and every now and again they'd say 'reverse the beats' ... We used to work always to the right, you know, round the block. My whole job was to walk, try property, and make your points every half hour.

In the countryside, and in urban townships where there were no police boxes, constables had to ask to use subscribers' private telephones or ring in from public call boxes:

> the main problem was the distance between things, and you had to work it out that you had to be at certain places at certain times and you worked your beat accordingly. The only way they could communicate with me then was by public telephone. We had no police boxes as such, no call boxes ... The station knew where you were, you had to wait five minutes by the phone box and if they wanted you they phoned you – always assuming the public were not using that phone.[17]

Change in working practices was gradual, however radical the intention, and every innovation or deviation from the old beat system was either hotly contested or simply not implemented. Thus police boxes in the towns gave rise to complaints that this led to the lengthening of beats so that it became a physical impossibility for the constable to do more than walk as fast as permitted between boxes, giving him only one thing to think about: 'I must not be late at my next box'. Several respondents agreed that the box system reduced their capacity for crime prevention, since instead of placing themselves where instinct told them they would do most good, the constable

---

17 Interviews with Inspector Outram, Inspector Archer, Chief Inspector Eyre and Inspector Smith. The latter refers to conditions in the late 1940s in the West Sussex police.

had to be sure that he was at the box at the time laid down.[18] A mechanical system thus might impose greater constraints on constables' freedom of action than had sergeant supervision. At the same time there were others who observed that under the old system many had spent the greater part of their tour in 'looking for the sergeant', and that the larger suburban beats could now be covered by bike and motor patrols.[19] Here were the seeds of change. Nevertheless, the extent of the mechanization of beat work was, and remained, rudimentary before the war. Some areas, whether through apathy or parsimony, kept altogether outside this field of contention by having nothing to do with mechanical innovations: in 1933 nearly 200 police stations and about half of the 5000 rural police houses were not on the telephone at all.[20] This situation points up the snail's pace at which alterations in the organization of police work took place, whether or not individual forces and officers were in favour. Mostly, they were not. Typical of the pre-war police hierarchy were the views of the Chief Constable of Birkenhead, Captain Dawson. In his presidential address to the Chief Constables' Association, Dawson commented on the increasing urge to displace police by the use of traffic signals, telephone boxes and 'other devices of a mechanical character'– not as an aid to the police but as a manpower substitute. His view on the preventive purpose of policing would have gained approval from his nineteenth century counterparts. Police boxes, he believed, would never prevent a crime, and prevention after all was the best cure for crime and first in importance among police duties. Similarly, the chief constable of Somerset described the result of his own experimental scheme of motor cycle beat patrols as unsatisfactory for the efficient supervision of a district. The conference agreed that the presence of a police constable, or even the knowledge that there was one in the vicinity, had a far greater deterrent effect on malefactors than the possibility of an officer arriving at great speed, and that good patrolling, rather than

---

18 Supervision in the MPD in pre-box days in theory meant two fixed point meetings with a sergeant per tour of duty, but in practice it seems that one was the norm. This left the constable much more on his own than under the box system. *Written communication from Sergeant Martin and Sergeant Tome, Metropolitan police.*

19 *Police Review*, 2 May 1930; 22 and 29 July 1932.

20 *Police Review,* 14 July 1933. Similarly, police boxes were not used at all in Liverpool. Instead, a system of street pillar telephones that the police shared with the fire service was installed in 1908 and continued in use until the 1950s. *Communication from Superintendent Clarke*, Liverpool City police.

good detection, was the best preventer of crime.[21] This view of policing was
to remain the prevalent one across the board until well after the war.

## Amalgamation

Similar arguments were raised in the long struggle over the amalgamation
of police forces, first recommended in 1919 by the Desborough
Commission, strongly supported by the Home Office and its civil servant in
evidence to the Select Committee on the Amalgamation of Police Forces in
1932, and strongly resisted by most others connected with the city and
borough police.[22] The Home Office took the view that, quite apart from
financial savings, amalgamation would bring about an increase in efficiency
through the extension of detective branches – since criminals recognized no
police boundaries – and the co-ordination of technical equipment and
information. Opposing views were vociferous but based more on sentiment
than on logic. These stressed chiefly four points: 1) the importance of
preserving 'that local interest which experience has shown to be so fruitful
in establishing friendly relations between the police and the public'; 2)
amalgamation would be the thin end of the wedge leading to nationalization
and from there to militarization; 3) the practice of appointing chief
constables in the counties from outside the service who had no knowledge
of police work would cause great resentment in the boroughs; 4) the lack of
experience or understanding of detective work in county forces which, in
moving men from one division to another ignored the need for the careful
nurturing of local contacts.[23] These arguments persuaded the Select
Committee that the case for amalgamation had not been made out. It saw no
compelling reason to upset the status quo, and therefore rejected the Home
Office proposals, preferring instead to rely on voluntary amalgamation
(except for boroughs with populations under 30,000). However, voluntary
amalgamation meant no amalgamation at all. Naturally, much of the
resistance was from borough councils reluctant to see a curtailment of their
powers, and from borough police establishments frightened of being
swallowed up by county forces. The evidence brought out the degree of

---

21 Views of the chief constables of Birkenhead and Somerset, and of HM
   Inspector of Constabulary. *Police Review*, 7 July 1933.
22 In favour of amalgamation were the Home Office, HM Inspectors of
   Constabulary, the County Councils and the County Chief Constables. Against
   were the Association of Municipal Corporations, the Non-county Boroughs
   Association, the Police Federation and the Chief Constables' Association.
23 Select Committee on Police Forces (Amalgamation) 1932. *PP V,* 1931–32.

hostility and mutual misunderstanding between county and borough forces, with each side believing that they were the only ones to carry out proper policing. But what the evidence to the Select Committee also shows was the extent to which the old bogey of a militarized police could unite the opposition, as well calling forth an idyllic picture, painted by numerous witnessess, of the present harmony prevailing between local forces and their public, which a larger regional force would destroy. The point of interest is that their resistance against the big guns of the Home Office and county chief constables was successful, and that the classic argument against militarization and against encroachment by a centralizing and bureaucratizing state in favour of local forces under local control still held the upper hand in pre-war England.

## Mechanization

It was the car rather than the Home Office that was to have the greatest impact on the old system of beat policing. Social habits and patterns of crime and population had begun to move to a different timetable from the familiar one which confined wrongdoers and constables within established boundaries, and here the motor car was the harbinger of rapid change. The car brought the 1930 Road Traffic Act in its wake, and with it, an unending escalation in police work that took men off the beat into traffic divisions to chase car-borne criminals and traffic offenders. It was the insiduous advance of the motor car which above all else was to encroach on and eventually erode the pristine contours of beat policing and to contribute largely to perceived manpower shortages, the achieved increase in police/population ratios notwithstanding. But even here, and despite the explosive effect of the 1930 and 1934 Road Traffic Acts on police work, fundamental change on the beat did not take place until well after the war. Instead, police work connected with motorists was hived off into separate traffic divisions manned by specialist motor patrols, whose work is discussed in Chapter 4. The chief effect on the uniform branch was in the draining of manpower for extraneous duties (such as checking for car parking, lighting or licence offences) at the expense of beat coverage – so that in 1934 the Inspectors of Constabulary were already warning that the requirements of the Road Traffic Acts were crowding out the constable's primary duties, and might mean that beats would have to be pooled in the future.[24]

---

24  HM Inspector of Constabulary Annual Report, *PP X*, 1934–35.

Despite these pressures, the use of cars for non-traffic police work before the war was largely confined to the cities. The counties made very little, or no, use of motor vehicles, apart from the motor patrols that were financed by the Road Fund. In some county forces higher-grade supervisory officers used their own vehicles to make their rounds in return for a mileage allowance, while a divisional van for the transport of stolen goods and of prisoners slowly became customary.[25] But the main work of the country policeman was carried out on foot or by bicycle. The cities made earlier use of car beat patrols. In Sheffield, for example, divisional cars came in to use around 1938. Inspector Frome recalled that his division had three Morris Minor two-seaters that were used for policing large housing estates and outlying areas, thereby covering up the manpower shortage which was even then apparent – since one man in a car could cover estates that would really have needed three foot men to check all the property and shopping precincts.[26]

Police motorization was most advanced in the MPD. Here, a system of 'area wireless cars' was instituted in the early 1930s, each crewed by a driver, wireless operator and plain clothes policeman. These operated within a division on a regular twenty-four hour shift basis, and were able to receive and send out Morse code messages to Scotland Yard. Soon after, 'Q' cars were brought in, manned by uniform branch men working in plain clothes, a CID officer, and a driver and wireless operator drawn from the traffic division. These cars covered a wider area than the 'area wireless cars', in response to the need to be able to cross divisional boundaries, and were specifically concerned with crime.[27] In a sense, they could be regarded as embryonic crime squads. There were more divisional cars, too, by the time war broke out, when each main station had a van and most had a car for use by the duty officer.[28] Any further motorization, however, was to be severely disrupted by the war.

## Post-War Developments

The war called a halt to further alterations to the beat system. As far as policing was concerned, this can best be seen as an interim period when

---

25  Before such vans were available, prisoners had to be conveyed to court and prison by public transport.
26  Interview with Inspector Frome, Sheffield City police.
27  Deputy Commander Blake, who joined the Metropolitan police in 1935, recalled that there was one 'Q' car covering two divisions, on which all probationers spent a day.
28  Interview with Inspector Cooper, Metropolitan police.

makeshift arrangements were made to try and approximate as closely as possible to traditional policing patterns, while having to take on board all the new wartime tasks and untrained personnel that came the way of the service. Towards the end of the war, however, the Home Office established a post-war reconstruction police committee, which reported in 1947 that as far as the organization of the service was concerned 'it had no sweeping reforms or radical alterations in the present organization to suggest'.[29] Even so, its suggestion that rural beat constables be provided with cars was criticized by local police committees and by the Association of Municipal Corporations, on the familiar grounds that:

> much of the value of the rural resident constable will be lost if the area that he has to supervise is enlarged and his patrol is made by car instead of by bicycle. He is a preventer rather than a detector of crime and it is important that he should have an intimate and day by day knowledge of his beat and be available for advice and consultation[30]

Radical alteration to this model of policing was to come not from the recommendations of the police post-war committee but from individual forces, driven by the need to conserve manpower.

The pioneer here was Aberdeen. In 1948, its experimental scheme for pooling beats within a division and dividing the men into four teams, each aided by police cars with two-way radios, made a definitive break with the past. Each team, under the leadership of a sergeant, was given freedom of action over the policing of crime within the division.[31] This was a considerable change from the more common arrangement whereby a small number of mobile officers were superimposed on an area that was patrolled by beat constables in the traditional way. Supporters rejoiced that mechanization would replace foot slogging, and initiative would oust routine, and Aberdeen's example was soon copied by other urban authorities – while the Inspectors of Constabulary tentatively approved the opportunity for the more economical and effective use of selected personnel. The police service at this point was facing a grave crisis in recruitment that had led to the setting up of an independent inquiry to report on pay and conditions 'in the light of the need for the recruitment and

---

29 Quoted in Critchley, *History of Police*, p. 239.
30 *Police Review*, 28 May 1948.
31 The scheme was introduced in one section of the city in April 1948, but extended to the whole in January 1949. The police authority claimed that they would have needed to employ fifty more officers if the scheme had not been adopted. *Police Review*, 7 May, 18 June 1948; Working Party Report for the Oaksey Committee, 14 January 1949. *Appendix V, PP XIX* 1948–49.

retention of an adequate number of suitable men and women ...' (the Oaksey Committee).[32] Fortuitously, this was able to look at the newly instituted Aberdeen system.

The Committee found that over eighty per cent of constables outside the metropolis had been spending all their time during their first ten years on beat duties, and it received a great deal of evidence on the monotony of this work. In Aberdeen, however, the new system was said to have improved the morale of the men, and it was this aspect which was of interest to the Committee. A working party was consequently appointed to report on the system.[33] It gave a cautious welcome to the scheme, which it considered in the light of the recommendations of the Police Post-war Committee. This had stressed the importance of retaining the orthodox system of beat policing as a basic principle, even if supplemented by mechanized beats and mobile patrols. Strong evidence was therefore needed to convince the Oaksey working party to the contrary. It found little evidence of increased efficiency under the Aberdeen scheme despite an improvement in the mens' morale – which it thought might be only temporary – while the cost of policing remained the same. Further, it was thought that the scheme was unlikely to lead to reductions in establishment. On the other hand, there was no evidence that police/public relations had been impaired. But the working party decided that while the scheme might be suitable for Aberdeen, they were not convinced that it was suitable for general adoption. The method of policing an area should therefore be left to the discretion of the chief constable concerned.

How were these findings received? Hull and Eastbourne were amongst the first to adopt the Aberdeen system of team policing, while a great enthusiast was the chief constable of Salford, who had been recruited from Aberdeen in 1949. In London, team policing was introduced into four sub-divisions in 1951 because of the grave shortage of men, but the Commissioner made clear that in his view this was not an effective substitute for the man on foot.[34] Alternative methods were tried elsewhere, and impetus given to these experiments by the deficiencies in manpower which had made it difficult or impossible for some forces to maintain more orthodox beat systems.[35] These difficulties were brought about, or compounded, by the reluctance of recruits to accept the old terms and conditions of service that pertained before the war. Plymouth therefore

32  Oaksey Report 1948–49, *PP XIX* 1948–49.
33  Ibid., *Appendix V*.
34  Annual Report of the Metropolitan Commissioner, *PP XVII* 1951–52. Team policing was also introduced in Birkenhead and Halifax early in 1950.
35  Annual Report of the Inspectors of Constabulary, *PP XVII* 1951–51.

inaugurated a new seven shift system which decreased the amount of night duty and early turn for most of the force, in order to conform with the usual hours worked in other trades or professions. That this was the predominant motive is made clear by the chief constable's statement a year later that he intended to continue a slightly modified version of the new system because the men preferred it, even though he could neither claim that efficiency had been increased nor crime decreased by it.[36]

Worry over the dearth of recruits and over the capacity of the service to retain them was a major motive behind the drive towards mechanization and alterations to the beat. Nevertheless, the open admission of this fact by Plymouth's chief constable was probably exceptional. More common was the attitude of Bolton's chief constable, who made clear that beat reorganization was an expedient entirely due to the shortage of recruits, and not one implemented for their convenience:

> I have recently found it necessary ... to review the beat arrangements. This has become necessary in view of the present deficiency in the establishment, and the fact that the present rate of recruitment does not augur well for any substantial improvement of the position in the immediate future. Thus the object of the review has been to re-deploy the available personnel, and to this end I have been obliged to recommend that the rural and semi-rural territory in this area be supervised by car patrols ... I would emphasize that the introduction of this arrangement must be regarded purely as an expedient ... I do not fully concur in any proposals to displace the traditional system of beat working[37]

The *Police Review* summed up the rationale for these changes with its editorial comment that 'the need to conserve police manpower has probably been the most compelling of the reasons prompting chief constables to make experimental changes in operational methods.'[38] Police cars were cheaper than police officers. Nevertheless, when manpower shortages eased, several chief constables abandoned team policing and reinstituted the old beat system, since their stated priority was the maintenance of personal contact between the police and the public, rather than the increase in crime detection that was lauded by advocates of team policing.[39] The *Police Review* regarded it as something of a mystery why team policing should be

---

36  Memorandum by the chief constable of Plymouth, 1949; quoted *Police Review*, 20 January 1950, 23 February 1951.

37  Bolton chief constable's annual report, quoted *Police Review*, 6 April 1951.

38  *Police Review*, 10 October 1952.

39  Brighton, Halifax, Dudley and Walsall chief constables all recommended a retreat from team policing to their police authorities. *Police Review*, 7 March 1952, 23 October 1953, 29 March 1957.

a phenomenal success in Aberdeen, Salford and one or two other places, and a disappointment elsewhere.[40]

The reason is not hard to find. It was based on the deep-seated reluctance of chief constables to alter a conception of policing that placed overriding emphasis on prevention rather than the detection of crime. The customary and regular presence of a policeman walking the streets and making sure property was secure was assumed to act as a deterrent to criminals and as the best way of maintaining friendly relations with the public and of gathering useful information. The overwhelmingly positive public response to the police as an institution, revealed in Geoffrey Gorer's survey in the mid-1950s,[41] meant that there was little outside pressure for organizational change – the main one, as we have seen, being a labour shortage due to uncompetitive wages and unsocial hours. Until the nature of everyday demand for police protection of persons or property increased, a conservative and bureaucratic institution such as the police was unlikely to wish to alter its working habits. Nor were many constables themselves happy that their independent role and relationship with their public should be reduced by mechanization and team working. Most respondents, and not only the pre-war bobbies, were clear that mechanized beat work was a disaster for policing. 'Police force circles will tell you that the worst thing that ever happened was police in panda cars, it made men lazy' Inspector Archer recounted, and Detective Chief Inspector Knight and Chief Inspector Eyre agreed. In a word, motorization meant the loss of 'good guy' contact with the general public, as opposed to contact with lawbreakers and with those calling directly for assistance, and it was this restriction which was to have such profound effect on the perceived quality of the service. But the dispersal of inner city working class populations on to new housing estates and overspill schemes stretched police manpower to an extent that made motorized patrols inevitable as the only practical solution to the need to maintain a police presence. Even so, it was twenty years after the war before a thoroughgoing mechanized scheme was first devised and instituted. This took place in Kirby, a Liverpool overspill development with 60,000 inhabitants, in 1965. Here, the dynamic Chief Constable of Lancashire, Eric

---

40  *Police Review*, 28 May 1954.

41  Geoffrey Gorer (1955) *Exploring English Character*, Chap.13. Gorer describes the response to his questions on the police, based on c. 11,000 questionnaires sent to readers of *The People*, as the most surprising in the whole of the research survey. Where he had expected a considerable number of his anonymous respondents to express hostility to the police, he found that only five per cent were really hostile and three quarters were enthusiastically appreciative of the English police.

St Johnstone, decided that in order to overcome the shortage of police, all eleven foot patrols would have to go.[42] These were reorganized into five mobile beats, patrolled continously by a constable in a distinctively marked (panda) car and carrying a personal radio.[43] The effect, recalled one respondent who was stationed in Kirby at the time, was magic:

> They had built all the houses, no shops, no pubs, no clubs ... if they'd had any sense they they would have built the shops and the clubs first and made it a society, but they didn't ... young people were left to their own devices, they moved into crime in an enormous way and crime started to escalate in Kirby with the result that in 1965 the criminals were winning, there was no doubt about it. The men on foot in these areas couldn't cope with it ... Bill Portree was the deputy, and he had a notion, well let's keep a few vehicles that were ready for trading in and paint them brightly coloured, so that people would know they were about, and they put everybody into cars instead of on foot. The illusion was that the police were everywhere, and it reduced everything from crime to accidents. You can achieve wonders for a limited period but people get used to it...and they did have a notion that what will happen in the fullness of time is that your policeman in these vehicles will get divorced from the public and you'll lose your contact.[44]

Meanwhile, the Home Office was so impressed with the results that it offered financial support for the purchase of panda cars and personal radios to any chief constable willing to set up a similar scheme. This measure gave support to the rupture of many of the links connecting the policeman with the local community, and to the creation of a more inward looking police culture, whereby a constable in constant touch with his headquarters would ask for advice and receive directives rather than relying on his own initiative. Perhaps for this reason, the unit beat system of policing was regarded with some reserve and hostility by many serving officers. At the time, Cain noted the resentment of men who felt that their status derived from their traditional independence, and who were not attracted to the

---

42 Lancashire, one of the largest provincial forces in the country had already made considerable moves towards the mechanization of beat patrols under its Chief Constable, Eric St Johnstone (who took up the post in 1950). By 1957 the force had over 500 police-owned vehicles and more than half the force had been trained to drive. The watchword for the future, the assistant chief constable wrote in the first issue of the county force's magazine was 'mobility' and the aim was the complete mechanization of the force. Quoted *in Police Review*, 23 August 1957.

43 See the article by Colonel T.E. St Johnston, 'Mobility Answer to Police Shortage' *The Times*, 26 January 1966.

44 Interview with Chief Constable Wiseman, Lancashire police.

alternative being offered.[45] A similar view was expressed by Inspector Smith:

> PC Clinton at Rudderick was given a Velocet motorcycle. Now this is where the rot set in. He was given a motor cycle, I was on my push bike ... Something urgent needed doing, oh, send for Clinton, he's got a motor cycle ... and in the end Clinton was spending more time away from his beat than he was on it. The chief constable offered me a motor cycle on two occasions and I said, no thank you. I still feel it was the right decision, because seeing what had happened to Clinton I knew full well that if I had a motor bike I would be charging around all over the place and I wouldn't look after my beat. So I said, no thank you sir, I don't want one. Why not? It would be a lot easier for you. I said it wouldn't be. It would be a lot easier physically, but at the moment if I'm cycling along at a leisurely pace in a funny pointed hat and somebody wants to talk to me, they can see me coming. You can put your foot down, no need to get off the bike even, and you can natter, that's how half police work is done ... Unit beat policing was foisted on chief constables because they were so short of policemen ... if a chief constable accepted unit beat policing he would be given panda cars, he would be given personal radios ... and I think they accepted it with open arms ... I've still got a copy of a report I put in, in 1969, telling the chief constable what a load of rubbish it was. Because once you give a policeman a personal radio one would think that you've got marvellous technology and you can get hold of a constable any time you like ... They didn't look at the fact that, yes, its brilliant but what it does is to take away the initiative of that constable[46]

It took many years of experimentation, resistance and manpower shortages to arrive at this point of fundamental change to the century long system of beat policing. In most cases, neither chief constables nor men were wholeheartedly in favour, and the changes were often made against their better judgement. It cannot be emphasized too strongly, therefore, that in the eyes of the majority of policemen this juncture became the turning point which was to mark off the 'golden years' of policing most decisively from the period that followed.

---

45  Cain, *Society and the Policeman's Role*, p. 241.
46  Interview with Inspector Smith, West Sussex police.

# CHAPTER THREE

# Prospects and Careers

Whatever the nature of the system, advancement within it was always a police priority, although no one ever thought it was easily come by. Promotion, the chief goal of many a rookie and a topic of paramount concern, was widely held to be slow, hard and uncertain. On the plus side, every pc – once past their probationary period – was eligible for the highest posts, which is why the idea of direct recruitment to these ranks from outside the service was so fiercely resisted and resented. But in practice, given the small proportion of chiefs to Indians at any one time in each force, recruits believed that only a limited percentage would ever move beyond sergeant, or even constable, since the waiting period for promotion had been known to stretch out over years and decades. There has, however, been little historical research to date to put precise figures on the English policeman's chances of promotion.

The outstanding exception is the article by Haia Shpayer-Makov, whose calculations for the Metropolitan police early in the twentieth century provide a benchmark.[1] Shpayer-Makov found that after serving their probation, only a quarter of the sample drawn from a decade of recruits ever rose above the rank of constable. She analysed the factors that were associated with a stronger chance of promotion, and found these included previous non-manual occupation (especially as clerks) and better levels of education. For a later period, Reiner's study confirmed that there were indeed consistent differences between the promoted and the non-promoted that correlated with the pc's previous job. Thus, despite the stress laid on an ethos of equality of conditions and opportunity, a tendency for those in supervisory grades to have attended secondary school and to have held non-manual jobs prior to joining the police held good over the half century covered by the two studies.[2]

---

1 Haia Shpayer-Makov (1991) 'Career Prospects in the London Metropolitan Police in the Early Twentieth Century', *Journal of Historical Sociology*.

2 Reiner, *The Blue-Coated Worker*, pp, 155–7. Shpayer-Makov's claim that differences in the success rate between non-manual and manual workers were not maintained later in the century is based on a mis-reading of Reiner here. While Reiner states that there was little difference between the grades as regards non-manual *class* origin, it remained the case that previous non-manual *job* experience continued to advantage those aspiring for promotion. Shpayer-

A distinguishing feature of the police service was that all who enrolled in it had to start at the bottom as probationary constables and to serve a minimum number of years before they could sit the qualifying exams for the next step up the ladder. In our period, this was two and four years respectively, with only a few of the highest posts open to outside or direct recruitment. As Shpayer-Makov notes, the fact that every officer started off on the same footing without fear of competition from outside nominees meant that the system of promotion offered more equal opportunities (to men) than that of most other work organizations. Nevertheless, given the pyramidical structure of the organization, many who qualified for higher positions never managed to achieve promotion, and clear structured differences between the promoted and non-promoted remained. She has calculated that promotion rates for those entering the Metropolitan police between 1889 and 1909, and excluding those who left within the first five years, was around twenty-five per cent (starting from twenty-three per cent in 1889 and rising to thirty-one per cent in 1909).

The norm calculated for the present study looks very different. This has been derived from data in the police registers for Birmingham City, for Cardiff City and for Warwickshire County police forces in the 1930s, with a sample taken from all three.[3]

---

Makov has used the previous occupation of recruits to stand for their social class origin, but – as Reiner shows – the two are not necessarily the same. The police records on which Shpayer-Makov built her case unfortunately do not note father's occupation, so that her conclusions regarding social class origins within the promotion system remain somewhat flawed.

3 Access to police personnel files is highly restricted for outside researchers. In the present instance I was fortunate to be granted access to the Birmingham files, courtesy of the deputy chief constable, and to the Warwickshire files (which have been deposited at the WCRO) with special police permission. For Cardiff, I am indebted to the South Wales police museum curator, Jeremy Glenn and his staff, who kindly extracted the data for me. The careers of one sixth of all recruits to the Birmingham police in the 1930s were noted (n=103); while for Warwickshire, details for all recruits entering in four sample years in the 1930s were extracted (n=122), as were those for all recruits to Cardiff City in the 1930s (n=68).

Table 3.1a: *Promotion rates for 1930s entrants: Birmingham City, Cardiff City and Warwickshire County police*

|              | Constable | Sergeant | Inspector & above | transferred /died | resigned/ dismissed |
|--------------|-----------|----------|-------------------|-------------------|---------------------|
|              | %         | %        | %                 | %                 | %                   |
| Birmingham   | 17        | 13       | 9                 | 7                 | 54                  |
| Warwickshire | 18        | 14       | 20                | 3                 | 45                  |
| Cardiff      | 12        | 56       | 18                | 4                 | 10                  |
| n =          | 46        | 69       | 44                | 15                | 119                 |

Table 3.1b: *Promotion rates for 1930s entrants, excluding those transferred/died/resigned/dismissed: Birmingham City, Cardiff City and Warwickshire County police*

|              | Constable | Sergeant | Inspector & above |
|--------------|-----------|----------|-------------------|
|              | %         | %        | %                 |
| Birmingham   | 45        | 32       | 22                |
| Warwickshire | 34        | 27       | 39                |
| Cardiff      | 14        | 65       | 21                |
| n=           | 46        | 69       | 44                |

Tables 3.1a and b show the enormous improvement in the chance of promotion for police recruits in the 1930s. One apparent reason for these improved prospects in comparison with Shpayer-Makov's figures is that the present study excludes all those who died or resigned for one reason or another.[4] Whereas I exclude *all* resignations/dismissals prior to promotion, however long the recruit had served, Shpayer-Makov has only taken resignations within the first five years into account – which has the effect of reducing the promotion rate, since her potential pool of recruits is thereby greatly increased. However, this is not a realistic basis from which to calculate promotion rates since resignations continued for many years beyond the probationary period, as did the time before the first promotion took place. The average period of service before promotion in Shpayer-Makov's sample was eight to nine years. This had risen considerably by the later period. From the 1930s to the early 1960s, the average time it took to

---

4    Although men could be and were dismissed, the great majority who left were entered as resigning (although this could be an enforced resignation as well as a voluntary one).

be made sergeant was twelve years, with a further eight years to inspector. An informant from the West Sussex police, who was promoted to sergeant in 1960 after thirteen years service, reported you were thought lucky if you got made up in less than that time. The longest it took for anyone in the study sample to become sergeant was twenty six years – four years before his retirement – for one Staffordshire pc, while the shortest was four years for a post-war Lancashire pc, who ended up in the very highest position and was picked as a high-flyer from the start. However, most rates clustered around the average, with little discernible variation between urban and rural forces.[5]

The change in promotion prospects between the turn of the century and fifty years on appears to be based largely on the fact that the present study takes into account the very high rate of resignations, dismissals, transfers or deaths, which gave an improved chance of promotion to those who remained, even though this promotion might be long in coming. There were very rarely any promotions prior to ten years service. If one takes the average length of service as twenty-seven years (since officers could retire on pension after twenty-five years, but could go on for thirty) this works out – over a seventeen year period – not to a one in four chance of promotion but close to one in two and a half.[6] In addition, there was some slight structural change in the proportion of supervisory to other ranks. Thus, the average sergeant to pc ratio over the seventeen forces represented in the study rose from around twelve per cent in the mid 1930s to around fourteen per cent in the mid 1960s; while that of inspectors and higher ranks over the same period rose from an average five per cent to seven per cent [7]. In many ways, the 1930 intake was unlucky in the length of time it took to achieve promotion, since it found the promoted ranks filled with a majority of men who had joined shortly after the First World War and who were therefore

---

5    Maureen Cain had found a difference of three years in the promotion rates from constable to sergeant in favour of the urban forces in her study, with an average wait of twelve years in the city and fifteen years in the county before the first promotion. Waiting times seem to have lengthened by the late 1960s from those in the period under discussion here, probably representing a renewed promotion blockage after the early post-war round of promotions. See Cain, op.cit., p, 151.

6    The formula can be expressed mathematically as follows:

$$1: \frac{(4 \times 17)}{27}$$

I owe this formulation to David Fowler, of the Mathematics Institute, University of Warwick.

7    Source, *Annual Reports, Inspectors of Constabulary.*

not due to retire until the 1940s. Pre-war economies further reduced such chances – as in Liverpool, where fifty supervisory ranks were abolished shortly before the war.[8] The war itself then put an end to any promotions, so it was not until the early post-war period that a great rush of retirements made room for the men who had been waiting to move up the ladder. So although the wait was long, and many may have given up hope, the actual prospect was not as bleak for the 1930s cohort of recruits as presented in police mythology. Indeed, in the early post-war period the prospects were exceptionally good, as they had been after the First World War. Well under half of the 1930s entrants remained at constable level for the whole of their careers, even though at least three-quarters of the force at any given point in time was made up of such men. Chiefly as a result of the two World Wars, this wave-like process of promotion and stagnation was one that was to bedevil the service over long periods and give rise to strong feelings of resentment and sense of injustice. In periods of stagnation promotion was seen to be too slow, whilst at other periods it came in a rush, and tended to leave some long-serving pcs by the wayside, with younger men promoted over their heads. At the same time later recruits found themselves confronted by a solid block of newly promoted men whom they saw as an immoveable barrier to their own future promotion.[9] The figures in Tables 3.1a and b also make clear that there were extreme variations in promotion rates between different forces, with a very small percentage of the 1930s cohort in Cardiff remaining at constable level throughout their career, whilst a very high proportion in Warwickshire achieved promotion to inspector level or above. This is partly due to the fact that police establishments increased steadily (although unevenly) throughout the period in all forces, and with it the number of supervisory posts. But differences between the three forces under discussion still remain puzzling. If we take Birmingham as the 'norm' as far as these three are concerned, (since a decreasing proportion of promotions the higher one goes up the scale is what one would logically expect) then we need to understand why a similar distribution of ranks did not occur in the other two forces. As far as Warwickshire was concerned, part of the explanation lies in the fact that its establishment increase after the war was very much greater than in the other forces, and led to substantial internal reorganization.[10] New sub-divisions,

8   See Roy Ingleton (1994) *The Gentlemen at War: policing Britain 1939–45*, p. 7.
9   'Too many Chiefs and not enough Indians' is how pcs in the Warwickshire force expressed the promotion blockage they perceived in the post war years once the first wave of promotions was past. Information from WPC Gilbey, Warwickshire police.
10  Figures for increases in establishment are as follows:

such as administration or women police, were created that made space for the establishment of new supervisory ranks. These sub-divisions might encompass sub-inspectors, inspectors, chief inspector, superintendent and chief superintendent. Amalgamation with borough forces in the 1960s brought new additions. In the amalgamation with Coventry, for example, Warwickshire gained an inspector and created a new post of superintendent (later done away with) for women police.[11] In this way, the high proportion of promotions to inspector or above in Warwickshire may have been a one-off occurrence consequent on expansion and reorganization. High post-war vacancy and resignation rates will also have boosted the promotion chances of those who remained.

The outstanding feature of the Cardiff force, in contrast, was its stable workforce and extremely low vacancy and resignation rates throughout the whole period, due not only to a lack of alternative employment prospects but also to the close, harmonious work relations within the force that were commented on by most informants. 'Cardiff was like a family really ... Cardiff was the happiest police force in the country ... the Chief Constable (Mr Wilson) looked after the men's well-being' were the sort of comments made.[12] No one made similar comments about Warwickshire, where the pre-war Chief Constable, Commander Kemble, had a reputation for ferocious discipline, with the result – according to one informant – that 'Warwickshire was the most vicious and hard force in the country'.[13] Given the low resignation rate and late date of amalgamation with Glamorganshire (1969), as well as the moderate increase in establishment, the high proportion promoted to sergeant in Cardiff remains puzzling. Part of the explanation may once more lie in organizational factors. Until 1941 the police had automatically been required to act as firemen here. After that date, the firemen were separated from the police, leading to a loss of fourteen per cent of the 1930 intake. This was implemented without loss of establishment among the regular police, so that some of the higher posts formerly filled by firemen/police could have accrued to the regular police

|  | Cardiff | Birmingham | Warwickshire |
|---|---|---|---|
|  | % | % | % |
| 1935–1947: | 17 | 23 | 31 |
| 1947–1957: | 12 | 1 | 16 |
| 1957–1964: | 12 | 13 | 35 |

Source: *Annual Reports Inspectors of Constabulary*

11  Information from WPC Gilbey, Warwickshire police.
12  Interviews with PC Lench, Inspector Slater and Inspector Moody, Cardiff City police.
13  Interview with PC Price, Warwickshire police.

force, and may help to account for the large number of sergeant posts. But whatever the explanation, it is clear that the police forces of England and Wales remained as unstandardized in their members' promotion prospects as they did in so many other aspects of their work organization and ethos.

On what did promotion depend, other than the chance of joining a force where the prospects were good? Partly one needed to pass the relevant exams, but this was a minimum requirement rather than a qualification leading automatically to higher things, and not all who passed their sergeants, and indeed their inspectors exam, moved on beyond constable. Supply was only one part of the equation. The question therefore needs to be asked whether some had intrinsically greater promotion prospects than others. What was the background of the men who were promoted? Were there any particular features, such as previous non-manual occupations mentioned by Shpayer-Makov, that proved advantageous? The following table indicates the position:

Table 3.2: *Social Class Origins, Previous Occupation and Policeman Father by Rank*

| Rank Achieved | Inspector+ | Sergeant | Constable |
|---|---|---|---|
| Social Class Origin | | | |
| Non-manual | 9 | 4 | 3 |
| Skilled manual | 18 | 10 | 8 |
| Semi/unskilled | 6 | 8 | 8 |
| Previous Occupation | | | |
| Non-manual | 12 | 5 | 2 |
| Skilled manual | 7 | 8 | 4 |
| Semi/unskilled | 14 | 9 | 13 |
| Policeman Father | 7 | 1 | |

The information contained in Table 3.2 points to a number of interesting correlations. Firstly, social class origin does not seem to have made as much material difference on achieved rank as holding a non-manual job prior to joining the police, or having a policeman as father. This finding corroborates that of Shpayer-Makov and of Reiner[14]. The chief finding, however, is that if high social class did not confer much benefit on a police career, neither did lower social class origin prove a barrier to those achieving the rank of Inspector and above. Upward mobility to this rank applied to thirty-two per cent of the male sample from manual class

14  Reiner, op.cit., p, 155.

backgrounds, and to twenty-eight per cent of the sample who had previously held a manual job. Thus there was substance to official pronouncements that joining the police was a career based on equal (male) opportunity.

If social class had little positive influence, what other factors entered the equation? How did the promotion system actually function? The picture, as so often in the organizational history of English policing, is somewhat confused. In the counties, promotion was in the hands of the chief constable. In the boroughs, both the Desborough (1919–20) and Oaksey (1949) Committees, which had reviewed the power of watch committees to appoint, promote and act as disciplinary authority, recommended giving borough chief constables the same exclusive powers as the county chiefs. But these recommendations had not been put into effect, and the 1960 Royal Commission itself reversed these former recommendations by supporting the existing powers of watch committees, since 'We consider that the need to justify a (promotion) proposal to a committee is salutary'.[15] However, the RC did lend its support to Oaksey's proposal for the setting up of promotion boards composed of senior police officers, to ensure that police recommendations were based on a fair appraisal. Up to this time, little progress had been made in that direction, with the Police Federation reporting only twenty-four forces where promotion boards had been established, while in sixty forces the chief constable consulted informally with his senior officers, and in sixteen no consultations were held at all.[16]

In our period, therefore, it seems that promotion boards were the exception rather than the rule. It was already an advance that promotion exams for sergeant and inspector had to be passed before a man could be considered for advancement. Before the First World War, promotion – outside the Metropolitan police – was largely based on seniority tempered by fitness. Since that time, compulsory educational exams meant that many senior men found themselves left behind, with the result that 'promotion has almost come to be fitness hampered by seniority'.[17] The *Police Review*, in a discussion of the situation, concluded that although qualifying promotion exams improved educational levels and raised the social status of the police, there was something to be said for the old system, which was based on an assessment of 'the whole man' and took into account his capacity for leadership and responsibility, qualities which lay outside the scope of written examinations. Many chief officers, especially in rural areas, will have agreed. Sergeant Hulme, from the Stafforshire constabulary, recounted

15  *RC on the Police 1960–62*, vol. 11–12, pp. 628–9.
16  Ibid., Evidence submitted by the Police Federation of England and Wales, p. 1027.
17  *Police Review*, 12 June 1931.

that that the chief constable there used to draw a line down the list of names put forward for promotion, and promote whom he wished.[18] One reason no doubt, in a conservative and tradition-bound service, was the fear and suspicion in which book learning and academicism were held, particularly by supervisory officers whose formal educational experience had not lasted longer than their first fourteen years. The passionate outbursts against the Hendon college boys of Trenchard's ill-fated officer class scheme make this clear time and again. Such men, in the view of the majority of pcs, had no idea what policing entailed, and all their book learning was no substitute for the years of hard won experience that went to make the *practical policeman*, who was the ideal bobby as far as established officers were concerned. Exams were therefore a concession to the modern world, as well as a way of automatically limiting the supply of candidates for what were always going to be a limited number of places.

Exams, it must have seemed to many chief constables, were enough of a concession without the need to introduce promotion boards in addition. But doubtless the main objection was that supervisory officers, and chief constables in particular, saw the bestowal of promotion as an important aspect of their own prerogative of patronage and discipline. This was certainly how the system was viewed by the men. According to Inspector Hay, there were three ways in which you could get promotion: having the same religion as the chief constable; marrying into a police family, preferably a superintendent's daughter; and if all else failed, working hard and coming to the superintendent's notice:

> In those days, the police force consisted of two things. One was Catholicism and one was Freemasonry. If you had a chief constable who was a Roman Catholic, all the promotions came from that side of religion. If the next one ... was a Freemason, a Freemason would get it. So if you weren't either, and I wasn't, you had to do it by hard work, you had to show yourself and come to the top that way.[19]

Others mentioned the advantage of sharing the chief constable's interests. Thus Sergeant Craig recounted that the best way to get promotion under Chief Constable Dain in Norwich was to put in spare time at his Lads' Club, of which he was the proud initiator, and with which he had won nation-wide recognition:

> ... some of the promotions were very hard to justify, you had little faith in some of the sergeants and inspectors because you wondered why on earth they had ever been promoted ... looking back, you can see how most of the promotions were made and why. Mention has

18 Interview with Sergeant Hulme, Staffordshire police.
19 Interview with Inspector Hay, Birmingham City police.

been made of the Lads' Club. That was a sound route to promotion.
If you were willing to give up your spare time and assist in the Club
then that was a certain door to early promotion. Most of the
promotions were done for that reason by the old chief constable, I'm
quite sure of that myself ... Later on, with the new chief constable,
the great thing was sporting activities. That was the main reason for
promotion.[20]

Sports were certainly a useful way to get preferential treatment with chief
constables who were keen that their own football, or swimming, or rowing
teams should come top of the police league table. Favouritism based on
qualities or connections that had nothing to do with the job thus clearly
played a part in helping or hindering some men's careers. More important,
however, were those factors that related more directly to internal police
requirements. A major concern here was to ensure the supply of suitable
candidates, which first surfaced as a problem in the early post-war years.
Similarly high productivity, the willing acceptance of orders to move from
one place or specialism to another, and above all the ability to keep in the
superintendent's good books, were all regarded as necessary features for a
well-ordered force. Above all, it was the chief constable who set the tone
and made the policy decisions that filtered down to every pc in the force.
The extent of the autonomous power and influence of these men throughout
the period can hardly be sufficiently stressed. Whether responsible for large
urban forces or county or borough forces made no difference: their word
within the force was law, their style and preferences prevailed. Thus, Chief
Constable Dain was able to focus the attention of his force on work with
juveniles in the police Lad's Club; Chief Constable Martin took up the
challenge with his juvenile liaison scheme in Liverpool; Commander
Kemble was obsessed with traffic offences, and deployed such large
numbers on traffic duty that his figures for traffic offences were the highest
in the country;[21] Chief Constable Wilson, who was much admired and
revered by his Cardiff force for the concern he showed for his mens'
welfare remained staunchly and adamantly opposed to the admittance of
women into the service; the chief constable of Colchester, Colonel
Stockwell, selected men on the basis of their brawn and boxing prowess –
as opposed to Birmingham's chief constable Dodd, who cared less for
physique than meticulous attention to correct procedure in accordance with

20  Interview with Sergeant Craig, Norwich City police.
21  Chief Constable Kemble was a martinet who would brook no opposition, to the
    extent that the *Police Review* called for a Home Office inquiry into his fitness to
    exercise 'the very autocratic powers vested in county chief constables'. *Police
    Review*, 5 September 1941.

the law;[22] while Colonel Eric St Johnstone, an ardent modernizer, was instrumental in pushing forward a policy of policing by panda car. Each chief constable's views and predilictions thus found expression in what could have a very material effect on policing routines and relations with the public.[23]

Within this orbit of power, outside pressures exerted their influence. The need to attract and reward men returning from the war was liable to become a source of grievance. The promotion of younger men over the heads of longer serving bobbies caused much resentment in a service where seniority was still basically regarded as the fairest way of deciding who should be promoted. This unwritten law was severely dented at the end of the war when the need to attract and retain returning police officers meant that many who had attained some rank in the services were offered promotion over the heads of the older men. One who suffered in this way was Sergeant Dunhill:

> The old chief constables, Sir Charles Rafter and CC Moriarty ... their idea was that nobody got promoted until they'd got at least ten years service in ... Then the war came and the chaps that had gone back in the services, they'd probably gained rank in the services, and when they came back they expected to gain some rank in the police. The chief constable ... promoted them after they'd done about four years service. Well, I was in between the two and was being used as acting sergeant, office man and everything else and eventually I had an interview with the chief constable ... and they did start promoting the older men after that, and I received congratulations from some of the older chaps.[24]

Inspector Archer had a similar tale to tell:

> We had a new Chief Constable, Eric St Johnstone, oh, he sorted the old lot out alright. He had no use for the old type superintendents, used to treat them like dirt... The only snag with him was that if you'd been in the army and got a rank you automatically got

---

22 Dodd, one of the first chief constables to emerge from Trenchard's officer class training scheme, was not interested in keeping to the height requirements so much as recruiting men of the right moral character. His recruits accordingly became known as 'Dodd's dwarfs' – but any hint of transgression of the rules was enough to deny men the chance of promotion.

23 While this typology does not clearly conform with the county-borough distinction between chief constables posited by Reiner, it is certainly the case that the scope of their autonomous decision making turned them into 'lonely men of power'. See R. Reiner(1991) *Chief Constables: Bobbies, Bosses or Bureaucrats?* p. 344.

24 Interview with Sergeant Dunhill, Birmingham City police.

promoted – at our expense, I mean some of us had had to stop here
and keep the force going.[25]

The promotion of younger men was not only resented because it was 'out of
turn' but because those who had had to wait many years accepted that
promotion and years of experience ought to go hand in hand. Sergeant
Lane, for example, believed that nowadays men were made up much too
early. 'You get some today made up in their twenties, and they don't seem
to have grown up. I don't think they've had enough experience of the
outside world, they don't know how to speak to people'.[26]

But even in the old days, it was not so much the ability to speak to people
that counted, but rather how you got on with your senior officers. Lack of
promotion was often ascribed to being too outspoken, to answering back, or
to having a 'face that didn't fit'. Conversely, being in the right place at the
right time, and prepared to go out of one's way helped considerably in the
promotion stakes. Superintendent Batey was given an early start up the
ladder by his transfer to the Chief Constable's office very early on in his
career. He had three years at headquarters, with the result that

> I had lost all fear of rank. Because you know, the superintendent, he
> holds your whole life in his hands. If he recommended you, you got
> on. If you upset him, he didn't recommend you and you didn't get
> on, it was as simple as that. There was no promotion board or
> anything to go into, it was just his say so ... But I was promoted
> after six years. And I was no more fit to be a sergeant than fly to the
> moon in the light of what a sergeant did and should do. The average
> in those days was eleven or twelve years before you were made
> sergeant ...[27]

Chief Constable Wiseman, who also soared swiftly to the top, owed much
of his success to his willingness to work all hours of the day and night. By
pure coincidence, his path crossed that of the new Chief Constable, Eric St
Johnstone, whose personal assistant was going on holiday.

> I happened to be at headquarters one Saturday morning as a very
> young chap, and Eric said to me 'my PA's going away on holiday, I
> want you to come and look after me'. Yes sir, I said ... So then I had
> to go home to face my wife and three kids with the car already
> packed to go on holiday ... Well, Eric St Johnstone was the sort of
> person who was incredibly forward looking, and absolutley dynamic
> in everything he did. He believed in bringing on young people and
> creating opportunity. But he expected absolute dedication in return.
> That wasn't difficult, it was the easiest thing in the world. I suppose

25  Interview with Inspector Archer, Durham City police.

26  Interview with Sergeant Lane, Sheffield City police.

27  Interview with Superintendent Batey, Staffordshire police.

> I had the attitude, if the chief wants to stay there seven days and seven nights a week then I would too. It was a pleasure, it was a privilege.[28]

On the other hand, many of those who were not prepared to accede to the wishes of their superiors found that their chance of promotion had evaporated. This was particularly the case when men refused a new posting, on the grounds that they did not want to upset their families, and especially their childrens' educational situation. PC Seaforth, PC Walker, Sergeant Foulkes, Sergeant Carling and Inspector Astley were all denied further promotion on these grounds. Others felt that they had stayed too long in specialist divisions where the chances of promotion were less than elsewhere – either in traffic, in CID, or on a suburban beat where there was little chance of being noticed. Those in one specialism tended to see more openings for promotion in another, on the principle that the grass is always greener on the other side. But occasionally there were examples of downright vindictiveness that held up or put a stop to a man's promotion, and which gave meaning to the excessive awe and fear in which many superintendents were held. Sergeant Richards gave his superintendent as an example, who told a young station sergeant:

> 'Quite frankly, you're a smart alec, you've got your degree, but you're not getting any further while I'm chief superintendent'. [29]

As Sergeant Richards pointed out, there was no redress to that in those days. PC Waterford is another case in point. He had had a run-in with his superintendent in which he had proved him wrong, and ever after this had been held as a mark against him. PC Waterford had long passed his sergeant's exam, but found when he finally made the promotion board that a man who had several times failed his exam was promoted over his head. PC Waterford was sure that:

> Sandy got passed and I got cooked. Now the only person who could cook me was the superintendent who sat on the board ... he didn't take any part when it was any of his men, but it didn't stop him putting his poison in ...[30]

While some higher ranks thus abused their position to bully, coerce, corrupt or keep down those serving under them, the fear they inspired rested directly on their power over the pcs career prospects. This was especially so in urban forces where there were more cases to be had for the asking than in

---

28  Interview with Chief Constable Wiseman, Lancashire police.
29  Interview with Sergeant Richards, Metropolitan police
30  Interview with PC Waterford, Metropolitan police.

rural areas, and where promotion and productivity tended to march forward together. Sergeant Dunhill described the pressure this exerted on pcs to bring charges:

> When I passed my promotion examination in 1938 you got your top rate of pay two years early, you got it after eight years service instead of ten ... the wording of it was 'subject to special zeal, intelligence and proficiency'. In actual fact it meant getting a certain number of cases. And I was the subject of this. I applied for this rise and I was turned down because they said I'd only had twenty-eight cases in the last twelve months ... The Superintendent said 'I'm afraid you haven't got your rise because you don't have sufficient number of cases ... there's another chap here, he's got 128 for the same period, you've only got twenty something'. I said, 'Yes, but they're only children playing football in the street'. And of course he went up in the air 'It's nothing to do with you, it's all cases as far as you are concerned'.[31]

The rationale behind this system was explained by Sergeant Martin:

> Discipline on the beats was terribly, terribly strict. It was the system. The system of promotion in those days was by selection, it wasn't competitive, I mean nowadays they work out that this year they need 150 sergeants, so all the constables sit an exam and the first 150, subject to being approved, get in. In those days, if you got through your promotion exams, you were added to what they called the zone of selection, and you came up every year from your division. You might have fifty or sixty who were eligible for promotion and they only wanted one or two. So those who had got to sergeant, to get to inspector, they had to show what great disciplinarians they were, they would go up and they would be asked 'How many defaulters have you had?'. That meant that the sergeants were really just out to catch the pcs ... It was the system. The higher up the tree, the bigger dictator you had to be ... there weren't many nice inspectors. They had got there purely by putting the boot in.[32]

Thus, although the chances of promotion in the period under discussion were much better than they appeared at first sight to the 1930s cohort of recruits, promotion was still perceived by this group to be governed by chance, by favouritism and by the personal predilictions of senior officers who held the pcs fate in their hands; where even the sergeant could be looked on as 'a holy being'[33] and where the chief constable was 'monarch of

---

31  Interview with Sergeant Dunhill, Birmingham City police.
32  Interview with Sergeant Martin, Metropolitan police.
33  Interview with Chief Inspector Sheen, Norfolk police.

all he surveyed'.[34] The desire for promotion thereby became a potent means of enforcing discipline in a service that gave full play to the whims and prejudices of the divisional superintendent, and where there were few sources of redress or courts of appeal over his head against any real or imagined injustices.[35]

---

34 Interview with Detective Inspector Aylesham, Durham County police.

35 The Police Federation, the nearest approximation to a trade union for the police, was a toothless body, especially in the pre-war period, which did not begin to carry some weight until after the 1960 Royal Commission. Indeed, several informants remarked that too great an involvement in the Federation was a sure way of blocking a pc's promotion chances.

# CHAPTER FOUR

# Policing the Motorist

We now turn to consider the work of the specialist branches, starting with that of the traffic departments. The car, which changed life for many people, changed life drastically for the police. The implications for traffic policing will be considered here in relation to policy and reorganization after the passing of the 1930 Road Traffic Act, even though traffic regulation had long been a task undertaken by the police. We tend to think of traffic problems as something that has grown up with the growth of motorized traffic, but traffic regulation in urban areas formed a large part of police work since the very inception of statutory police forces in Britain. Keeping traffic flowing while enabling drivers to load and unload and cabbies and street sellers to conduct their business without causing obstruction has been one of the perennial balancing acts required of the police. Similarly, the typical response has always been a mixture of resentment and acquiescence. Nor was passive resistance the only reaction in pre-car days. Just as the Automobile Association (AA) was formed as protector of the motorist against the traffic laws, so by the turn of the century street sellers and costermongers had banded together to found trade protection societies in several towns, to preserve their right to free trading, and to provide legal assistance against vexatious prosecutions.[1] What the motorcar did was to export these and other traffic problems to the countryside and small towns and villages, and to extend police/driver encounters to a wider, more middle class and more vocal public. The motorcar driving public was different to that of cab drivers and costermongers, and one where the police were not so sure of their ground in expecting an automatic acceptance of their authority. It was also the scale of the problem and the seriousness of the damage inflicted that was new. But, largely because the law now drew a social group previously unaccustomed to police attention into its net, both police and public were slow to adapt to the criminal and public order problems this entailed.

At first, motoring was seen as a rich man's sport, with offenders against the traffic laws and the 20 mph speed limit stigmatized by the press and the Automobile Association as 'road hogs'. According to *The Times*, such

---

1   See C.E.B. Russell and E.T.Campagnac (1900) 'The Organization of Costermongers and Street Vendors in Manchester' *Economic Review*, X.

people were drawn from a class that possessed money in excess of brains or culture.[2] In other words, since gentlemen were unlikely to break the law and drive without due care and consideration, it could only be cads who would behave in this manner. This optimistic assumption was supported by most of the motoring public and even by some police officers, who felt embarrassed at having to chastise or summons members of a class with whom they were normally on deferential terms. Thus as late as the end of the 1920s, the Chief Constable of Staffordshire warned his men against too rigorous an application of the traffic laws. Too often, he said,

> (motorists) are treated as if they were running off with someone's purse or were suspected of being incendiaries, or what not. Such people are not malefactors: they may be persons of the utmost respectability of character and position, by accident brought, so to speak, into collision with the law: and common sense requires that they should not be treated as possible criminals.[3]

But even where the police were not given such partisan instructions, they were generally aware of and extremely sensitive to the fact that police/motorists encounters were changing the positive image of the police held by the respectable majority of the population. Indeed, as they told the Royal Commission on the Police in 1929, they would have preferred that some other body such as the motoring organizations take over the management of traffic.[4] This suggestion was not taken up, but the police's difficulties with motorists were acknowledged by the Minister of Transport, Herbert Morrison when he introduced the Road Traffic Bill in 1930. Its main proposal was the abolition of the 20 mph speed limit, on the grounds that:

> It is an exceptional thing in Great Britain for a law to be almost universally disregarded ... The police ... are in an impossible position. Nominally they have to enforce the law. In fact they know that the law is not supported by the general body of public opinion, and they tolerate breaches of the law which now exists. This is not a fair position in which to place the police. If the law is there, the police should be expected to enforce it ... If the public do not expect it to be enforced, ... well the British police have enough common

---

2   W. Plowden (1971) *The Motor Car and Politics, 1896–1970*, p. 43.

3   Staffordshire Constabulary Archives, Chief Constable's Memo Book, 27 September 1929. Quoted in Clive Emsley (1993) '"Mother, what *did* policemen do when there weren't any motors?" The Law, the Police and the regulation of motor traffic in England 1900–1939'. *Historical Journal*, 36, 2.

4   Plowden, *The Motor Car*, p. 378.

sense not to be too meticulous in enforcing laws which are not in accordance with the general body of public opinion.[5]

With the passing of the Act, the police were absolved from enforcing a non-regarded speed limit, but at the cost of having to decide what constituted dangerous driving and of distinguishing it from the new offence of careless driving. Unfortunately, the move from the general application of an unpopular law to discretionary power over motorists did nothing to restore good police/driver relations. On the contrary, it exacerbated fears of arbitrary police power; and even the Police Federation paper, the *Police Review* foresaw trouble in basing cases on the judgement of one pc.[6] It also immediately provoked the sort of objections that were to characterize pc/motorist relations from that time onwards. 'Will the Under-Secretary arrange that the police pay less attention to motor cars and more to burglars' was the cry raised in parliament.[7] At the same time, a new breed of 'road hogs' (or an early manifestation of 'ton-up boys') emerged, who were able to cock a snook at the police if they tried to catch them. These were gangs of motor cyclists who used to race each other on the newly built bypasses around cities, and whom the police in their Morris cars were unable to catch.[8]

For the police, however, the chief impact of the 1930 Road Traffic Act was not so much on police/public relations as on the police organization itself, since in tandem with the lifting of the speed limit, the Home Office had made clear that all but the smallest forces would be expected to set up motor patrol units to monitor and advise the motoring public. Unwittingly, by recommending the establishment of police motor patrols to supervise the working of the Road Traffic Act, fundamental change in the form of motorization was introduced into the service. There were two aspects to this: first, the development of specialist departments with their own traffic policing policy; and more importantly, motorization as a way of maximizing the use of police manpower, with all the consequences this had on policing strategies.

---

5   *HC Debs 5s*, 235, 10 Feb, 1930.

6   *Police Review*, 12 December 1930.

7   *HC Debs 5s,* 251, 15 April 1931. This comment came after it was revealed that there had been 350 burglaries in the MPD in 1930.

8   Jock West, the motor-cycle racer, described how groups would meet on Sundays to lay bets and race each other up and down the Bexley Heath or Rochester by-pass, ending up in a pub get-together. The police were totally unable to catch them, but would get their own back by issuing summonses for some other traffic offence. Private communication, courtesy of Steve Koerner.

If we turn first to the development of specialist traffic departments, these owed their existence chiefly to grants from the Ministry of Transport's Road Fund for the establishment of police motor patrols, as part of the implementation of the Road Traffic Act. These grants provided for 1000 vehicles (one third cars, and two thirds motor bikes) for the various police forces, giving an average of five vehicles for each of the 183 separate forces in England and Wales. Local police authorities were, of course, free to supplement this number, and several had already done so. In the metropolitan area, for instance over 300 pcs were appointed to motor patrols in 1930;[9] while other forces might make do with only a few motor bikes. But by 1938 Merioneth was the only force without a police patrol car.[10] Nevertheless, whatever the level of motorization, it was the universal introduction of police vehicles into county and borough forces that was noteworthy, and the effects were soon noticeable within the service. For a start, recruiting took this new orientation into account. Recruits had to pass certain minimum standards of height, physical fitness and education in order to get in to the police, and in the early 1930s, at the height of the depression, only a small proportion of applicants were successful out of the hundreds who applied. But the study sample shows that driving skills or knowledge of car mechanics stood applicants in good stead, while the possibility of working in a police traffic division motivated several to apply in the first place. PC Selby is a good example. He did an apprenticeship as a motor mechanic, but was thrown out of work in 1931, when someone suggested to him that he join the police, since they were looking for mechanics and drivers. So he joined Neath Borough police and was soon receiving special increments above the basic police wage because he was on car maintenance, as well as acting as police driver. Another recruit, the son of a pc, who had grown up with motor bikes and had taught himself to drive on his father's Triumph joined the police in 1934 specifically in order to get in to the traffic department. As he recalled, motor cars were the thing, and it was more or less the ambition of all young recruits to apply for traffic. Driving a police car at a time when few working class lads could afford one was certainly seen as the next best thing to car ownership.

The idea of the motor patrols that came in with the abolition of the speed limit was as an extension of the general principle of preventive policing, on which policing in Britain was based. These patrols were intended to supervise motorists and prevent accidents by guiding and checking rather

9   Report Metropolitan Commissioner of Police, *PP XVI* 1930–31.

10  *Police Review*, 22 July 1938.

than actually arresting people,[11] and the police were instructed to issue warnings instead of summonses for minor traffic offences. In the metropolis, 79,000 cases were dealt with in this way in 1930, with only 19,000 cases reported for process.[12] But this softly softly approach did not prevent public criticism, with the usual jibes in Parliament over whether, in view of the need for economy, it would not be better to employ the police in catching criminals rather than in joy-riding and harrassing the motoring public for purely technical offences.[13]

This perception, that the police were ignoring 'real' crime in their pursuit of motorists, was to bedevill police/public relations for decades to come. Ironically, large sections of the police shared the public's view in the matter. Beat policemen, in particular, did not consider the work of the traffic department to be real policing. Inspector Archer gave voice to this view when he said that:

> There's a terrific divide ... The traffic pc, he liked to sit down all the time, they were tired men, very tired, they were not pcs, never have been. A traffic pc, he's out on the road and he knows what he's looking for, he's out to pinch motorists ... We were the practical men on the job, these fellows ... well, these fellows were never pcs.. One night I was standing in the police station in Durham and there was a chief inspector on traffic and a superintendent and another fellow and I'd been called in off the streets from north Durham 'you're wanted at the police station, there's a drunk in charge been brought in'. And I said, 'What's the matter with you people, have you got cloth hands or something'? The thing was, they couldn't take a charge, they didn't know anything about it. You were either a working man or you weren't in those days, these were traffic men, see. 'Oh, no, we don't do this, we're specialists, we don't accept charges' was their attitude.[14]

Police on the other side of the divide naturally took a different view, although they too were conscious that they were different from the other police. Sergeant Tome of the Metropolitan police sought to join the traffic department because he thought it would be better than the soul destroying work of the beat; and indeed he found that the traffic were a close knit little community where discipline was less harsh than elsewhere. Working in traffic also allowed pcs wider use of discretion than on the beat, since they were encouraged to educate road users rather than charge or summons them. How this discretion was used was very much up to each pc or his superior

11  *HC Debs 5s*, 279, 1933.
12  Commissioner report, op.cit.
13  *HC Debs 5s*, 257, 1930–31, 194–5; *HC Debs 5s*, 260, 1931–32 2034.
14  Interview with Inspector Archer, Durham County police.

officer to decide. Inspector Ford's rule of the thumb was that he would advise, unless they argued; and this seems to have been the common attitude. But the leeway to bring in traffic offenders was there, since finding such people was as easy as falling off a log. They were there for the taking, no rear lights on bicycles, no parking lights, number plate obscured, the list was endless. Quite often pcs were told by their sergeants to go and book a few lawbreakers. Car offenders were the easiest. One young pc, for example was brought in to see his chief inspector, who said to him

> 'Now look, lad, you can't go on like this, you've been here nearly a year and you haven't been to court yet.' 'But I've only seen trivial things' said the pc. But the Inspector replied 'these trivial things are still offences.' So the lad went out and the following year he had 365 cases in court, bicycle not right, rear lamp off, parking on the wrong side of the road, anything ...'[15]

But strict surveillance and prosecution brought its own dilemmas. The 1930 Road Traffic Act had not been able to ameliorate the problem of road accidents, so that when the number of road casualties began to rise in the first few years after the lifting of the speed limit, pressure mounted for its reintroduction. In consequence, a new Road Traffic Act in 1934 brought in a 30 mph speed limit in built up areas. The police response was mixed, since many felt it would put them back to the position of having a speed limit which would be unenforceable in practice[16] and would mean a great deal of extra work. Others, however, welcomed the restrictions under the Act, and there are numerous accounts of the ways in which traffic pcs came to maximize their checks on motorists. The Warwickshire chief constable is simply an extreme example. He was particularly keen on such checks, and put half his force on traffic duties. Not surprisingly, the county soon had the highest rate of motor prosecutions in the country, at more than double the national average, there was an outcry, and the local police committee was eventually forced, after several more years of intensive police action against motorists, to set up an inquiry because of the number of complaints received.[17] This showed how intolerable intensive police surveillance of motorists was felt to be.

---

15  Interview with Superintendent Clarke, Liverpool police.

16  Plowden, *The Motor Car,* p. 275.

17  *Police Review,* 7 Feb, 1936; 29 Jan, 1937.

## The Courtesy Cops Scheme

Meanwhile, the government waited to see the results of the new Traffic Act. With more cars coming on the roads, a rising number of road casualties was more or less inevitable, and the government was soon faced with the now familiar dilemma of effective enforcement and a disgruntled public versus good public relations and less effective policing. The chief constable of Cardiff was in no doubt about his choice. He had operated a plain clothes patrol for the first six months of 1936 and prosecuted 963 offenders, as against thirty-eight offenders in the subsequent six months when his officers were put back in uniform. In his view, motorists would break the law if they were satisfied that they were not likely to be caught; the result of his experiment convinced him that he was justified in reverting to plain clothes patrols.[18] Other authorities, including the government, were not prepared to face the outcry against such 'un-British methods'. In 1937, therefore, the Home Secretary announced an experimental motor patrol scheme to be carried out in Lancashire, Essex and the MPD. Its purpose would be to educate road users in the proper observance of the new Highway Code, rather than to increase the number of cases taken to court. 800 men were to be recruited and trained, with the cost borne by the Treasury. The scheme was dubbed 'the courtesy cops' and it ran from early 1938 to the beginning of the war, with key recruits receiving training in London from the former racing driver, the Earl of Cottenham. The scheme was  pronounced a success: in Lancashire there were reported to be forty-six per cent less accidents in the first six months than for the corresponding period the year previously, prosecutions were reduced by fifty per cent and nearly half a million people were advised or cautioned; while the county force was augmented by 331 men, ninety-two cars and fifty motor bikes, at an estimated cost of over one million pounds.[19] This was a major investment on the part of the government. Whether it was more than a public relations exercise is open to doubt, despite the reduced accident figures just quoted. For one thing, it only operated for a short period in a limited area. To have extended it throughout the country would have meant saturating the roads with police cars and increasing the police establishment to a level that would have been financially unsustainable. As it was, there were sceptics about the scheme among the police. Inspector Brierley was in the Essex traffic division before the scheme started, and he recalled that:

---

18  *Police Review*, 26 Feb 1937.
19  *Police Review*, 28 October 1938; *Auto*car, 28 July 1939.

When I first joined, if an offence was committed, it was committed. But then ... we had the courtesy cop scheme. That was when discretion came in, yes, let's be nice to the customer for about 12 months. But up until that time, and after, no. *Were you on the scheme?* Yes. *And what did you think of it?* I thought it was excellent, it did a lot of good, more particularly with public relations ... *Did it improve the public's driving habits?* No. *And how did the motorists react to the police stopping them?* I think, as I recall, it was annoyance at being stopped in the first instance and relief for not being booked after that.[20]

Other criticisms, of the men who entered the scheme, came from another Essex pc who was already in the traffic division. He had this to say, when asked if he had anything to do with the courtesy cops:

Yes ... there was a big increase in the Traffic department to fulfill the needs of the courtesy system, and I felt that then we got fellows coming off the beat who weren't really particularly interested in driving as such, and that sort of work, ... they'd found beat life too difficult for them, and they were coming in to traffic for an easier life ... they hadn't really the great interest and background of a traffic department officer. *Do you think the scheme was any good?* Well, that's difficult to say. I think it could still have been done by a traffic department without filling cars with people who had no interest in, shall we say, the real side of police work. For instance, the superintendant who took over the department ... he wasn't really interested in catching the thieves aspect of our job, he was more interested in how many times you had stopped somebody and told them to clean their number plate or their windscreen ... And I felt the balance wasn't there ... You'd probably stop 20 or 30 drivers, and you didn't do any more when the courtesy scheme came along. You did it for more trivial things, just to keep the records.[21]

With the coming of war most traffic problems and schemes like the courtesy cops fell into abeyance and were not revived until the 1950s when there was a major road safety drive. This followed on the Select Committee report on the prevention of road accidents, which reiterated that the main object of police policy should be to educate and help rather than prosecute motorists, especially over technical offences. A modified form of the courtesy cop scheme was instituted in a number of forces, but this time without Treasury support. Coverage by traffic police was therefore proportionally much sparser than in the pre-war experimental period. Wolverhampton, for example, set up courtesy patrols on twelve major roads in the town and reduced the number of car accidents on these roads by more

20  Interview with Inspector Brierley, Essex County police.
21  Interview with Inspector Chambers, Essex County police.

than three-quarters. However, when drivers became aware of the police presence there, they switched routes, so that the overall accident rate was not reduced.[22] Preventive policing by car could only have worked – and even this is not certain – if set up on an immense scale, and would have been terribly expensive. As it was, motorists continued to complain of police harrassment over trivial offences, while the traffic police became tired of hearing the same excuses time and time again and lost their previously deferential attitude towards drivers. More commonly now, if a motorist threatened to pull rank, this would decide the pc in favour of a summons. In addition, the traffic pc was conscious of his authority in a way that underlined his difference from the beatman. 'In those days, when you didn't own a car, and you drove a big limousine with big signs on top, you were the real bees knees' one pc recalled. Another noted the difference, when he moved from beat work into traffic:

> It was a different sort of policing. One felt one had more power in some peculiar way. The people with whom one was dealing were passing in a car from A to B, as opposed to having regular people on the beat whom you met every day, and so in that sense one didn't have quite the same attitude ... one booked a motorist for speed, for driving licence or whatever, without the same kind of feeling that, oh, he's one of my locals, I'll handle him a bit gently ...[23]

It seems clear that the creation of a specialist traffic police had done little to improve police/motorist relations, which remained edgy at the best of times, however much the police were instructed to be nice to the customers. At the same time, it brought out a distinct difference of attitude between the beatman and the traffic cop. This difference was exacerbated by the impact of motorization on the police organization as a whole.

## Mechanization as a Substitute for Manpower

Naturally, the rise in car ownership, especially among criminals, stimulated police motorization. By the start of our period the police were asking for fast cars to help them deal with 'motor bandits' and 'smash and grab raiders', categories that had replaced road hogs as the new motorized scapegoats.[24] But the main impact of police motorization was not on new means of catching criminals, but as a substitute for police manpower. Quite

22  *Police Review*, 7 May 1954.
23  Interviews with Chief Constable Wiseman, Lancashire police and Inspector Chambers, Essex County police.
24  Further discussed in Chapter 8, p. 136.

apart from the need to police motorists, the growth of the suburbs which expanded dramatically in the inter-war period, stretched police resources to the limit. Established beats were being depleted to help cover outer areas as well as new traffic and other duties. The Inspectors of Constabulary began to point out the undesirability of sacrificing any more police patrol men[25] and warned of the danger of overloading the traditional beat officer with tasks that crowded out his primary beat duties. They foresaw a time in the near future when country beats would have to be pooled and mechanized. However, police authorities were hesitant in introducing such measures, and a pre-war experiment in Somerset with motor bike beat patrols was abandoned, after the chief constable concluded that service under the old system outweighed any financial savings to be made by mechanization.[26] The scenario forecast by the Inspectors was not to be fulfilled until the post-war period, when a new system of beat working was instituted in Aberdeen in 1948 in what was described as 'the first real departure from the beat system' since the inception of the full-time British bobby. The driving force behind this move was the shortage of recruits in the aftermath of war, that was to intensify in the late 1950s as the economy started to pick up. The Aberdeen system, mentioned in Chapter 2, was the first in a series of experiments in 'team policing', whereby a number of pcs under a sergeant in a wireless patrol car were made responsible collectively for the supervision of a division. Its origins are of some interest. It was devised by the chief constable, after he noted that men demobbed from the forces did not relish the prospect of resuming monotonous beat working, especially at night. He himself had served in the Camel Corps during the war, each of whose units operated as a self-contained team, and he decided to apply this principle to the police. In Aberdeen this meant that an area of ten beats was now policed by a single team, consisting of four pcs and a sergeant, with a wireless car at their disposal. One or more of the pcs was set down at different points, either to patrol or to deal with a specific matter, and was later picked up by car and transferred to another area. This put an end to the routine patrolling of the beat and the examination of lock-up property, and changed the function of the sergeant from supervisor to team leader who directed his men to any trouble spots. The car itself was described as a mobile police station.[27] It was enthusiastically received by police spokesmen favouring mechanization over foot slogging; while the Aberdeen police committee maintained that the new system had saved them from having to

25  *Police Review*, 27 Feb 1931.
26  *Police Review*, 7 July 1933.
27  *Police Review*, 30 September 1949.

employ fifty more men.[28] Other advantages were that men were posted to areas where they were most required; pcs had more interesting work to do; there was more discussion between pcs and sergeants; and an element of surprise against wrongdoers was added, that had been missing under the old routinized beat system. Government authorities were impressed, but a working party of chief constables and HMIs carefully concluded that each police chief should weigh the matter up in the light of his own circumstances. In the hotch potch of police authorities that made up the English police presence, it cannot be said that team policing immediately swept all before it. Some chief constables, notably in Plymouth, Halifax, Eastbourne and Salford became early converts; but others, as in Hastings tried and then abandoned team policing. Nevertheless, it was an important innovation and the forerunner of the panda car and unit beat policing system that came in generally in 1966, and that changed the face of British policing from a dominantly preventive to a fire brigade mode. It is of some interest, therefore, to retrieve the views of the practioners. The comments from the oral history sample were uniformly negative. Two very senior officers who joined after the war, and were therefore not indoctrinated under the old system, gave their reasons, as follows:

> It is a super system of policing. The only thing it can't cope with is human nature. When you put a police officer in a tin box and call it a car, human nature being what it is, he doesn't get out that much ... what happens in practice is that you send them by radio to deal with an incident and the flashing blue light's going ... and when you arrive at an incident there's a certain amount of nervousness, wishing it wasn't you going there ... when you arrive in your tin box and actually pull out of it, you become aggressive, or tend to ...[29]

The other officer, for his part, described the new mobile unit system as the ruination of policing:

> It was supposed to make more use of manpower and save increasing manpower which was costly. It was supplemented by a residential beat man ... but gradually you found that with courses and training and courts and sickness you took the residential man in to cover the car, because it was essential to have someone on mobile duty then because there were vacant places where the policemen used to be, it still had to be dealt with. So in fact it degenerated into just a mobile control, and if it was a busy place the policeman in the car lost touch because all he was doing is what they they are doing now,

28 *Police Review*, 7 May 1948.
29 Interview with Chief Constable Wiseman, Lancashire police.

> answering calls, and he didn't have time to chat to somebody and get to know what was going on.[30]

Finally one pre-war pc gave his view of the changes:

> When my children were children, they were proud that their daddy was a policeman. It was a marvellous feeling really. You were Mr All Powerful, there's no doubt, although you were only a very ordinary bobby ... at six o'clock in the morning and at ten o'clock at night there were twenty-seven policemen on the road in each division ... policemen all over the place, going to or from their jobs and all in uniform, all on push bikes. Now they're all in cars with anoraks on, you don't get to know who's who, they just sneak in and become policemen when they get there and drop it and come away again...[31]

In retrospect, it seems that most officers were not too happy with the new style of policing, and some certainly objected to it at the time of its introduction. Neither did this style particularly endear itself to the motoring public, as was shown in the social survey commissioned by the government as part of the Royal Commission on the Police in 1961. Its findings showed that those most critical of the police, apart from young males, were motorists. It seems that the car changed the face of British policing, as it did so much else, to the latter's detriment. Given the crisis in police/public relations in recent years, desperate efforts are now being made to overcome the impact of the car by trying to get back to the bobby on the beat style of policing. But how far this is a realistic goal in today's circumstances must remain a very moot point.

---

30  Interview with Superintendent Hearn, Durham County police.
31  Interview with Sergeant Freeth, Hull City police.

# CHAPTER FIVE

# The CID

What image did the public hold of the detective officer in the period? And how did he himself view his position? In much twentieth century fiction – if this can be taken as a symbol of the public's view – the figure of the detective is placed at the core of police work and portrayed as its chief raison d'être in the fight against crime.[1] In practice, there has been little historical work on the detective branch of policing, researchers having been kept at bay by the secrecy in which the records are shrouded. Full knowledge of the work of the detective branch has also been withheld from other departments within the police organization. Furthermore, the CID made a virtue of its secret mode of operation and readily agreed with its fictional counterpart that this was necessary and intrinsic and that detective work gave it superior status over the uniformed branch.

From the late Victorian period onwards, the CID had become a feature of urban, and above all metropolitan police forces, with a well established reputation for incompetence and for venality and corruption. The emphasis on prevention and distrust of undercover police work that was characteristic of most police authorities had kept detective departments small and lacking in technical training and expertise; some smaller forces managed without any detectives at all, while in no force in the 1930s was the proportion more than six per cent of the establishment.[2] Meanwhile, scandals involving corrupt practices erupted with monotonous regularity as the pressure for results during various clean-up campaigns pushed detectives and plain clothes officers towards the use and acceptance of illegal methods and inducements.

The situation at the start of our period is well illustrated by an assessment of the Metropolitan CID that was made in the early 1930s by the Home Office. This found that a complete and reliable system of crime recording was wanting, and that the way in which cases were entered into the crime book or suspected stolen register varied not only between divisions but

---

1   But see Reiner's typology of fictional images of the detective which shows that detective heroes tended to be amateurs rather than professional policemen. Robert Reiner, (1985) *The Politics of the Police,* Chapter 5.

2   Home Office (1938) *Report of the Departmental Committee on Detective Work and Procedure,* vol. 1, p. 59.

between stations within the divisions, to the extent that 'CID headquarters are not in a position to obtain reliable statistical information as to the general state of crime throughout the Metropolitan Police District'. This casual observation at a stroke puts into question the validity of all prior statistics of crime. But although the problematic status of the statistics has been raised time and again, historians have been extremely reluctant to abandon them, on the premis that they must show *something* relevant about trends in crime. The view taken here is that the only thing that they reliably show is police practices. Recording practices apart, CID was further found to be almost entirely separate from the uniform branch, with a very wide gulf between the two. The CID were neither under the officers in charge of a district nor under the superintendents, but came directly under senior CID officers at Scotland Yard, and the divisional detective inspector. The CID felt themselves superior to the uniform men, and the uniform men were estranged from the CID, and resented having to hand over a case entirely to CID when they had made a good arrest. The situation was a thoroughly unsatisfactory one, in which sub-divisional inspectors had men in their districts for whom they were responsible but about whom or about the work they were doing they knew nothing. In addition, it was found that in some cases CID areas of control did not coincide with the subdivisional areas. Moreover, the discipline of the CID was not in the hands of the superintendants and officers in charge of districts, who thus had no control over its CID officers.[3] These findings clearly set out the nature of the problems involved. As we shall see, these remained remarkably resistant to subsequent measures of reform. Meanwhile, the Metropolitan report overlapped with, and perhaps stimulated, a broader look at the CID in the country as a whole.

## The Committee on Detective Work

In 1933 the Home Secretary set up a committee of inquiry into the work of the detective branches.[4] The final report in 1938 was hailed as equal to that of the Desborough Committee in importance and the foundation for all subsequent developments in the field.[5] It began by grappling with the thorny

---

3   *PRO: Mepo 12/5*, 'Correspondence on the reorganization of the CID, 1929–1934'.

4   *Committee on Detective Work.* The report was published in five volumes, of which only volumes 1 (an overview of the system) and 5 '*The Application of Science to the Investigation of Crime*' were on sale to the public.

5   Critchley, *A History of Police*, p. 210.

question of whether a detective force on a national basis was necessary, but managed to side step the issue by deciding that

> it should be possible to secure the main advantages of unified control without any radical departure from the present police system, provided that the necessary local improvements are made in matters such as training, equipment and detective strength: (and) that the local forces unite effectively for common action in matters which are of common interest ... In detective work ... too much importance is still attached to force boundaries. Every opportunity should be taken for establishing personal contact between detectives in different forces ...[6]

To this end, training courses for detectives were to be put on a more uniform basis. The inquiry had found that while most detectives in the larger forces received some form of specialized instruction, this was limited in scope, whereas in smaller forces any form of training was the exception rather than the rule.[7] The report recommended improvements in record keeping, the first essential being the maintenance of a crime complaint book in which all crime complaints were to be entered, which it was hoped would obviate the practice of writing off complaints as 'no crime'.[8] Standardized forms of crime reports and crime registers were to be kept. Improved communication systems, and the means to collect and disseminate information on criminals between forces were to be extended, and the work of the scientific branch expanded. The committee also stressed the need for greater cooperation between the uniform and detective branches within the different forces, and for uniform constables to be associated with detectives in crime inquiries.

The report revealed that crime was a highly localized affair, three quarters of which was carried out by persons living in the police district in which the crime was committed. It also found that a high proportion of local crime was detected even though little or no provision had been made for a specialized detective branch. Nevertheless, its emphasis was on the importance of inter-force and regional cooperation and a better standard of training for detectives. Not much was done immediately at Home Office level to implement the recommendations in the report, coming as it did shortly before the outbreak of war. But these began to be addressed soon after the end of the war. In particular, a number of regional detective

---

6  *Committee on Detective Work,* vol. 1, pp. 38–9.

7  *Committee on Detective Work,* vol. 2, p. 3. The report noted that 'we have not found any existing course of instruction for detectives which we could regard as satisfactorily meeting all requirements'.

8  *Committee on Detective Work,* vol. 3, p. 8.

training centres were set up, where all entrants to CID had to undergo a three month training course. Standardized ways of recording crime were instituted, and more detectives were appointed. Cooperation, however, was another matter. Although regular district meetings of detectives from within the region were encouraged, the innate parochialism of police culture and the tenacious hold each force kept on the integrity of its own reputation and territorial boundaries leaves the degree of voluntary inter-force cooperation open to question. At the same time, more specialized training did little to bring detectives closer to their uniformed colleagues.

## Relations with the Uniform Branch

While the proportion of detectives within each force grew, it is not clear how far this was due to Home Office pressure, how far to a growth in organized crime and to changes in policing styles on the ground. In the early 1930s, when only two per cent of cases involved theft of property valued at over £100, and seventy-five per cent valued at under £5, the bobby on the beat uncovered, and frequently cleared up, many of the incidents involved. At this time, detectives made up around six per cent in the major urban forces.[9] By the late 1950s and 1960s, motorized policing had gained ground, the proportion of detectives had increased twice and threefold in several areas, and the gap between preventive policing and crime busting had widened. Instead of improving, relations between the uniformed and plainclothes branches – never very good – became minimal in some forces such as the Met as it moved towards the situation of 'a firm within a firm'. Relations, however, had been unequal from the start. Detectives did not need to fit in as did uniformed men. They had a degree of freedom from routine and supervision that the others lacked and they received allowances not given to policemen in other branches. They were on intimate terms with the sorts of people that uniformed officers tried to steer clear of, and they thought they were better than the other pcs. Detective Inspector Aylesham admitted as much. When he was transferred as a pc from uniform to detective 'I still had the same rank, but it was an elite body, the CID, and it was always considered that you had to have a

---

9   *Committee on Detective Work,* vol. 1, pp. 30, 59. These percentages applied to the Metropolitan, Birmingham, Liverpool and Manchester police. Some divisions within these forces, such as C division in central London, had a much higher proportion. Here, Deputy Commander Blatchley estimated that a quarter of the strength in the late 1930s were in the CID. Interview with Deputy Commander Blatchley.

little bit of grey matter on top to be a detective'.[10] From the other side of the divide, PC Lench observed that the CID 'were a lordly lot on their own, a branch apart, you didn't associate with them'; while in the metropolis, the CID was seen as a department where 'you didn't know what was going on and you didn't want to know'.[11] Sergeant March expressed the feeling between the two the most forcefully. Above all, he resented the assumption that transfer to the CID should be regarded as equivalent to a promotion. As Federation representative for the uniformed sergeants' branch,

> I had argued for many years and I fought against it tooth and nail as representative, about the two police forces, and gradually we did get it knocked into the heads of the CID that they were not, as they chose to call it, the brains of the bloody job, they were just part of it.[12]

Not everybody wanted to be part of the CID. Chief Inspector Tate, for example, tried it but decided that he preferred the uniform side 'because I was proud of the uniform, and I liked to be seen trying to be of help to the City population'.[13] Others felt they had no choice but to transfer back to uniform if they were to achieve further promotion, since CID as a smaller branch than uniform appeared to have fewer openings for promotion.[14] For most, however, a transfer 'back to the blue' was meant, and regarded, as a demotion and a punishment.

## Selection for CID

How then were police officers selected to become detectives? To start with, none were eligible until they had done their probationary years on the beat in uniform. After that, the most usual route was through plain-clothes attachment, which was a dry run method of trying out officers to see if they were suited to the work. Those not considered suitable were simply posted back to uniform without explanation, adding fuel to well aired tales about

---

10 Interview with Detective Inspector Aylesham, Durham County police.
11 Interview with PC Lench, Cardiff City police; PC Waterford, Metropolitan police; and Sergeant Blake, Metropolitan police.
12 Interview with Sergeant March, Metropolitan police.
13 Interview with Chief Inspector Tate, City of London police.
14 Interview with Inspector Roper, Birmingham City police. Roper was one of those who had to transfer back to uniform against his wishes three years before he retired, in order to get made up to Inspector.

barriers due to masonic or religious influences.[15] Nevertheless, it was
chiefly men who volunteered or expressed a desire to go into CID who were
posted as aids, although it could take many years before they achieved that
goal – as in the case of Superintendent Spender. He realized that he first
needed to get into the plain clothes branch, chasing the bookmakers and
prostitutes and the indecency offences, before he could be considered for
CID. 'That's how I got in', he related

> You went down initially for three months aid to CID, no allowances,
> that was the first step. It took six and a half years. I was attached to
> CID for four and a half years, then went back to the division until I
> was called in ... it was dead men's shoes, vacancies were filled up
> from them ... But you had to pass the exams, they weren't taking
> you as a detective unless you were qualified for promotion.[16]

Once in, you had to be shown the ropes, and these were very different to the
routines pursued by officers on the beat, or to the practices learnt on
training courses. Inspector Hay, from Birmingham City police, provided a
most comprehensive account of initiation into the work, which will be
quoted at length.[17]  Although he had no particular desire to join the CID,
Hay was posted to 'Plain Clothes Nights' soon after he had completed his
two year's probation, on the chief inspector's recommendation.[18] This was
to last one month, directed each week by a different detective. In this way,
he was able to sample a full range of detective styles of work:

> The first one was a gem. We worked from the central detective
> department and did not budge out until 11 p.m. He had instructed
> the other two (plain clothes) to patrol the other end of the division
> and ring in every hour or so. Our little walk was to a large pub in
> the city centre. Three rings on the bell did the trick and we were
> soon inside to join a room full of people. Everyone was very
> friendly and pints of beer kept appearing in front of us from various
> sources without us doing any paying. I had to keep going to the
> phone every hour and ringing in, but we had an undisturbed night
> and carried on drinking. The next night we were in a different pub,
> again with free beer ... it must have been the best week I'd ever
> spent.

---

15  An example was Sergeant Dunhill, who found plain clothes work much more
     interesting than walking the beat, but who was transferred back to uniform after
     his three month attachment. Interview with Sergeant Dunhill, Birmingham City
     police.
16  Interview with Superintendent Spender, Sheffield City police.
17  Hay, *The Saga of a Practical Copper*.
18  Hay's comment was that he could now see that there was more than religion to
     get you on in the police force. *Practical Copper*.

The detective for the second week was a card addict and every night saw us helping the two night duty clerks with their work so that we could all play cards ... The third week saw an energetic type. We would leave the office at 10 p.m. and walk round the division for eight hours, with him pointing out to me where all the well known criminals lived ... I was certainly glad to see that week out and dreaded what my fourth partner was going to be like ... but he turned out to be the best of the lot. He wasn't too heavy a drinker, not too fond of exercise, and intended to use his week of nights as a chance to catch up on his sleep. We would wander round the city until about 1 a.m. and then would go into a large hotel, claim ourselves a large chair in the lounge, and that was it until 6 a.m. Headquarters apparently knew where we were and if we were wanted they would telephone the night porter, who would wake us up. It seemed too good to last and the week went very quickly ...[19]

## Inside the CID

Unusually, given his short length of service, Hay was transferred into CID proper shortly after his month's plain clothes work, and sent to a suburban station to work with the detective sergeant there. The difference in relations between ranks in the CID and the uniform was immediately noticeable. Where the sergeant was regarded as a 'holy being' by the uniformed pc, here things were on an entirely different footing. Hay was astonished. Sergeants, he said, had always been the uniform pcs natural enemies, put there by someone 'so that we could pull the wool over their eyes'. Now here was a sergeant who told Hay to call him by his first name, so long as they were on their own, and who was to spend all day and every day with him for the next two years on close and equal terms. It became clear that the CID was run on entirely different lines to the uniform branch.

The difference has been well captured by Dick Hobbs. In his book on detectives and criminals in the East End of London, Hobbs portrays their symbiotic relationship through the concept of entrepreneurship which defines the individualistic and opportunist style of both sets of partners. It is a style based on wheeling and dealing, on the buying and selling of stolen goods, on getting by, that had its roots in the poverty, overcrowding and criminality generated by the East End's particular economic structure and history. Hobbs goes on to argue that these characteristics of East End culture have parallels in the culture and work practices of CID officers,

---

19  Hay, Ibid.

which he characterizes as an organizationally deviant branch of the police service that decrys team work and relies on individualistic enterprise.[20]

A similar account could be given of the Birmingham CID, or indeed of the CID in any other large urban centre. The style relied on formalized relationships with members of the targeted population, on the basis of favours expected and received and on the skill with which this was done – a skill which certainly merits the term entrepreneurial, whether applied in London's East End or in a Birmingham suburb. Hay's detective sergeant, Tom, was a past master:

> He had worked the area for many years and knew everyone. Two mornings a week we would walk along the main street just before dinner because we knew the local bookmaker visited his branch shop about this time. We would always be walking along smartly just as he was getting out of his car. To my everlasting amazement, Tom would never get within six feet of him, but after we had passed the time of day we would walk off, and Tom would give me 10/-, half of what the bookmaker had given him. This would have done credit to a professional conjurer.[21]

They would also collect £1 notes from the registers of metal dealers in the area, whose books they examined once a month to make sure they were not buying stolen property. But it was after they had recovered the proceeds from a succession of burglaries that Hay really saw the master at work:

> Tom set all of the property up in our office as though he had a stall on the market, and then we invited the losers to come in and view. Tom would be dancing attendance on them, letting them see the property and marking that which they identified as their own. Right on the corner of the table was an upturned trilby hat with a £1 note in it. When the visit was over, Tom would look at it in some surprise and comment that a previous viewer had left this note, which was not necessary, but much appreciated. It took a very strongminded man then not to put his hand in his pocket and do the same. We shared £40 for this case.[22]

## Competition for Cases and Cooking the Books

Where the uniformed officer might be judged by the absence of public misdemeanours and disorder on his beat or patrol, the detective needed to

20  Dick Hobbs (1989 edn) *Doing the Business: Entrepreneurship, The Working Class, and Detectives in East London*, Chapters 5 and 8.
21  Hay, *Practical Copper*.
22  Hay, Ibid.

justify his existence by filling his record with cleared up crimes. It was this pressure to show results that opened the path to a range of illegal ways and means which lay at the heart of the department's reputation for corruption. This came into play even before entry to CID proper. As Inspector Cooper recalled, when discussing the fabrication of evidence, 'there *was* fabrication. The people that were aids to CID, it was an open invitation, because if you didn't get enough results you didn't get made CID'.[23] Moreover, once in, the pressures were stepped up, and who can say how many were able to resist? Supplementing their income through contributions from grateful members of the public or through sweeteners from the targets of unenforceable laws – such as bookies, publicans or prostitutes – was one thing. Corruption in the interest of forwarding their careers was yet another, that had an insidious effect on the operational norms existing within a number of CID departments. Some senior officers were quite open about this. Superintendent Carling had a spell as aid to CID when he was stationed at Limehouse as a young man, but this ended after the detective inspector told him 'You're alright picking up little jobs, but I don't think you'd do for this department ... you're too bloody honest'.[24]

The whole focus of CID departments on getting results exacerbated rather than forwarded a state of cooperation with the rest of the force. Instead, it induced bad feeling, since nearly all uniformed officers could recount instances where their cases had been 'pinched' off them by CID. It was, of course, normal procedure for criminal cases to be handed over to CID for processing. Nevertheless, uniformed officers wanted some credit for uncovering these cases. Sergeant Home offered one example:

> CID men used to pinch jobs off uniformed policemen. I remember arresting somebody breaking into a shop and on him he had a diary of several other break-ins he had done ... I reported it and the CID took over, and the next thing I knew he had been dealt with and I wasn't mentioned. It did create bad feeling because you got the impression that you were just being cut out ...[25]

This was not just an urban phenomenon. Rural stations before the war had largely operated without the benefit of designated detectives, but their subsequent appointment began to affect rural as well as the urban forces. Inspector Astley was stationed at Crawley, which was a small station with a sergeant and five pcs before the war:

23 Interview with Inspector Cooper, Metropolitan police.
24 Interview with Superintendent Carling, Metropolitan police.
25 Interview with Sergeant Home, Sheffield City police.

> We had no CID at Crawley. What appealed to me about the county
> force, you did all your own crime ... later on the CID became more
> prevalent and they used to take over anything where they thought
> there was a chance of clear up, and leave the uniformed branch to do
> anything that they didn't think was going to be cleared up at all ... it
> created quite a bit of bad feeling.[26]

Detectives, however, were not primarily interested in good relations with
the uniform branch. They were driven by the numbers game, by the need to
get confessions and a good clear-up rate.[27] Their whole career structure and
modus operandi militated against an open and interactive relationship with
colleagues, whether at local or regional level. Gone was the corporate
bonding of the peer group that had been such a strong feature of the
probationary years on the beat. Instead, the CID system fostered an
individualistic, competitive outlook that did not easily yield to official
admonishments in favour of a frank and open exchange of information and
aid. Such unrealistic invitations were treated with the contempt it was
thought they deserved. Inspector Hay had much to say on this subject:

> In order to pass on snippets of information regarding local bad lads,
> we used to have a CID conference every Saturday morning and all
> CID officers had to attend unless they had a very good reason not to.
> It was the biggest load of rubbish that was ever thought about. If
> you had some good information you kept it to yourself, not pass it
> out to two hundred other people who might beat you to it by
> collecting the prisoner before you did ...[28]

If cooperation within each force was problematical, this applied even more
strongly to contacts across force boundaries. The *Committee on Detective
Work* had stressed the special importance of closer contact between large
city forces and the forces policing the adjoining areas. Force boundaries,
they stated, ought to be no more a hindrance to effective cooperation
between detectives than they were to the criminal in the flight from his
crime.[29] The reality was that if a detective ventured into foreign territory,
even just to make enquiries, hackles were immediately raised. What's he
doing here? was the usual response. Thus, Superintendent Spender
described neighbouring Doncaster, in the force adjacent to his, as a walled

---

26  Interview with Inspector Astley, West Sussex police.
27  This is where violence against prisoners, that most of my informants agreed was
    most prevalent in the CID, came in. This is discussed more fully in Chapter 10.
28  Hay, *Practical Copper.*
29  *Committee on Detective Work,* vol. 1, pp 47–8.

city as far as detective enquiries were concerned.[30] Every force, and every detective within that force jealously guarded their own villains, who each represented a possible good case to be chalked up in their favour. Inspector Hay, for instance, defined a good villain as one who committed lots of offences 'so that they could arrest him again and again', to keep up their reputation.[31] These league tables operated at all levels. Sergeant Dunhill, who was manning the telephone switchboard, overheard two detective chief inspectors from different divisions discussing the month's figures. 'How many have you had this month? 'Oh, I've had 130 arrests'. The other man replied, 'Dear, oh dear, you'd better get the whip out, that's not enough. The Selection Board want 200 at least'.[32]

Everything was geared to getting cases in the complaints book. But this did not mean that everything was entered. The 'rubbish' cases, where there was no chance of a clear-up, were left to the uniform branch or simply not recorded. You did not note down what was not important, such as an attempted break-in – that was simply ignored or 'cuffed'.[33]

## The Creation of Crime Statistics

The theory and practice of 'cuffing' has been cogently presented by Young. He describes how the manipulation of 'crimes' was made on an almost daily basis, where the classificatory differences between crimes and offences was continually used to redefine them in a manner suitable to the practiioners. Undetected crimes were reduced to offences, or simply lost from the account altogether, whereas detectable crimes were always welcomed. At many police stations, the crime book was locked away and only the detectives were allowed to record crime, in an effort to stop uniformed 'wollies' putting in certain types of crime. Thus, what was eventually recorded was carefully controlled, and varied according to departmental

---

30 This attitude remained endemic and characteristic. James McClure, for example, states that police divisions in Liverpool were administered as territorial entities, where bobbies rarely, if ever, crossed into neighbouring divisions. James McClure (1980) *Spike Island: Portrait of a Police Division*, p. 19.

31 This meant that the detectives got a lot of respect from wrongdoers: 'we always spoke up well for them in court, because a good criminal languishing in prison was no good to us, if we could get him out on probation, we might have the good fortune to catch him again'. *Practical Copper*, p. 88.

32 Interview with Sergeant Haines, Metropolitan police.

33 Information from Detective Superintendent Spender.

opinion about desirable or creditable levels of recorded crime. These levels were low in the 1950s, but rose rapidly in the 1960s when detectives were encouraged to record as much crime as possible.[34] 'Cuffing', as with so much else concerning the compilation of criminal statistics, varied according to season and to orders from above. The Crime Complaints book that was the main instrument used to try and overcome these distortions did not prove much of an obstacle, and was fated to remain as much a book of fiction as of fact.

Orders from above in connection with the recording of crime could have an encouraging or a disheartening effect on the work motivation of the detectives. It all depended on whether management wanted more or less crime in the records. Thus, Inspector Hay described the system in operation when he first joined Birmingham's CID:

> in those days the CID had what they called the Blue Book. The Blue Book was most important, you put all your own cases in there. And you weren't allowed to put in cases that had been handed over, such as shoplifters, it had to be one where you'd caught them by your own means. And every six months these books were sent in to the chief detective inspector on the division, and he put a report in on the amount of cases you'd had during the six months, which was most important. So in those days, thirty was our average each over six months. By hook or by crook you kept up to that. If it got towards the end of six months, and you were down, you worked day and night to get some.[35]

These books were a speciality of CID in Birmingham, and the basic record on which promotions were decided. However, when a new chief constable was appointed in the late 1950s, he decided to do away with them, to the dismay of the detective department:

> He said that it was not a good way of getting promotion, because you went out to get as many thieves as you could in order to beat your opponent ... he decided it was unfair ... I always thought that this was the most retrograde step I ever witnessed in the force, because until then most of us had carried out our duties to serve the public ... setting out to catch burglars etc ... but after a time we realized that we were the willing horses, but not being singled out for promotion, so naturally the workers decided it was not worth the candle, and catching thieves became a thing of the past ... The

34  Malcolm Young (1991) *An Inside Job: Policing and Police Culture in Britain*, pp. 323–5.
35  Interview with Inspector Hay, Birmingham City police.

popular saying then was 'catch no-one and keep your nose clean' and you were eligible for promotion.[36]

The uniform side took a rather different view of the scaling down of crime reports during this period, claiming that CID used to 'no crime' events (such as attempted break-ins) in order to improve the look of the clear-up rate. Sergeant Minch, when discussing entries into the Crime Complaint book (or Yellow Peril, as it was commonly known) described the tussle between the two branches over crime definitions, and the reasons behind this:

> Crime went down before the war, because it wasn't recorded ... If a woman came in the police station and said 'I've had my purse stolen', years ago that would have been recorded as lost property, but because of the Yellow Peril book it had to go down as suspected crime. It went to the CID and the CID's job then was to try and write it off as 'no crime'. And that was one of the areas of friction between the uniformed and the CID branch, because we wanted more crime reported. We wanted to say at the end of the year that crime's gone up ten per cent because we haven't got enough policemen. And the CID, because their gaffers kept saying 'we're having too much crime', they tried to write it off. [37]

Similarly, Detective Inspector Ellworthy noted that they were the first division, in Sutton Coldfield in the 1950s, to record a thousand crimes a year:

> But we were our own worst enemy. Because we always used to make a point of looking good on paper at detection ... we recorded a thousand crimes a year, but our true figure would have been half as much again, if we'd put the real figure in, but we didn't. [38]

As these examples show, the statistics of crime rose and fell according to whether the department was in favour of more, or less, recorded crime.[39] Management's directives and policies thus made a direct impact on the morale and work styles of the CID. In our period its members responded most positively to competitive pressure for more cases of cleared up crime,

---

36  Ibid.
37  Interview with Sergeant Minch, Birmingham City police.
38  Interview with Detective Inspector Ellworthy, Warwickshire police.
39  It also depended on how a crime was defined. In Birmingham, all stolen cars were deemed to have been 'taken and driven away' if the vehicle was recovered within 48 hours and any crime report was cancelled, whereas in the MPD all stolen cars were recorded as such even after recovery. The Home Office therefore proposed a new category of crime, entitled 'Unauthorized Takings and Thefts of Motor Vehicles'. *PRO: Mepo 2/8564,* 15 May 1949.

since this corresponded well with their own image of the lean, keen detective, energetically fighting crime and criminals as he climbs up the promotion ladder, gathering admiration and tribute on the way, and giving the public good value for money. However, the more the branch became bogged down in bureaucratic rules and regulations as police authorities struggled to keep the CID under control, the more disheartened its members became. Bureaucracy killed the entrepreneurial spirit that brought joy to the hunt for villains. According to Superintendent Spender, this downgrading of criminal investigation started when they started to pay overtime to detectives, after the 1964 Police Act, which – ironically – took all the rewards out of being a detective:

> The system is such that you'll get an inefficient detective who gets more money than the efficient detective. Because it takes him longer, he's slower in detecting the same amount of crime. I could get a prisoner arrested, sorted out, searched, booked and locked up in two hours. But it's like a go slow. If it takes four, why do it in two hours ... we get two hours more money. So there's no incentive to get the job done and get on to the next job. It's alright talking about ambition and satisfaction in doing a job well, but incentive is money ...[40]

Formerly, promotion had been the sole organizational incentive; later, money entered in to complicate matters. Both had immediate effect on the norms and trends expressed by the crime figures. But then, as Superintendent Spender said, 'you can make the figures mean anything'. The *Committee on Detective Work's* simple faith that a uniform system of recording crime complaints would overcome 'write offs' and the downgrading of crimes, and supply the chief constable with the means for the effective supervision of detective work proved to be sadly misplaced.[41]

---

40  Interview with Detective Superintendent Spender, Sheffield City police.
41  *Committee on Detective Work*, vol. 3, pp. 9–10.

1.  Tea with the police matron in the station house (early 1930s).  *Birmingham Police Museum.*

**2.** Road safety instruction in schools (1950s). *Birmingham Police Museum.*

**3.** Monthly police Sunday church parade, Birmingham (1930s). *Courtesy of Sergeant Dunhill.*

**4.** Chasing sheep from the local school on the occasion of a royal visit (1950s). *Essex Police Museum.*

**5.** Nuneaton Traffic Division (1950s). *Warwickshire Police Museum.*

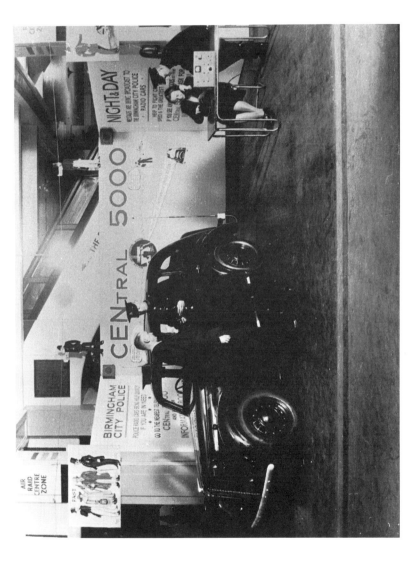

6. The first radio cars in Birmingham: an exhibition at Lewis's department store (1950s). *Birmingham Police Museum.*

7. The CID at work (1950s). *South Wales Police Museum.*

8. Birmingham wpcs and their supervisors (1930s). *Birmingham Police Museum.*

**9.** The Metropolitan police holding back demonstrators in Cable Street on the occasion of the BUF march, 1936. *Metropolitan Police Museum.*

10. Removing barricades in Cable Street, 1936. *Metropolitan Police Museum.*

**11.** The oldest woman in Glamorganshire being issued with her gas mask, 1939. *South Wales Police Museum.*

12. Metropolitan police in wartime. *Metropolitan Police Museum.*

# CHAPTER SIX

# Policewomen and Police Wives

A career in the police service in the 1930s – the first decade in which women were to be accepted as fully fledged police officers – involved a clear rift with many of the norms that governed women's lives. To begin with, there was the difficulty of moving from the private to the public sphere at a time of job scarcity, when disapproval of female waged employment was high. If this applied even to sectors where women were not in direct competition with men, how much more was this likely to be the case in careers that had traditionally been entirely reserved for the latter. Not only was policing regarded as an exclusively male preserve, but its whole ethos and work practices were centred on concepts of masculinity and its prerogatives. Above all, policing relied and rested on the exercise of authority, and the expectation of submission to that authority; and authority was the attribute of the masculine *par excellence*. So how could women expect to enter and function in this terrain?

The rest of this chapter will seek to answer these questions and to demonstrate how the few women who entered the service fared, and what areas of work they undertook. In addition, the role of women police officers will be compared with that of police wives, to try and discover what divided them and what they had in common during what has been termed the 'latency' period of the feminist movement.[1] Although an earlier generation had gained some success in promoting the acceptance of women within the police, by the 1930s the high tide of suffragist and feminist campaigns and activity had turned, leaving a modest body of achievement behind. The impetus and fervour behind earlier feminist campaigns and causes had waned, and left exposed the essentially unequal and subordinate position of women in all spheres of public life. Drawing on broader societal norms, women involved in the police service from the 1930s to the end of the war, whether in an official or unofficial capacity, were therefore expected to provide what was essentially an extension of the supportive and caring tasks

---

1   Martin designates 1930–45 as the latency period in the history of the introduction of women into the police service. See S.E. Martin (1979) 'POLICEwomen and WOMENpolice: Occupational Role Dilemmas and Choices of Female Offenders', *Journal of Police Science and Administration*. This designation and periodization is also used by Frances Heidensohn (1992) in *Women in Control? The Role of Women in Law Enforcement*.

that they normally performed in the domestic sphere. As policemen's wives, they were expected to uphold their husband's professional standing and to adapt their behaviour accordingly and – in rural areas – to help him in a number of unpaid tasks by manning the telephone, conveying messages and running police errands. As women police officers wpcs were, until the integration of the sexes in the 1970s, largely organized as a separate, specialist branch that focused on work relating to women and children. It was on this basis – and on this basis only – that wpcs found acceptance in the service, and their usefulness as police officers was regarded as strictly limited to such work. In this way, the main bastion of police masculinity remained unsullied and unbreached until several decades after the Second World War.

## The Pioneering Years

Was this what the pioneers for women in the police service had hoped for? A small body of literature on the history of women in British policing, largely based on the memoirs of those involved in the first half of this century, lays stress on the founding years just before, during and immediately after the First World War. This has been seen as the heroic age when pressure from a number of dedicated women actively sought to open up the police service as a career opportunity for women. Two distinct organizations were set up.[2] The Women Police Volunteers (WPV), founded by the suffragist Nina Boyle at the outset of the First World War, sought to place women in police forces around the country as full-time officers engaged on general police duties; while the Voluntary Women Patrols, launched by the National Union of Working Women (NUWW), was a more middle class organization that concentrated on the policing of working class girls and women in the cities, and largely relied on unpaid, part-time

2  Policewomen's memoirs include: Mary S. Allen (1925) *The Pioneer Policewoman;* D. Peto (1970) *The Memoirs of Miss Dorothy Olivia Georgiana Peto, O.B.E.* (M/S); Lilian Wyles (1952) *A Woman at Scotland Yard*; Edith Tancred (n.d.) *Women Police 1914—1950* ; Joan Lock (1968) *Lady Policeman.* Apart from Heidensohn, there are few substantive works aside from articles on the British women police, other than John Carrier (1988) *The Campaign for the Employment of Women Police Officers*; and S. Jones (1986) *Policewomen and Equality.*

volunteers.[3] The feminist impulse as the motivating force behind these initiatives has usually been stressed at the expense of any countervailing views. However, a recent revisionist account by Philippa Levine makes clear the complex nature of the motives that engaged the membership, with feminism as only one part of what propelled women into police work in the period of the First World War.[4] An early split within the ranks of the WPV illustrates the point. A separate organization, the Women Police Service under the leadership of Margaret Damer Dawson and Mary Allen, was set up that was prepared (as was the NUWW) to implement the wartime Defence of the Realm Regulation 40D, that permitted the detention and prosecution of infected women accused of sexual relations with members of the armed forces, and against which Nina Boyle of the WPV, and many other feminists protested. However, the WPV, which kept its feminist credentials, was rapidly sidelined, ignored by police authorities precisely because of its continued commitment to a feminist perspective.[5] It was in this context of acceptance of an authoritarian stance over the monitoring of women's sexual and moral behaviour that the two remaining organizations began to gain recognition from a number of police authorities and from their parliamentary champions, and that pressure for statutory recognition for women police officers mounted. As Levine rightly insists, this makes clear that it was only by virtue of shedding their feminist allegiances that police authorities were prepared to countenance the continuation of the women police organizations. She might also have added that the one work area policemen were happy to relinquish concerned sexual and domestic cases, since the sexual prudery and sexual unease common to their class and period inhibited many officers in their dealings with the opposite sex. Apart from their dealings with prostitutes, where respect was not called for, pcs were often uncertain as to how other women should be treated, finding the line between "angel" and "whore" difficult to negotiate. However, despite the recommendation of a Select Committee (the Baird Committee) in 1920 in favour of the employment of women police – reinforced by the report of the Bridgeman Committee in 1924 – cut-backs under the Geddes Axe of 1922 frustrated plans for any expansion and indeed reduced the small number of policewomen already employed.

---

3  For an account of the early women's policing organizations, see Alison Woodeson (1993) 'The First Women Police: a force for equality or infringement?' *Women's History Review*.

4  Philippa Levine (1994) '"Walking the Streets in a Way No Decent Woman Should": Women Police in World War 1', *Journal of Modern History*.

5  Ibid.

A renewal of government economy measures during the depression of the early 1930s meant the outlook for women police recruits at the beginning of our period remained bleak. In 1935, the number of wpcs in the seventeen forces considered in the study on which this chapter is based came to 105, with nine out of the seventeen forces employing no wpcs. The lopsided nature of these figures emphasizes the reliance of would-be female recruits on the interest and goodwill of the chief constable, who was under no compulsion to employ any women if he chose not to do so.[6] In contrast, fifty-two police matrons were employed full-time in these forces, with a further 732 matrons on call. These figures make clear that the long established practice of calling on a policeman's wife or a local woman of good repute to help the police in searching and looking after the rare female prisoner was deemed quite sufficient for police purposes, in what they saw as the chief area where women had a positive contribution to make. At a Home Office conference in 1931, called to consider draft regulations for wpcs, it became clear that the majority of chief constables were opposed to employing women 'precisely because the only activities they were fitted to perform and for which their employment offered any advantage were in the nature of welfare work and not police duties at all'.[7] In view of the proposed government economy measures, even the Metropolitan Commissioner, who favoured the idea of women police more than most, decided to hold wpc numbers (already at half the pre-1922 number) at their existing level. The argument ran 'It would not be easy to defend additional expenditure ... for what every one but a few enthusiasts regards as more of a luxury than a necessity while other economy measures are still in force'. Elsewhere, it was suggested that wpc posts should be abolished or reduced.[8]

A career in the police in the decade before the war thus seemed to offer limited prospects. Nevertheless, the decision by the Secretary of State in October 1931 to issue statutory regulations for women police on the same basis as those prescribed for men in the Police Act of 1919, was a considerable step forward.[9] Women police campaigners, who had been pressing for these regulations for a decade, knew they were vital to

---

6   By 1939 only forty-five out of 183 police forces in England and Wales were employing women, and a sixth of those women had not been sworn in as constables. See Joan Lock (1979) *The British Policewomen: Her Story*, p. 172.
7   *PRO: HO 45 15202/591766/2*, WPC Draft regulations, Minutes of the Central Conference of Chief Constables, 10 July 1931.
8   *PRO: HO 45 15202/591766/15*. Proceedings of the 8th Police Council, 21 October, 1931. *PRO: HO 45 17526/10*, Conditions of Entry of WPCs, 20 December 1933 .
9   For a detailed account, see Carrier, Chapter XVIII.

acceptance of a full role for wpcs in the service. They were passed (after rejection by the 7th Police Council the previous year) by a strongly divided 8th Police Council, which was only placated by the fact that the employment of wpcs remained a voluntary option, open to each chief constable to accept or reject.[10] However, the important point was that the regulations gave attested policewomen uniform conditions of pay, service and pensions, even though their starting pay of 56/- was below that of the men. Candidates had to be unmarried or widows, to resign on marriage, to be over twenty-two and under thirty-five and to measure at least 5 feet 4 inches. They were to be issued with a uniform, and to work an eight hour day, but it was left to the chief constable to decide on their precise duties. These were largely confined to cases involving women and children, especially after the National Council for Women (NCW) ensured that the *Children and Young Persons Act* of 1933 required a policewomen to look after all children in court.[11] This situation remained largely unchanged until the outbreak of war and beyond.

## The Early, 'Post-Regulation' Wpcs

What was the career trajectory, the attitude and the motivation of these early wpcs, the first who could lay claim to the title of police officer? What form of self-image did they hold? How far did they share the outlook and values of the founding members of the womens' police service? Did they see themselves primarily as POLICEwomen or as policeWOMEN?[12]

In the period between regulation in 1931, and 1948 when policewomen were first admitted to the Police Federation women police continued to be organized on a specialist and separate basis. However, even after Home Office recognition in 1948 that 'the law does not know policemen and policewomen but only police officers', their role in the police was to remain

---

10 The Police Federation, strongly opposed to the introduction of wpcs remained unplacated and convinced that their work could be done by police matrons. Carrier, p. 240.

11 *PRO: HO 45 17526/24 and 4*, WPC regulations, 20 July 1933. As an example of a typical police authority, Coventry City, which employed three wpcs attached to CID at the start of the war, issued a list of their duties, thirteen of which related to dealings with women and children. The fourteenth and last item on the list was clerical duties.

12 This conceptualization is from S.E. Martin, 'POLICEwomen and policeWOMEN'.

strictly gendered until the 1975 *Sex Discrimination Act*[13] This is the single most important factor influencing their outlook, as well as their reception. By ensuring that wpcs remained unintegrated into the main body of police, by assigning and largely confining them to gender-related tasks, the police authorities not only confirmed their marginal and subordinate status but thereby also muted the hostility of the general body of policemen, as well as the incidence of sexual harassment. This does not imply that the idea of women police officers was well received inside the service, only that most men never had much, if anything, to do with wpcs in the course of their day. Women did not undertake traffic duties, nor did they often patrol with the men. Their most likely contact would have been as plain clothes officers attached to CID. Here, indeed, resentment could become vocal. The following, facetious comments from an article in *Police Review* gave it expression:

> The year 1933 will go down in police history as the year when the all-conquering female achieved her final conquest by being officially admitted into the mystic rites of criminal investigation. Hitherto, crime investigation has remained an essentially male ritual. Policewomen, it is true, have occasionally been permitted to play a subordinate part in it by typing reports, answering the telephone, playing tennis with CID officers, and making tea for the police cricket team. Now, however, they wish to detect crime for themselves, and much as it grieves one to record the fact, their claims have been recognized by the authorities and women Detectives have recently been appointed in several police forces.[14]

Nevertheless, a sense of threat and harassment, which are paired responses in the field of sexual politics appear to have been largely avoided in the 'latency' period through the simple fact that not only were wpcs few and far between, but because the job continued to be modelled on the traditional female role, and the work related to a separate sphere.[15]

My women informants were clearly aware, and approved of, this fact. They were thus able to combine acceptance of a subordinate standing vis à vis their male colleagues with a sense of relish of their special position, and of their specialist skills. This response was the norm, whether the women

---

13 Jill Radford, 'Women and Policing: Contradictions Old and New' in J. Hanmer, J. Radford and E.A. Stanko (eds 1989) *Women, Policing, and Male Violence*, p. 43.

14 'Eve goes sleuthing'. Article in *Police Review,* 29 September 1933.

15 Joan Lock, for example, described the attitude of the men at her central London station in the 1950s as excellent. She was one of twenty young women among 600 young men, they got preferential treatment, and were treated like pets. Lock, *The British Policewoman*, p. 197.

were organized into a separate women's branch, as in the Metropolitan police, or whether they worked with and were supervised by men, but assigned to specialist duties. Take, for example, WPC Proudfoot, who was the first of two attested policewomen recruited into the Coventry City force in 1938. The strict confinement of her duties to gender specific tasks and a lack of acknowledgement of her general policing capacities was readily accepted by her:

> I think at first they did treat us as a sort of novelty, what can they do, sort of thing. It was quite obvious they didn't know what to do with us ... We'd go along to the CID office and we'd say, what can we do? And sometimes it would be one of these detectives going to interview someone and they'd say 'you can come along with us this morning'. Or maybe there's some females coming up in court, 'go to court'.

*Did you interrogate female suspects?*

> Yes. But quite often, especially if it was very important, the detectives would do it; sometimes we did have a case ourselves, but any important cases, like abortions and that sort of thing where there is a lot of medical evidence, usually one of the detectives would take it. The chief inspector would detail a detective and a policewoman, so you would be there with them, but *they* would be taking the case ... They would be interviewing and we would think of something to ask them, and they would. But taking it through the court would be the detective, yes.[16]

Looking after lost children and any female prisoners was automatically part of their duties. But in addition, writing policemen's reports or listing stolen property was work that the wpcs did 'to help the men when they came on', which the men otherwise would have had to do themselves.

Doing, or being asked to do the men's typing for them as a favour was standard practice even in a city like Birmingham, which had a long established, separately run wpc section. Here, the women had their own building and women supervisors to organize and oversee their work. WPS Willow was one of a new batch after a long gap, so that when she joined in 1933

> there were only old policewomen there, they were all fifty, sixty, we were the first lot of youngsters that came in before the war ... The

---

16  Interview with WPC Proudfoot, Coventry City Police. WPC Proudfoot had to resign from the police on her marriage in 1941, so she only had a few years in the service. Nevertheless, these were most important to her and despite a subsequent career as a security officer, at heart she still felt that she was a policewoman. As she said 'The police has always been with me. It still is'.

> sergeant, they used to call her old mother Miles, she was seventy
> odd when we joined. She was eighty nearly when she finished and
> she was one of the first policewomen, she and Mrs Lipscombe were
> the first two that walked around Birmingham, the first two
> policewomen in 1917 ... there was about seventeen of us when I
> started.

WPS Willow described the set-up:

> We weren't in a police station. We were in a little house in Newton
> Street, next door to us was Lost Property and Hackney Carriages,
> headquarters was on the other side, we were in the middle. Mrs
> Miles' office was in the front room and we were all in the kitchen at
> the back ...

WPS Willow joined the police because she wanted to look after women and
children. This fitted in perfectly with the work the women were required to
do. At first,

> We just sort of mingled with the older women. We didn't have any
> duties, we didn't have any beat or anything. We just used to go, and
> sometimes we'd patrol the city in twos, and then if somebody had
> been to the office and complained about the conduct of husband and
> wife, we went out to interview them, two of us. An older woman
> and us recruits ... and sometimes they came in to the office to
> complain about their daughters who wouldn't come in at night.
> Nothing criminal, it was all sort of domestic we did, for ages and
> ages.

The system worked through word of mouth. People slowly became aware
that there was a women's section where they could go and take their queries
or complaints. Basically, much of this work was case work with families,
with the women police going back to keep check on cases that never came
to court. However, as war approached, the nature of the organization began
to change. The women were now posted to divisional stations, which
Willow liked because there were only two of them in her division and 'we
more or less had our own way'. Much of her work was in plainclothes in
connection with prostitutes and brothels. Here, 'you always had a
plainclothes man with you, you were only more or less a witness to what he
was doing'. The arrangement worked well, in her view, since when it was a
man and a woman arresting a prostitute there wasn't half the trouble that
there was when it was two men, and the presence of a wpc allegedly
reduced the likelihood of bribery and corruption between the prostitute and
the constable. At the same time, as soon as the women police began to work
with the men, a process of downgrading of wpcs was immediately in
evidence. Not only were the men in charge when they were on duty with a

wpc, but they continued to assume (correctly) that the women would do their office chores for them.

> Some of them used to come in and ask us to do their typing for them
> ... I always typed their reports for them... I didn't mind so long as I
> was helping them. I enjoyed my service with the men.

The testimony of WPS Willow is of particular interest since she built her career in the service, achieved promotion to the rank of sergeant, worked as a training officer for new recruits and served for twenty-nine years before leaving to get married. She provides a good example of how the women's section developed in the years prior to full integration in 1975. Her work certainly changed, to include patrol and beat work, but her attitude remained firmly focused on police duties connected with women and children.

The war brought surprisingly little change in this regard. Women, who were such an abundant source of labour, were only recruited in tiny numbers, supplemented by a slightly larger group of Women Auxiliary Police Corps members. It was this latter group who were specifically recruited to replace policemen who had joined up, and although they were issued with a uniform, and some were attested, their numbers were restricted to ten per cent of the force and their work to clerical and driving duties.[17] Regular wpcs rather despised and resented these women, whose uniform could so easily be mistaken for their own (since only the caps were different). Edith Tancred, Director of the Scottish Training School for Policewomen, wrote that the National Council of Women (successor to the NUWW) regarded untrained wapcs in smart police uniforms but without police powers as misleading to the public, and as not serving in any way to meet the need for more attested women constables.[18] It is quite possible that the setting up of the Women's Auxiliary Police Corps had indeed been regarded by the government as one way of increasing police labour resources without committing themselves to a greater women police establishment. But the Home Office also remained cautious about increasing their number because of the lack of suitable candidates; and although the

---

17  *PRO: HO 45 19532/825059/1,* March 1940. The Home Office issued the terms and conditions under which the WAPCs could be employed. Although their wages were to be paid by the Treasury, Buckinghamshire, for instance, decided to set up such a corps on a voluntary, unpaid basis. Whether they thought that payment by central government would be the thin end of the wedge regarding the entry of women into the service, or whether they believed they would attract a better class of women if the corps was made up of volunteers remains a moot point.

18  Edith Tancred, *Women Police,* p.25.

inspectorate declared that 'the war had made clearer than ever before that there is a field for women in the service', the actual figures, and their increase, was derisory.[19] Despite widespread and sustained efforts by local police authorities to attract women into the service, the supply remained negligible.[20]

## The Post-War Wpcs

The early post-war years saw continued difficulties in the recruitment of women for the police service. In the metropolitan area annual recruitment during the year after the war only rose by twelve, which left the total figure of 149 at less than half the establishment.[21] Women, even after the lifting of the marriage ban, were not coming forward in sufficient numbers or of a calibre to suit recruiting officers. Potential policewomen, together with women in so many other spheres, were it seems retreating back into the home. The dearth of applications, even from single women, encouraged a degree of scepticism over the suitability of married female applicants. Thus, a Home Office official was able to comment after the removal of the marriage ban, that 'the most serious difficulty is the question of the action to be taken where the married wpc does not give proper attention to her duties because she is preoccupied with her domestic responsibilities'.[22] It was some years before numbers began to pick up, due to a combination of factors, including Home Office encouragement and the admission of women into the Police Federation. But even though there was an increase of over ten per cent in the number of women employed by the seventeen forces in the study, the figures here had only increased from 105 in 1935 to 1491 in 1964. Women police constables remained a very small minority.[23] The

---

19  *PRO: HO 45 18816/801044/96*, Appointment of WPCs 1937–41. *PP XIV 1945–46*, Report of Inspectors of Constabulary for Year ending September 1945. The figures for policewomen in England and Wales show an increase from 282 in 1940 to 418 in 1945.
20  *Police Review,* 13 October 1944.
21  *PP XIII 1946–47*, Commissioner's annual report for year ending September 1946.
22  *PRO: HO 45 252/6/1,* WPC Recruitment, January 1946.
23  In 1939 there were a total of 246 policewomen in the country, amounting to 0.4 per cent of the total police establishment in England and Wales. By 1963, there were just over 3000, comprising about 3.5 per cent. Figures in Clive Emsley, *The English Police,* p. 149.

question is how far their outlook on police work had changed by the post-war period.

Frances Heidensohn has discussed what she calls the hidden histories of the changing attitudes and the broadening out of their prescribed roles among women who served in the 1970s prior to integration.[24] She sees these women as readily preparing for and responding to integration when it came. However, her sample was drawn from women who were currently serving in the police, so that the few pre-integration women included must have been at the very start of their careers. In the present instance, even those wpcs who joined in the 1950s and 60s continued to believe in the value of separate spheres, and to accept as just their lower pay scale and lack of equality with the men. WPC Haver thought women could never be equal to their male colleagues because of the physical differences, while Sergeant Gilbey recalled that:

> We were classed as a department, whereas now they're integrated with the men. Quite honestly, the girls I've spoken to feel it's not really so good for the job as when we were our own department. Another thing, you see, now they work shift work. We never worked nights unless it was a specific job ... occasionally discussion would arise with the women and they would say, we should get equal pay, we should do the same as the men ... But I didn't agree with those things. I didn't agree with equal pay. I felt that as a woman you couldn't expect to do the same work as a man could do, and I felt we wouldn't get the respect from men if we had equal pay.[25]

Sergeant Gilbey was probably correct in her assessment that respect (as a proxy for the absence of sexual harassment) depended on the wpc's separate and unequal status. But she was not the only one to resent integration. WPC Halsey retired prematurely when she realized that the women police department was going to be disbanded, while a much younger women, WPC Miles, said of integration:

> Well, that finished me, didn't it? When was it, about 1973, when they turned police women into policemen in skirts, that was the end as far as I was concerned, because they wanted me to start working hours that I would never have agreed to in the first place. If I'd had to work the men's hours I would never have joined ... and they did it unilaterally without so much as a by your leave ... it made me very, very angry and very, very bitter. Apart from that, they had taken

---

24  Heidensohn, *Women in Control?* p. 119.
25  Interview with WPC Haver, Birmingham City police; WPS Gilbey, Warwickshire police.

> away from me the main satisfaction that I got from my job, which
> was in effect being a uniformed social worker.[26]

Women police in the period of the 1930s to the 1960s were proud of their
minority status, they enjoyed the public attention this brought them, they
felt cosseted and protected by the men, and privileged in the freedom from
street supervision and routine in their daily work. None of them complained
about any form of sexual harassment from their male colleagues. WPC
Miles' view that there was no sexism, only back chat and bandinage, was
typical – although WPC Lake added that their own attitudes were more
accepting, so that they may not have recognized the sexism for what it
was.[27] However, sexism appears chiefly to have taken the form of a
conventionally 'chivalrous' response to the alien and constricting presence
of women in the workplace, strongly related to their scarcity and novelty,
that wore off as familiarity and a more strident feminism were later to
breed more overtly expressed hostility and harassment. In WPC Miles' day,

> I used to feel sorry for them sometimes, because they were so
> careful about their language. When the women weren't there, the f's
> and c's used to fly like snowflakes in a storm, and sometimes they
> would forget that you were there and I used to feel really sorry for
> them, because all of a sudden it would be 'I'm sorry, Sheila'. And
> I'd say, 'Oh, don't worry about it'.[28]

But while denying any sexism, the women also felt strongly that they were
professionals in their own areas of work, who used different, less
confrontationist and also less colluding methods than the men to get results.
Wpcs offered neither physical violence nor deals to their customers, as was
common amongst the men, since their relationship to the public was
premised on strictly gendered lines on both sides. Thus, their whole
experience was not only separate, but entirely different to that of their male
colleagues. Few of their careers were for life, despite the lifting of the
retirement on marriage ban after the war, and it would seem that they were
quite satisfied with their conditions of work, and their relations with male
colleagues.[29] In this they differed significantly from their pioneering
predecessors *and* from the generation of wpcs who followed after
integration. Their attitudes, despite their unusual job choice, meshed closely
with that of other women of their age and the (upper working) class from

26  Interview with WPC Halsey, Essex police; WPC Miles, Metropolitan police.
27  Interviews with WPC Miles and WPC Lake, Metropolitan police.
28  Interview with WPC Miles.
29  Instructive as it would be, it is impossible to establish a 'true' resignation rate
    for wpcs to compare with that of the men, since marriage and pregnancy made
    resignation more or less a foregone conclusion.

which they were drawn. These were not women with a mission. Their motivation had little or nothing to do with any feminist aspirations for equality but more with a consciousness of job opportunity, a desire to get away from home, and a certain rebelliousness at the boredom of provincial life. It is also notable that four out of the seven wpcs in the sample had fathers or close relatives who were policemen, while one joined as a wartime auxiliary and then went over to the police proper, and one was allowed to join in preference to her own wish to join the WRENS. There was thus little element of shock or surprise involved for the family, and no one reported much in the way of adverse comment from friends. Further, having sown their wild oats, the majority settled down to domestic life after marriage and the birth of their children, in company with the vast majority of their peers. Carrier and others have criticized this generation for not actively ascribing to earlier or later feminists' aspirations for equality of opportunity, work, pay, status and promotion, or of any consciousness that their work with women and children might be oppressive rather than protective.[30] It would, however, be anachronistic to have expected such aims or consciousness in the main body of women police of the era.[31] In the 1930s era of high male unemployment the earlier feminist effort in promoting women's employment gave way to a defensiveness about women's right to paid work at all – a defensiveness that promoted an outlook best described as that of 'conservative modernity', in Alison Light's telling phrase. Women of this generation who would not have dreamed of calling themselves feminists were nevertheless linked, she suggests, by resistance to the 'feminine' as it had been thought of in late Victorian or Edwardian times.[32] Although Light is referring to a group of middle class women authors, her depiction of their outlook as a deferral of modernity but one that demanded a different sort of conservatism from that which had gone before, accurately sums up the stance of the wpcs of the time. Caught between the progressive achievements of the pioneering women's movement and the inhibiting force of high levels of male unemployment, we can best

---

30 Carrier, *The Campaign for the Employment of Women*, p. 257; Woodeson, 'The First Women Police'.

31 However, as already mentioned, the feminist credentials of some of the earliest police women have been called into question by Levine, so that where Carrier describes these women as 'poacher turned gamekeeper', Levine insists that many were 'gamekeepers' all along. Levine, '"*Walking the Streets in a Way No Decent Woman Should*"'.

32 Alison Light (1991) *Forever England: Femininity, Literature and Conservatism between the Wars,* p. 10.

describe this first generation of attested wpcs as 'staunchly innovative in a conservative mode'. [33]

This is further illustrated by the movement for reform. This move towards reform and integration proceeded from above, not below – starting with the decision agreed between Sir Robert Mark and the head of the Metropolitan Women Police, Commander Becke, to abolish the women's section there in 1969.[34] Ironically, the move towards integration has not entirely favoured the situation of women police officers. The hostility of the men when women were brought into direct competition for jobs, and the 'glass ceiling' in the promotion stakes, has become much more overt, while women's loss of their former expertise in the field of work with women and children is emerging as a matter of regret. There are now signs that women are being reinstated and having to relearn practices in specialist areas dealing with rape, domestic violence and child abuse, in which their predecessors had built up a great deal of knowledge and experience. For all their acquiescence in the limitations of their work and career opportunities, Heidensohn believes it is fairer to judge this earlier generation of policewomen as having unique and innovatory roles in which their male colleagues did not share,[35] rather than as women who were only performing half a task. A less positive, but probably more realistic view would be that the specialist and separate position of women police in the latency period was the only way in which they could have functioned without too much hostility and hindrance from their male colleagues, and that their return to these specialisms is a sign of women's weakness within the male-dominated bastion of police work, and not one of strength – however great their expertise.

## Policemen's Wives

In contrast, there was little that was innovative about the role of policemen's wives, whose work was rarely given any public acknowledgement. Police wives, especially in rural areas, were nevertheless deeply embroiled in police work and relied on for their police services by the authorities, and even more so by their husbands. So while there has been a certain amount published about policewomen, there has been very little work focusing on the experiences and perceptions of the wives of policemen as a group who were closely affected by their husband's choice

---

33  Light, op.cit., p. 10.
34  Lock, *The British Policewoman*, p. 201.
35  See Heidensohn, *Women in Control?*, p. 121.

of career.[36] Nevertheless, their position is one that well merits further research, since the outstanding characteristic of the situation confronting police wives was the extent to which they found their lives moulded and constrained by their husband's occupation. This leakage from the husband's policing role did not take place sporadically or only on certain symbolic occasions, but was ongoing, insidious and all-embracing. What was it that brought this about?

First and foremost the wife's situation was structured by the fact that her policeman husband was a public servant whose behaviour came constantly under public scrutiny; and insofar as she was identified in the public's eyes with her husband, she was subject to the same scrutiny. In this respect, the position of the policeman and his wife was equivalent to that of the parson, the doctor and the teacher, with whom country police wives in particular often compared and identified themselves. But the comparison lacks several components that led to the greater constraints experienced by police wives. Policemen did not have the professional qualifications and social status that gave these groups autonomy within their own spheres. Instead, the constable was subject to strict and continuous supervision and discipline, and was liable to be called to account for any shortcomings, with possibly dire material consequences. It is in the degree to which police wives shared responsibility for many of these shortcomings, in the eyes of the authorities, that their situation differed from that of their more fortunate sisters. Further, their position as women within a male-oriented occupational environment could lead to their outright exploitation by the authorities, an exploitation that might well be facilitated and reinforced by their own husband's views on women and work. The lives of police wives were thus doubly constrained by their public and representative function, and by the service role into which they were unwittingly forced. Their response was generally acquiescent. Police wives mostly came from respectable working class or lower middle class backgrounds and could well rank above their husbands in social origin. Policeman might marry women working in unskilled occupations but – at least in the immediate pre-war period – were more likely to marry former nurses, secretaries or teachers. The link between nurses and policemen was particularly pronounced and was commented on by the police themselves, who felt that their ways of life had a lot in common. In many instances, the class discrepancy between policemen and their wives was more apparent than real, since white collar jobs such as nursing or secretarial work were growth areas for female

---

36 One exception is the section on police wives, based on questionnaire data, in Maureen Cain, *Society and the policeman's role*. Her findings are similar to mine.

employment in the inter-war period. But even where there were social class differences, a policeman was still regarded as a most desirable marriage partner, since his work brought security and a reasonable wage at a time of high unemployment. Women in white collar occupations thought themselves lucky to land such a catch, while the police authorities were happy to welcome such respectable spouses for their employees.

## Police Wives' Representative Function

The representative function of the policeman's wife was fundamental in structuring the lives of police families, since it invaded even the remotest corners of the relationship. It was required and expected that police marriages should uphold the ideals and set an example of respectable family life. Any major deviation from the norms deemed necessary for the success of this model were therefore regarded as serious lapses that were liable to bring discredit on the force. Great care was taken to guard against this likelihood. From the start, the representative function of police families was given direct recognition by the police authorities in the conditions they laid down in the years up to the Second World War before giving policemen permission to get married. First of all there was a marriage ban which prevented recruits from getting married at all until they had served for several (normally between three to five) years. No married men could be recruited into the service, while recruits in many forces lived together in section or station houses under the eye of the station sergeant, in conditions not unlike those of army barracks. This gave the police authorities the time and close supervision they thought necessary to mould the men to fit their requirements, while the waiting period gave prospective wives their first taste of the restraints that the service would inflict on their lives. One wife observed philosophically that the ban was in fact good training for the country policeman's wife whose husband was often absent on long tours of duty,[37] while a male apologist for the ban gave as his reason that

> if it were not for the marriage ban the majority of newly joined recruits would undoubtedly take advantage of their comparatively settled position and marry the first pretty face that attracted their attention. This would make it impossible for them to give proper attention to their training and in addition the success of such marriages is doubtful. In the opinion of one who has made a close study of the opposite sex, no man should seriously consider getting married until he is twenty-five. At least five years should be spent

---

37 *Police Review*, 27 May 1938.

> investigating the wiles, mentality and charms of women ... at the end
> it should be possible to separate the chaff from the grain and choose
> something that will turn out fairly well.[38]

Choosing something serviceable, in the guise of someone who would uncomplainingly accept the difficult conditions that went with marriage to a policeman, was clearly no easy matter. But towards the end of the 1930s criticism of the ban was becoming more vocal. By the end of the 1930s, largely because of the recruitment difficulties experienced by many police forces as unemployment started to recede, the marriage ban for men was abolished in 1939.

However, the second condition regarding marriage persisted for much longer, and concerned the vetting of the prospective wife before permission to marry was given by the chief constable. This normally involved a home visit by an inspector, in which not only her own comportment but her address and family circumstances would be taken into consideration: those whose fathers were publicans, for example, could forget all about their wish to marry a bobby.

The final condition of marriage to a policeman was that the wife had to give up all forms of paid employment. Few wives complained since it was so much the norm for the majority of women in the period that it was taken for granted. Wages for single men were quite adequate when compared with those for other working men, but couples might have a financial struggle, particularly since wives were not permitted to try and extend their budgets by taking in lodgers, or sewing, or any of the usual working-class wives' means of self-help. Even unpaid work outside the home was prohibited. In Manchester in 1931, for example, PC Taylor was threatened with dismissal unless he stopped his wife from helping out, unpaid, in her mother's dress shop.[39] After the imposition of a pay cut in 1931[40] as part of the government's economy measures police pay began to fall behind industrial wages and many married couples found it harder to make ends meet despite their rent allowance. The police federation paper, the *Police Review,* started

---

38  *Police Review,* 6 May 1938.
39  Manchester City Police Personal Files, December 1931. Quoted in JoanneMarie Klein (1991) 'A Hot Meal at any Hour: Police Marriage in Manchester, Birmingham and Liverpool 1900—1939'. Paper given to the *Southwestern Historical Association Conference*, San Antonio.
40  The situation was actually slightly more complicated. At first a ten per cent pay cut was proposed in September 1931, which was scaled down after protests to five per cent, with a second five per cent cut in November 1932. Five per cent of the cut was restored in July 1935, but the other five per cent remained as a police grievance up to the start of the war, when pay rates were frozen.

a weekly column entitled 'The Thrifty Housewife' that gave tips for cheap recipes and household savings.[41]

Having made sure that all conditions had been met, the police couple were now free to marry. They were not, however, usually free to choose their own lodgings and were always liable to be transferred to another division at a moment's notice to suit the exigencies of the service rather than their own convenience. Normally, the police were either assigned to police accommodation, or if they found their own, as was the case in most urban forces, the lodgings would be vetted in the same way as police wives, to see that they were not in unsuitable (i.e. disreputable) neighbourhoods or premises. If it was a police-owned house, there were other restrictions, reminiscent of those on council tenants, but rather more stringent. Mrs Kay recalled her move to a police house, one of the first to be built for the Glamorganshire force, and all the restrictions this entailed:

> A big list came round one day, I can't remember half of them, but you weren't to put a nail in the wall, you couldn't wallpaper or paint, you didn't have to put coal in the bath. I'd never heard of that before, and it really tickled me.[42]

More irksome, perhaps, was the condition of some police housing which had been rented by the police authority rather than bought or built by them, especially police houses in rural areas. These were often unmodernized, damp, and vermin-infested. Mrs Clore recalled her first house which had no running water or flush toilet: 'It was one of those awful things where you had to bury it in the garden' she confided;[43] while Mrs Spiller complained that her house was terribly damp. 'What few wedding presents we had, among them were three upholstered chairs and one beautiful fur rug and eventually that came up in pieces, and there was mould growing on the chairs in the front room'.[44] Improvements paid for out of the police families' own pocket brought a poor return, since men were liable to be posted to a new station at a moments' notice. A country policeman's wife described her situation as it was in 1936.

> Our first house cost nearly £50 to be made habitable. £25 alone went to clean it and free it from bugs. There was no bath and not even a kitchen sink — just a tap and a bucket and a hole in the wall ... after the transformation there came another dread — that of having to shift ... then, after four years, the blow fell and another received the benefit of our money and labour. What is my position now? We

---

41  *Police Review*, January 5 1934.
42  Interview with Mrs Kay, Glamorganshire.
43  Interview with Mrs Clore, West Sussex.
44  Interview with Mrs Spiller, West Sussex.

came to a house quite as bad as the first with an outlook fit to break
the heart of any woman·[45]

There was little time and no choice of house when a transfer was ordered.
Mr and Mrs Spiller were given a fortnights' notice to move house with their
two month old baby, while PC Proudy and his wife found that they had
been transferred at a few days' notice to a house without gas or electricity,
so that she had to do her cooking over a coal fire. He said 'I'm not going to
stand for this' and went down to have electricity run to the house, which
they were going to pay for quarterly on their bills. But when he was taken
ill and sent to hospital, his wife was summarily evicted. Spending money on
a police rented house might well therefore be money down the drain, while
complaints or requests for improvements or repairs usually met with a stony
response from the police authority, which above all was concerned to keep
down expenditure on police 'extras'. A prime example of the cheese-paring
that might be involved comes from the Monmouthshire police authority in
1938, when a question arose over the need for police wives to answer the
phone when their husbands were out on night duty, and the committee
solemnly debated the rival merits of supplying wives with bedside telephone
extensions or with dressing gowns. Since the cost of dressing gowns was
assessed at £2 and extensions at 5/-, a decision was taken in favour of
telephone extensions.[46]

While her housing conditions thus might prove disastrous, the  police wife
nevertheless was required to keep up appearances, and in country stations
was subjected to impromptu visits from the sergeant or inspector to make
sure that everything was in order on the domestic front. Mrs Spiller
remembered that the sergeant was a frequent visitor. The chief constable
would also drop in to the cottage at any time of day on his way to the next
town. The sergeant would then call to see what he had wanted. On
reflection, Mrs Spiller thought he was a very insecure person. 'But at the
time you don't think of that', she said, 'you are in awe of them, he was the
sergeant and you didn't offend the sergeant ... Another thing', she went on,
'how a policeman's wife kept her house went towards her husband's
promotion stakes.' When asked if that was spelled out, she said 'Only the
odd remark, nice to see that *some* policeman's wives keep their place
looking nice'. Other wives corroborated this experience. 'We always had to
dress tidy and look tidy', said Mrs Kay. In Warwickshire, the chief
constable would make an annual tour of inspection of police houses, to see
that they were being kept up to the mark. Mrs Ellworthy remembered how

---

45  *Police Review*, 1 May 1936.
46  *Police Review*, 18 November 1938.

he would don a pair of white gloves and run his finger along the skirting board to see if it had been dusted.[47] Wives were held responsible for the standard of housekeeping. But equally, the authorities were concerned that wives should be able to make the right impression socially if their husband moved up the hierarchy. Thus, when interviewing an applicant for the Metropolitan police college, in the short-lived attempt to train an officer class in the 1930s, the interviewer asked whether the applicant's wife would be 'competent to uphold the standing and dignity of the rank, and able to mix with the standard of society his rank would entail him meeting'.[48] A police wife noted the effect, when she wrote that

> I find myself married but without a husband, with little freedom, conscious always that I must put my husband's profession before my natural inclinations, and above all remember that I have 'a certain position to uphold'.[49]

That position was clearly delineated by her husband's, so that when the Eastbourne chief constable's wife entertained police wives to tea, she gave each of them a label to wear indicating their husband's rank, in order that no social gaffes should be committed.[50] But whatever the rank, upholding the standing of a policeman's family was of prime importance. At the first sight of marital scandal or public discord, the husband was liable to get transferred to a different station, or in extreme cases forced to resign. Separation was viewed slightly more favourably than divorce, which could in some forces be grounds for dismissal, as could getting into debt. The records also show instances of policemen being ordered by their chief constable to pay their wife's debts or to keep up maintenance payments in separation cases on pain of transfer or dismissal. The authorities would not countenance the desertion of a wife by a police husband, and in such cases he would have to leave the force.[51] Police wives thus gained some compensation for the intrusion of the police authorities into their lives, in that neglect or abuse by their husbands was not tolerated by their employers. The imposition of standards of respectability on the police couple also had its compensations in the social standing and respect that was accorded police wives, which went some way to counteract their social isolation and the suspicion and reserve that they frequently encountered in

---

47  Interview with Mrs Ellworthy, Warwickshire.
48  *Police Review,* 29 March 1934.
49  *Police Review,* 25 March 1938.
50  *Police Review,* 16 February 1951.
51  JoanneMarie Klein, *'A Hot Meal at any Hour'.*

their social dealings. Mrs Proudy described the consequences. The police wife she met at their first posting had said to her:

> Mrs Proudy, you are a young woman, if you take my advice you'll say nothing about anyone to nobody. So we kept ourselves to ourselves, we never mixed with the public, as the saying is. Never got friendly with anyone' [52]

In these circumstances, police wives usually made friends with other police wives. Mrs Kay again:

> More or less you kept to yourself, you mixed with policemen and their wives, and you didn't seem to mix with outsiders, not a lot ... it was just sort of handed down. But I know I often wouldn't say I was a policeman's wife, other people didn't like the police, and that was it.

In country stations, however, there might be no other police families nearby to socialize with; but here the respect with which the policeman was regarded by the community was extended to the wife, and highly valued by her, as Mrs Clore explained:

> The majority of people would show you respect, they would never be unkind and rude, as I've seen them be to other people ... you met the doctor and his wife, and the teachers and their wives and you had a very nice relationship in that type of person. Of course, you also met the ordinary public ...

Thus while the representative role of police wives enforced very real hardships and constraints on their lives, it did have some compensatory aspects.

## Police Wives' Service Role

The same cannot be said of the police wives' service role, which stemmed from broader societal attitudes on gender divisions regarding home and work. It was these attitudes that were of prime significance in long delaying the full acceptance of policewomen into the service, while prolonging that of police wives as unpaid policemen, as they were quite frequently referred to in the 1930s. There seems to have been little overt response to the plea of one wife, who wrote to the *Police Review* in 1936 that

> No policeman's wife need act as matron or cleaner if she does not wish to do so. Her marriage to a constable does not enter her in a contract to do this, and no Chief Constable has authority to order a

---

52  Interview with Mrs Proudy, Glamorganshire.

> wife to take messages or to remain at home for this purpose. A
> policeman cannot be dismissed if his wife refuses to do these things
> ... my advice to  wives is: refuse to be a policewoman until you are
> sworn in as such and receive the usual wage. Refuse to be a cell
> cleaner, since the wives of many unemployed would be glad to be
> paid for this work. Above all, get rid of the inferiority complex
> towards superior officers which many wives have.[53]

Few dared to follow her advice at the time. The war brought changes here
at a time of great manpower shortages, as it did in so many other spheres
affecting womens' work. But long term change  was a slow process, and it
was not until many years after the Second World War, when circumstances
and attitudes had altered more generally, that the views cited above gained
wider acceptance. Meanwhile, police wives continued to act as unpaid
police assistants. Any payment that was offered was derisory, and confined
to the work of police matrons. Towards the end of the nineteenth century
campaigners for the appointment of matrons to deal with women prisoners
in police stations had succeeded in persuading the Home Secretary that this
was desirable. Police matrons were appointed (sometimes unpaid in the
early years, at which point they were the wives or widows of policemen) to
deal with all cases of female prisoners held in police cells, whether to
search, to guard or to feed.[54] Since female prisoners were thin on the
ground in most areas, this often simply meant calling in a woman who lived
locally when the need arose who, for a few shillings, would perform the
tasks required. But equally often, in the absence of any women police, the
job fell to the wife of the station inspector or sergeant. Mrs Proudy recalled
that when the inspector was away, her husband took over the police station,
and she then had to act as police matron.

> I had to go with him to arrest the person, down to the station and
> search them, on one occasion there was a telephone call and a
> woman was picked up for stealing, a dreadful person, and I had to sit
> alongside her in the car, it was hard work, she was so filthy dirty ...
> She was put in a cell and I had to sit with her all night.

For this she was paid 1/- per call, and another 1/- if she also cooked dinner
for the prisoner. Mrs Proudy provides an extreme example, not so much of
the exploitation of wives that went on in many county forces, but of the
callous way in which the authorities might ditch them once their services
were no longer required. In other respects, her story stands as testimony to

---

53  *Police Review*, 24 December 1936.

54  See Lynne A. Amidon (1986) 'Ladies in Blue: feminism and Policing in the late
    19th and early 20th centuries' *PhD thesis*, State University of New York at
    Binghampton, p. 43.

the experiences of countless other police wives. In common with all police wives in detached country stations, whilst living there Mrs Proudy was regarded as a proxy policeman. She recalled:

> We were real servants to the police station there. We couldn't go out without telling them, we always had to ring and tell them if we were going out, because I had to be at the telephone ... One night there was a call at three in the morning and it was the station asking is Proudy about? I said no, he was out on the chicken run as we called it, it was near Christmas time, you know, watching the farms. Well, he said, there's a car been stolen in Cardiff coming this way, and you go out and watch which direction it takes. I said not on your life, not at this time of the morning, there are no lights in Lisvane, I'm not going to risk being knocked down ... My husband said I shouldn't have done it, I should have told them it wasn't convenient, shouldn't have told them the way I did.

So she did not even have her husband's support for her small defiance of police expectations. But when her husband fell ill, the station was in a great hurry to dispense with her services. As soon as it was discovered that Proudy would need a long stay in hospital, she was evicted since – as the Superintendent told her 'I want you out of the police station, we must put a man in there'. She was forced to put her furniture in storage and return to her parents until her husband came out of hospital, without the slightest consideration being shown her by an authority which clearly thought it owed her nothing.

Husbands, like their employers, also tended to expect a degree of subservience in their wives that went beyond the norm. The rigours of the shift, which meant that half the time the husband was working nights, and the wife had to keep the children quiet during the day, while getting meals for them by day and for him by night, already imposed a heavy strain on family life. But in addition, as C. H. Rolph – himself for long a City policeman – wrote in one of his books: 'the consciousness of authority spoilt one in ten of policemen'.[55] Mrs Spiller would have agreed. Her husband rarely took her out, since he believed that her place was in the home. 'I was the wife at home with the children. That was my position according to him, and that has been so throughout our married life'. Another wife summed it up as follows for Ted Willis when he was gathering material for the script of the *Blue Lamp*, 'I can't stand the hours, and I can't stand the arrogance that goes with the uniform'.[56]

A police wife before and shortly after the Second World War had a husband who was protected from unemployment – unless he put a foot

---

55  C.H. Rolph (1988) *Further Particulars*, p. 59
56  Interview with Ted Willis, January 1992.

wrong – and had a regular wage packet and the prospect of a pension. The police authority would also protect her and her children from maltreatment or abandonment by her spouse. However, as we have seen, she paid a heavy price for this security. The epitaph on police wives in the era must come from Mrs Dicey, interviewed shortly before her fiftieth wedding anniversary.[57] When asked whether she would change anything if she had her life over again, she surprised herself, and her husband, by saying quite passionately

> Well, I don't think I would marry a policeman ... I never saw him, I mean its a wonder our marriage didn't go wrong, because he was never there ... it was *very* lonely, yes, especially at weekends when everybody else was at home, and holiday times ... My husband had one weekend off in seven, and then we were able to go out. But you might just be getting ready to go out and the telephone would go, there'd been an accident, and he'd have to go. You were never free. We were expected to do everything, if there was a road accident, they'd bring people down, we had to look after them, they came to the door with all sorts of things, you had to be doctor, solicitor and general factotum ... Nowadays police stations just shut up and put a notice on the door.

That's the difference. But it took many years until the police service arrived at this point, and police wives gained some measure of freedom in and for their private lives. Even so, they are still being described by one police analyst of the contemporary scene as 'reflections of the public image of their husbands' occupation and status'.[58] Whereas no force now expects police wives to provide their services free and unasked, the representative function of their role remains, and probably always will remain an ineradicable part of being a policeman's wife. Similarly, while no one officially questions the suitability of women to become police officers, their denigration and abuse by male colleagues continues, while their position within the current police occupational culture continues to be one of 'structural marginality'.[59]

From the men's point of view, a policewoman could only be made 'safe' and returned to her proper sphere if she left paid police employment and re-entered it, unpaid, as a policeman's wife. Then, all the female qualities that make her such a threat within the service would find their natural place and

57 Interview with Mrs Dicey, Warwickshire.
58 Malcolm Young, 'Police Wives: a Reflection of Police Concepts of Order and Control' in H. Callan and S. Ardener (eds 1984) *The Incorporated Wife*, p. 67.
59 The phrase is Malcolm Young's. See *An Inside Job*, Chapter 4, 'Women in the Police: a Case of Structural Marginality'.

setting.[60] Even male supporters of women in the police subscribed to this
view. Thus, Eric St Johnstone noted that

> I have always been a strong supporter of the women police ... but in
> recruiting girls, I insisted that we should select feminine girls rather
> than 'collar and tie' types. What one wants from a woman is the
> feminine point of view and intuition. The disadvantage of selecting
> the feminine type of woman is that they usually get married after a
> short while ... but all is not lost for they usually marry policemen,
> and make good wives ...[61]

The work situation of the pre-integration generation of women police, and
their own acceptance of their status and role meant that they avoided the
grosser forms of male hostility and sexual harassment. They are thus able to
look back with pride, warmth and affection on their former careers. The
recollections of policemen's wives, quite apart from whether they had
successful marriages or not, are far more critical. Ironically, it was
policemen's wives in their 'proper place' who bore the brunt of the dominant
and domineering male police culture, rather than their female police
counterparts, who were to some extent shielded from it.

60  Young, *An Inside Job*, p. 193.
61  Eric St Johnstone (1978) *One Policeman's Story*, p. 281.

# CHAPTER SEVEN

# Policing in Wartime

With the coming of war, the police service was put to its greatest test. The war drew men and women away from their accustomed tasks and responsibilities, broke up families and started an unsettling flow of population around the country because of war work, evacuation, homelessless, the internment of aliens and conscription into the armed forces. The police were expected to deal with many of the social consequences of these events, although no major institutional alteration was envisaged. None of the measures considered prior to the war involved any radical reorganization by way of nationalization or regionalization of the police. It was assumed that the British police forces would retain their individual identity and remain under local control.[1] But while the structure remained largely unaltered, it was clear that police duties and personnel would be radically affected. There was going to be strong competition from the armed forces and industry for police manpower, while the exigencies of war would inevitably place new protective and organizational tasks on the police. Fairly detailed plans and estimates to meet these requirements had been worked out in the years preceding the outbreak of war by a Home Office committee of selected chief constables and the Air Raid Precautions department of the Home Office, which helped to prepare the *Police War Instructions*. These instructions were issued in August 1939, and formed the basis of the standing instructions throughout the war. Their main focus was on the formation of police reserves; on measures of internal security such as the control of aliens and the prevention of sabotage; and on duties in connection with air raids and their effect on the civilian population. Target figures on the recruitment of temporary constables were set out, as well as the sources from which these might be met. For internal security, measures concerning aliens and subversive organizations were largely based on an extension and development of pre-war practices, since aliens were already controlled under the various *Aliens Restrictions Acts* which would simply need strengthening through Orders in Council. Similarly, the pre-war activities of the IRA had resulted in the *Prevention of Violence (Temporary Provisions) Act* (1939) which gave the police special powers, that were then

---

1    Sir A.L. Dixon (1963) *The Emergency Work of the Police Forces in the Second World War,* M/S, Bramshill Police Staff College Library.

extended under the Defence Regulations.[2] These regulations (even after amendment due to opposition pressure) enormously increased the powers of the police, so that they were now able to arrest without a warrant anyone suspected of breaching the defence regulations, and were given extended rights of search and entry. As far as enemy attack was concerned, the most difficult to forecast were estimates about the scale of requirements for dealing with the civilian population in the event of air raids. It was thought that this latter task would reach mammoth proportions, on the assumption of a general collapse of morale following enemy air attacks – to the extent that the Metropolitan Commissioner envisaged the need for 17,000 regular troops and 20,000 extra police to control the expected exodus from London and prevent panic.[3]

Soon after the outbreak of war, existing police reservists (a total of just under 3000 men, or about five per cent of the total of 60,000 regular police in England and Wales) were called up. Given the absence of air raids, sabotage or other enemy activity, the most pressing problem facing the police service at the outbreak of war became that of replacement manpower. There were three sources to draw on: the First Police Reserve, which consisted mainly of police pensioners who had been paid a small retainer on the understanding that they would come back to full-time service when called upon to do so, and who numbered around 10,000; Special Constables, who were a voluntary, part-time and normally unpaid body of men numbering around 131,000 just prior to the war; and the Police Reserves, to be made up of men over thirty not working in a reserved occupation, who would be encouraged to join the service as full-time, paid and uniformed officers. As we have seen, a small Womens Auxilliary Police Corps, mainly engaged in part-time clerical and chauffeuring duties was also set up rather reluctantly after pressure from the National Council of Women.[4] At the end of 1940 the composition of the police in England

---

2   On the relevant Acts, see F.H. Hinsley and C.A.G. Simkins (1990) *British Intelligence in the Second World War: Security and Counter-Intelligence*, vol. 4, pp. 22–3.

3   R.M. Titmuss (1950) *Problems of Social Policy*, p. 19;   PRO: Mepo 3/3066, Police War Diary 1939–45. Metropolitan police files give a far higher estimate of 45,000 for the extra police required. The highest number achieved was 27,074 on 16 September 1939.

4   Dixon, pp. 24–5. The Home Office were very cautious over the formation of this Corps, and decreed that they should only work part-time and might not exceed ten per cent of the authorized establishment. Their wages, like those of the war reserves, would be recoverable from the Exchequer, but they would be unattested (i.e. not sworn in as constables).

and Wales was made up of almost two thirds regular police, seven per cent First Police Reserves, and twenty-eight per cent War Reserves and Special Constables, making a total force of just over 88,000. What was the effect of this influx, and of the new tasks brought by the war, on the functioning of the service and on police organization generally? In particular, did the impact of the war bring fundamental change to the ethos, methods and objectives of the police and to its relations with the public? The extent and permanence of the social changes wrought by the war are a topic of fierce debate amongst historians, with revisionists modyifying earlier views that the war was a key turning point in class relations, in the distribution of wealth and political power, in welfare provision, in the role of women, and in many other matters.[5] The consensual image wrought by the war has also come under fire.[6] So far no one has looked at the police in this context.

One might have expected was that the sudden, large influx of untrained volunteers and the exodus of young regular police officers would have had the effect of turning a strongly hierarchical institution that relied on pettyfogging disciplinary methods of internal control into something resembling a 'peoples' police'. Further, that the common effort of the police and the ARP and civil defence forces in preparing for enemy attack and in dealing with the human consequences of air raids would strengthen the service aspect of police work, and by bringing the police into contact with a broader section of the public, improve relations between them. Together, it seemed likely that these would have a long term impact on the nature of the service in the form of less rigid internal discipline and closer links with a wider public. In the event, the research did not confirm these expectations. Both the chronology and causes of change were different. The impact of the influences for change will be discussed in turn, starting with that of changes in personnel.

---

5   Most of the debate over the supposedly revolutionary impact of the war has centred cn social policy questions and the origins of the welfare state or on its effect in swinging the country towards socialism. The major protagonists in favour of an 'optimistic' view of the impact of war are Titmuss, *Social Policy*; Paul Addison (1975) *The Road to 1945* ; and Arthur Marwick (1974) *War and Social Change in the Twentieth Century*. Among the growing band of revisionists on the left and the right are Corelli Barnett (1986) *The Audit of War*; Harold L. Smith (ed. 1986) *War and Social Change*; Penny Summerfield (1984) *Women Workers in the Second World War*.
    See José Harris (1992) 'War and Social History: Britain and the Home Front during the Second World War' *Contemporary European History*; and Angus Calder (1991) *The Myth of the Blitz*.

**The War Reserves**

Chief constables were asked by the Home Office to begin recruiting war reserves in the spring of 1939. The ARP were also recruiting volunteers prepared to offer full-time service. Their pay had been fixed at a flat rate of £3 per week, regardless of skill or the nature of their duties.[7] The same rate and main conditions of service were extended to the war reserves, since it was felt that a higher rate would create a very awkward situation for the ARP, who were drawing on the same pool of labour. War reserves had to be over thirty, they were sworn in as constables, had powers of arrest, and were (eventually) issued with uniforms. Visually then, there was little to distinquish them from regular policemen except for the letters WR on their collars, and their possible smaller stature.[8] But as volunteers they lacked training, discipline and the constraints that promotion and a distant pension might place on police behaviour. Until the 'trial by Blitz' when many war reserves proved their worth, they were almost universally despised, ignored or resented by the regular police. They were regarded as draft dodgers and known as 'cut price bobbies'. This response was underscored by circumstances in the first year of war when, in the absence of air raids or invasion, the numbers recruited proved totally at variance with the need for their services.[9] War reserves volunteered, or were recruited by regulars (who were offered time off for any recruits they brought in), until numbers swelled to such an extent that many beats were halved and halved again. 'We halved beats, we quartered beats, we invented patrols and traffic points', a Metropolitan police officer recalled.[10] Another described the consequences:

---

7   See T.H. O'Brien (1955) *Civil Defence,* pp. 204–5. A recruiting campaign for the ARP was launched by the Prime Minister in January 1939. The minimum age for volunteers varied between services from twenty-five to thirty.

8   War reserves in fact were issued with a flat cap rather than a police helmet. But since the police wore tin hats most of the time, this distinction was not often in evidence.

9   There were large regional variations, however. Whereas the Metropolitan force and some others had more auxilliaries than regulars by October 1939, other cities had a far lower proportion (Cardiff, with only two per cent being outstandingly low). The average for county forces was forty-nine per cent, and for cities and boroughs, twenty-two per cent. Dixon, op.cit. p. 141.

10  An informant recounted sorting out three likely fellows from amongst the stall holders and barrow boys on his beat. Ten other pcs did the same, so that on a particular day there was a queue of twenty-five to thirty would-be policemen at the station, and my informant had earned himself two days off. Interview with Sergeant Martin, Metropolitan police.

We were expecting people to be killed by the hundreds and thousands. That's why they had war reserves. We must have had 5-600 people at my station because they were expecting to be killed so quickly, you see. And so much so that ... each relief had three times as many (men). They came into the section house and sat down for four hours (otherwise) you would have had more policemen in the streets than pedestrians ... The war reserves came in with no training. There were all sorts, solicitors and road sweepers, and of course they had no uniform but they had a tin hat and a gas mask and a chair leg as a truncheon ... they were doing nothing, just walking around, and people got fed up with it, and gradually these war reserves would go back to their jobs and the police would let them go, because they just didn't need them.[11]

Here we see the first reason why the war reserves made little impact on the regular police service, in that the gap between reserves and regulars was too wide for the latter to be taken seriously in a situation where they were not regarded as performing any useful function. Reservists therefore felt justified in trying to combine policing with their own work, and disillusionment on both sides led to a rapid falling off in numbers.[12] This early police experience of close contact and co-operation with members of the public did not therefore result in a new harmonious relationship in which status differences were overcome or overlooked. Instead, reservists were made aware of their lowly standing and felt badly treated. 'Its always the bloody same, it never happens to the regulars' said one when he was called on duty during his rest day.[13] The result was that in London, for example, numbers dwindled from a peak of 27,064 in September 1939 to 15,472 in February 1941.[14] In the words of the chairman of the *Police Auxilliary Association*:

During the spring and summer of 1940 there was an amazing exodus from the ranks of the Auxilliary Police Force, for men, aware of official aloofness ... took the opportunity of leaving a service where precedent appeared rooted and beyond challenge, where tolerance

---

11   Interview with Inspector Outram, Metropolitan police.

12   Publicans and barrow boys were seen at their old workplaces during police duty hours, while market porters were renowned for wearing their police capes whatever the weather, to hide the alarm clocks that would wake them from their police duties so that they could be back in the markets on time. Interview with Sergeant Martin, Metropolitan Police.

13   *WCRO*, Misconduct Forms, Police War Reserves, 1 March 1941.

14   *PRO: Mepo 5/220*, Establishment and Strength of the War Reserve, 1941–48.

was stifled by tradition, and where the professional policeman was
too frequently 'out of sympathy'.[15]

The debut of the war reserves had not been impressive. However, after the
air raids began in earnest, they retrieved their reputation in the common
struggle against death and destruction, when 'differences were shelved and
comradeship discovered'.[16] But as the pressure on manpower increased, this
accord was often shortlived. By 1942, when regular police officers in their
twenties became liable to call up, older men were being directed into the
Police War Reserve as an alternative to service in the armed forces, under
the National Service Act of 1941.[17]   Altogether, nearly 5000 men were
enrolled and directed to those police forces that stood in greatest need of
manpower.[18] But as the number of regulars decreased, and those of the
reserve increased, there was corresponding pressure for better pay and
conditions for men who were now in a reserved occupation, who had
eventually received some measure of training and who were carrying out
normal police duties. Accordingly, while their pay scale continued to be
linked to that of civil defence workers, they received a pay rise that put
them above the starting pay of regular pcs. This renewed resentment among
the regulars and put the reserves on the defensive.[19] An informant recalled

---

15  *PRO: Mepo 2/7050. The Police Auxilliary – His Story and Troubles.* Pamphlet
    distributed to members of Parliament in the auxilliaries' campaign for better
    pay and conditions in 1944.

16  Ibid.

17  The basis for this decision was the loss of civil defence workers to the armed
    services and industry. Reluctantly, since it was unwilling to destroy the
    voluntary basis of the ARP services, the government ordered firemen and police
    reservists to stay in their jobs, and announced that men between thirty and fifty
    could volunteer for either duty as an alternative to military service. See Sir
    Harold Scott (1951) *Your Obedient Servant,* p. 121. Sir Harold Scott, who was
    to become Commissioner of the Metropolitan Police after the war, was
    appointed in February 1939 as Chief Administrative Officer of the London
    region with the job of organizing and coordinating all its civil defence and ARP
    services.

18  The peak year for the number of war reserves in England and Wales was 1941,
    when 29,719 were in post. After that, numbers declined steadily to 1945 when
    there remained 12,951 in post. See *PP XIV 1945–46:* Report from HM
    Inspectors of Constabulary for Year ending September 1945, p. 6.

19  As illustrated by one war reserve – rather pathetically signing himself
    'Intruder'– who wrote 'I agree that the Auxilliary should not be paid more than
    the Regular, but the statement that the Reserves are not, and cannot hope to be,
    as useful as the average regular constable, just puts into print the average

one war reserve asking a regular 'how do I do this?' and heard the regular reply 'You're getting more money than me. Why should I tell you'.[20]

The gulf between the auxilliaries and the regulars remained – the more so, since no sooner had a decision been taken to make auxilliary policing a reserved occupation than demand for labour for the war industries forced the Home Office to make concessions which allowed for the full or part-time release of police reservists to industry. Men once more began to leave the service, thereby preventing the forging of long term links and a community of outlook between them and the regulars. From a peak in 1941, the number of reservists fell by 2000 in 1942 and in 1943; by 8000 in 1944 and by 5000 in 1945.[21] So what was the effect on the force as a whole?

There was undoubtedly some impact on discipline. War reserves, whose career was not dependent on commendations from their superiors, were clearly little troubled by disciplinary threats. Indeed, they were not always clear that the disciplinary code of the police applied to the reserves.[22] The diary of a London war reserve in the summer of 1940 provides an illustration of the general attitude, first when he wonders as his alarm clock goes off whether he should get up, since 'I had not been late in a long time, so it would be excusable'. Being late for parade would *never* have been excusable in a regular. Second, when he notes seeing a very high police official, but 'did not know whether he was a police officer or St Johns Ambulance, so did not salute'.[23] The reserves brought a new 'civilian' outlook into the job that led regulars to comment on their bad influence in this respect:

> Well, they were not policemen in a sense. They hadn't had the training or the discipline or anything like that. They were glorified Special Constables ... the sergeants and inspectors, they had to make allowances for these people. They had to treat them with kid gloves. Because they were just as likely to say, well you can go and ... They

---

Regular's idea of the capabilities of War Reserves'. *Police Review*, 11 July 1941.

20 Interview with Inspector Outram, Metropolitan police.

21 *HMI Report*, op. cit. p. 7.

22 A war reserve, charged with an offence under the Discipline Code objected that he did not know he was offending against the code, since he had never been informed of its contents, and was unaware that such a code was in force for police war reserves. *WCRO, CR 2770*: Police War Reserve Misconduct Forms, 1 March 1941.

23 *Mass Observation Archive: Day Diary of a War-Time Policeman*, entries 11 July and 20 June 1940.

were like that ... they would do things that we wouldn't, you see ... discipline was bound to suffer.[24]

However, it was not only the advent of the war reserves that had an undermining effect on discipline. Recalled police pensioners (the First Police Reserve) were also not amenable to the pre-war disciplinary standards. They were old hands who had probably achieved some rank and who were not going to take kindly to the pettier forms of discipline were it to be applied to them. These were men past their 'sell by date' – in the phrase of one of my informants – men of around sixty who, according to another, were looking for a quiet life.[25] Supervisory officers were unlikely to try and throw their weight around with the police pensioners. In any case, they were overworked because of the additional administrative duties brought about by the war. They had less time, and little motivation, to walk the streets looking out for minor transgressions by pcs, since booking a few war reserves or police pensioners would not have gone very far to help them in the promotion stakes.

## Wartime Policing Tasks

Policing was affected by other things than changes in personnel, since the war disrupted normal police routines, outside the intense but intermittent effect of air raids, by the imposition of new tasks. Firstly, these involved a great deal of stretching and redeployment of police manpower. The *Police War Instructions* listed the main tasks as intelligence work, the control of aliens, and the protection of vulnerable points. But there were many others, ranging from the distribution of gas masks and gas attack training to the sounding of air raid sirens and the billeting of evacuees.[26] Police stations and vulnerable points, such as power stations, key war factories and communications centres had to be guarded; an aliens officer had to be appointed to each station for the registration of aliens; police, war reserves and ARP personnel had to be trained in anti-gas measures; and every police force was required to set up a Special Branch department to deal with espionage and fifth columnist activities. Traffic departments were also reorganized for war duties. Nevertheless, the underlying structure of policing based on patrolling the beat remained in place. This meant that

---

24  Interview with Inspector Cooke, Birmingham City police.

25  Interview with Inspector Astley, West Sussex Constabulary; and Chief Inspector Sheen, Norfolk Constabulary.

26  See H.M. Howgrave-Graham (1947) *The Metropolitan Police at War*, p. 16.

many officers actually experienced little change in police work outside any bombing incidents in which they may have been involved. And even the specialists frequently found that their wartime tasks were meshed with 'normal' policing through the simple expedient of greatly extending the hours of duty, for twenty-four hours if need be. For example, the pc who was bomb disposal officer for his county, was still expected to continue with his ordinary policing tasks [27]. Similarly, aliens officers soon had their task relegated to fit in with other routine work.[28] Initially, one officer recalled:

> when the war started we had an aliens officer at every station. And to start with he would deal with any aliens, but after a while they became a little bit thin on the ground, and the station officer had to deal with them. But what it was, they'd come in and say 'change of address' or something like that, which was nothing – fill in the book and Bob's your uncle. The only problem we did have was aliens weren't allowed to go into certain areas, so you had to send a telegram to the Chief Constable of that area and say, will you accept him, and that sort of thing. But not often, you wouldn't have one a month, I don't suppose.[29]

As far as vulnerable points were concerned, if unarmed these were often assigned to war reserves in order to relieve the regulars for normal police duty; if armed, this became just one more four hour point duty to be taken on board. In addition, police stations had to be guarded, for which the station officer was issued with a gun. It was probably more effective in scaring the natives than in warding off any would-be attacker. One pc recalled:

> There were more policemen injured by this station officer than by the enemy, I think ... Because some blokes, if they got a gun – and they were automatics, you see – the only way they could see if there was a bullet in, they would pull the trigger and that's what they used to do, instead of taking the magazine out ... And there was chaos then, because even if it did no damage and didn't hurt anybody, they're a bullet short and how the hell are they going to explain that, because they've got to hand the gun over with eight rounds of ammunition and they've only got seven. But at Bow Street, there was a gunsmith there who was very favourable to the police, and

---

27  Interview with Inspector Archer, Durham County constabulary.

28  One beat officer recalled having to call every night at a house where an eighty-five year old German woman lived, to make sure that she was at home at ten thirty p.m. She was always in bed asleep but he was required to go up and check. Interview with Inspector Hay, Birmingham City police.

29  Interview with Inspector Outram, Metropolitan police.

you'd go and see him and tell him the tale, and he'd let you have a bullet.[30]

Since very few policemen had been armed before the war, one would have expected that some instruction or training would have been given. However, no such training was forthcoming. Instead, police on armed duties were simply issued with a revolver and sent out on watch. But as the fear of invasion and sabotage receded, the guard on a number of vulnerable points was slowly diminished.

Special Branch work in local police stations was assigned to CID officers, whose work thus changed little, except that the object of their surveillance was now enemy suspects instead of criminals. The bulk of this work was focussed on the IRA, with a special watch kept on the reception ports from Ireland. Watch was also kept on any known or suspected communists, notwithstanding the status of Russia as an ally.[31] Government suspicion of pacifists and of British communist party activity remained as an undercurrent throughout the war, with the emphasis on counter-propaganda rather than supression, through the application of the defence regulations under the *Emergency powers Act*.[32] Known Fascists do not seem to have been regarded as an active threat after the BUF was banned and most of its members imprisoned in 1940, and were perhaps not so closely watched.[33] When Sir Oswald and Lady Mosley were released from detention in 1943, they were simply required to report to the police once a month and confined to a seven mile radius from where they were living, despite widespread

---

30  Ibid.

31  One Special Branch officer was posted to Holyhead, the port for Ireland, where he worked in conjunction with Immigration.  Although Special Branch kept watch on fascists, communists and crooks, the biggest group under surveillance, he said, were the IRA. Interview with Detective Inspector Pugh, Metropolitan police. Another CID officer, seconded to Special Branch, kept special observation all through the war on the 150 known communists in Hull. Interview with Detective Inspector Farrell, Hull City police.

32  The use of counter-propaganda rather than the criminal law  was the line chiefly taken by the government against communist activity. An exception was the supression of the *Daily Worker* for a period after the communist inspired 'People's Convention' meeting calling for a 'people's peace' at the beginning of 1941. See Neil Stammers (1983) *Civil Liberties in Britain during the 2nd World War*, Chapter 4.

33  See Colin Cross (1961) *The Fascists in Britain*. Cross states that at the August 1940 peak there were 1600 British subjects in prison without trial (under Defence Regulation 18b), of whom three-quarters were members of the BUP. By mid-1941 only 400 fascists remained in prison. Ibid.,p. 195.

indignation and almost unanimous disapproval at their release[34] – whereas a CID officer had to attend the local meetings called by the communist party in protest at the Mosleys' release.[35] Elsewhere, there were more vociferous protests and demonstrations, and Herbert Morrison, who had ordered the release, came in for much criticism from the Labour Party.[36]

The one group which experienced greater disruption was the traffic police, whose task in the war changed from keeping an eye on offending motorists to waiting on stand-by and acting as drivers for high up officers. Petrol for normal police work was not available since this had to be conserved for management purposes. An officer from a county traffic division recalled:

> We were very restricted, we were gated at headquarters. We had a deep shelter there, we used to have to sleep there, we not allowed to go anywhere unless we were called to an incident ... As soon as war was declared all the traffic department was on stand-by ... for relief in the divisions and other war duties. For instance, when the invasion was expected we were detailed to learn by heart and in the dark the evacuation routes where the local people were to be evacuated away from the coastal areas ... as things settled down we went back to nearly normal work until of course the air raids started, and then we were back to the original intention for us to stand by at headquarters for relief in the divisions ... It seems to be a blank period in my police service as such, because we weren't doing police work, we were doing more relief and rescue work, rather than police work, it wasn't work that you well remember.[37]

Similarly, a traffic pc from elsewhere remembered operating what he called a taxi service, in that:

> Everytime there was an air raid warning we had to go to the Superintendents and different ranks in the force and bring them all in to their respective headquarters from home ... Where bombs dropped and incidents occurred, they'd come across from Central for a car to go here and a car to go there ... if you were at home, you

---

34  *PRO: INF/1182,* Ministry of Information Home Intelligence Weekly Report No. 164, 25 November 1943.

35  There were fifteen people in attendance at the first meeting. The lights fused after fifteen minutes and the meeting ended with an audience of five. The second meeting was cancelled because nobody came. *Eric St Johnston papers,* European Centre for the Study of Policing: Report of Meetings, 17 December 1943 and 4 January 1944.

36  See A. W. Brian Simpson (1992) *In the Highest Degree Odious: detention without trial in wartime Britain,* p. 390.

37  Interview with Inspector Chambers, Essex County Constabulary. His comments are corroborated by another traffic man from the same force. Interview with Inspector Brierley, Essex County Constabulary.

> were on call eight hours before your time for duty ... on an air raid
> warning, you turned out ...[38]

Men from traffic might also be redeployed as driving instructors, or to run ARP instruction courses for civil defence workers, reservists and regulars. For the traffic police the war altered the whole focus of their work away from policing purposes. But for the rest of the police, these purposes remained as the bedrock of their daily routines, however much extended or disrupted by new tasks and bombing attacks.

## Relations with Civil Defence Workers

The last aspect to be considered in assessing the effect of the war on the police institution is the relationship of the police and the civil defence services and the response to air raids. For purposes of civil defence, Britain was divided into twelve regions, each under the direction of a Regional Commissioner responsible to a Minister of Home Security.[39] Within each region, an ARP controller had to be appointed by the local authority with wide powers over matters of civil defence. Nearly half those appointed were county or town clerks, over a quarter were chief constables, and most of the remainder were councillors.[40] London was a special case in that incident control was not placed in the hands of the police, but in that of a selected Incident Officer, who was usually drawn from the warden's service.[41] For the rest of the country, where controllers were not chief constables, police officers often acted as deputy controllers, while the wardens' service came under the general charge of the chief constable in about 200 of the 250 areas involved.[42] However, it was made clear that controllers would have no responsibility or powers over the police nor, where a chief constable was appointed controller, would he be acting by virtue of his office as a policeman. Chief constables thereby ensured that their independence from local authority control was preserved, but at the cost of friction and

---

38 Interview with Sergeant Freeth, Hull City police.
39 Under 'normal war conditions', the Commissioners' authority was limited to their coordinating role, but in the event of complete disruption of communications with government, they were empowered to exercise the full powers of civil government. See O'Brien, *Civil Defence*, p. 175.
40 Ibid., p. 315.
41 *PRO: HO 186/554*, Ministry of Home Security: Memorandum on Incident Officers and Incident Control, 7 May 1940.
42 O'Brien: pp. 176–77.

misunderstanding.[43] Given the absence of uniformity and clear lines of command, relations between the police and ARP workers could become strained when one side tried to exert authority over the other. Nor was the Home Office ever able to solve the problem, despite issuing a circular stating that a senior police officer was considered the best person to act as incident officer and to assume the general direction of the other services. But since wardens as well as police were being trained as incident officers, this created many difficulties. Chief constables were unsympathetic to indications that non-police incident officers might want to take control, while the ARP felt the police knew little or nothing about the ARP services, yet wanted to interfere.[44] In London, incident officers felt that they were getting very little help from the police.[45] In Leeds, an instruction to air raid wardens that all contraventions of the blackout regulations must be reported to the police led to the resignation of a number of wardens, who said they would not become messengers to the police.[46] In Sussex, where incident control was officially vested in the police, success was impeded by 'the antipathetic attitude of some ARP authorities who have never really accepted the Home Office circular, and are pressing for control by ARP Incident Officers',[47] while in Birmingham and Warwickshire there was considerable friction due, according to the Inspector of Constabulary, to bad relations between the respective chief constables and controllers.[48]

The Home Office never really resolved this conflict, and its own instructions compounded the confusion. On the one hand it instructed that the police should not take charge of the work of other services. What they were to do was take charge of the scene and clear up confusion between

---

43  This problem had been forseen and ruled on before the war. See *PRO: HO 186/88*, Central Conference of Chief Constables Held at the Home Office, 27 June 1939.

44  O'Brien, *Civil Defence*, p. 567.

45  *PRO: HO 186/2319*. Note from W.B. Brett, London Civil Defence Region to Mr Simpson at the Home Office, 9 May 1941. Brett noted that 'whereas some months ago the usual complaint was that the police tried to do the work of the ARP parties, the complaint now seems to be that very often they do not turn up at all'.

46  *Police Review*, 27 October 1939.

47  *PRO: HO 45/19509*. Letter to Sir A.L. Dixon from the South-East Region Controller, 10 December 1940.

48  *PRO: HO 186/554*, 'Incident Officers': Note by Mr Vince, 27 June 1941. The Inspectors of Constabulary also noted that friction could occur in county forces when a local pc took charge of an incident and had to give orders to the squire. Ibid.

services. On the other hand, it clearly stated that the police did not come under the control of an incident officer, unless he was himself a policeman.[49] Such advice did little to sort out priorities. Trouble could also erupt with the other services, as in London during the invasion scare in the summer of 1940, when the newly formed Home Guard were liable to challenge anything that moved, including the police.[50] Here, one over-enthusiastic branch of the Local Defence Volunteers ( nicknamed the 'Look, Duck and Vanish squad' by the police)[51] stopped and challenged policemen at rifle point during an air raid, while on another occasion police on patrol were made to proceed with their arms over their heads. The police also had their difficulties with air raid wardens, some of whom could act like 'little tin-pot Hitlers'.[52]  Nevertheless, the police and other services seem to have worked reasonably well together when an incident actually occurred, without too many questions about who was in charge. According to some, the police would just dive in and help where necessary. In this view, it was the ARP and not the police who were the people in control. According to others, it was the police who were the key authority, and who set up incident posts to liaise with everybody else.[53] The effectiveness and cooperation of the various services obviously varied from incident to incident but overall, relations between wardens and police – the two local groups who were always on the street during air raids – were mostly quite amicable. However, there was no special closeness between the two

---

49  *PRO: HO 45/19509* Police Control Policy 1940–44, 9 January 1940; 26 March 1943. *PRO: HO 45/19509/67*, 24 April 1943: As late as April 1943, the Ministry of Home Security was proposing a review of the position of the police as incident officers, because of the supposed failure of the police in that role – a proposal which was firmly resisted by the Home Office.
50  *PRO: Mepo 2/7013.* 'Local Defence Challenges to the Police 1940'. The Police Federation complained to the Commissioner who, perhaps because of his scant regard for the Federation, was inclined to treat the matter as a joke. But the Commander of the LDV was unrepentant, and replied to the Commissioner: 'So much has been said about Fifth Columnists and Germans in disguise that suspicion is general ... If you wish no policeman to be challenged I will issue such an order, but the time may come when no one at all may be allowed to approach a post without being challenged'.
51  Interview with PC Lewis, Warwickshire police.
52  An informant described walking up the road smoking in the middle of an air raid, with flames all around him, when a warden commanded him to put out his cigarette, because he was showing an illegal light. Interview with Sergeant Martin, Metropolitan police.
53  Interviews with Superintendent Carling; Sergeant Blake; Sergeant March, Metropolitan police; and Inspector Astley, West Sussex constabulary.

services, since the police saw themselves as the professionals, and were liable to ignore the wardens or regard them as a bit of an intrusion on their territory. It would not appear, therefore, that police relations with the civil defence services altered their view of each other or brought them closer together in the way predicted.


## Relations with the Public

On the other hand, the general public's opinion of the police rose during the war. For one thing, the police not only shared the dangers of the air raids, they were also on duty to guard people's property and homes on these occasions. In the event of an air raid, those on duty had to stay on the streets to report incidents and check the air-raid shelters, and this cemented the bond between them and the local population. Sergeant March remembered that during the Blitz

> I always made a point of visiting every air raid shelter ... on more than one occasion on my day off, I'd still go in and be warmly welcomed: have a cup of tea, have this, have that. The mere fact that they knew you were out there looking after their homes as far as possible, in spite of the bombs coming down and blowing them to smithereens, they respected you for it ...[54]

All this helped to generate good feeling, and as Inspector Hay recalled:

> Until a few years after the war, the relationship between the police and the public could never have been better. You were very good indeed with them. They thought the world of you, they came a little bit closer to you. Because remember, prior to the war, all this was you walking along with your white gloves on during the daytime, with your buttons all clean and looking round to see what was going on, if anyone was doing anything wrong, so you were more or less an object of fear ... but once the bombing started things changed drastically. You were then the friend for life, they got to know you, they realized you were human. That if they dropped a bomb you would be killed the same way as they were. This was the start of a wonderful relationship ... but sadly this was lost over the years, when they got a new generation growing up.[55]

The police were the first port of call for the bombed out and homeless, the lost and bereaved. During raids, they shepherded people into public shelters while themselves remaining above ground patrolling, protecting property

---

54  Interview with Sergeant March, Metropolitan police.
55  Interview with Inspector Hay, Birmingham City police.

and guarding it from looters. According to many officers, police morale was never higher than in wartime because of the high esteem in which they were held, and the sense of comradeship that came about through the fight against a common enemy. Former police officers thus fully subscribe to what Angus Calder (with some exaggeration) calls 'the myth of the Blitz', whereby factors making for a provisional, conditional and potentially fragile sense of national unity among those opposed to war or to the curtailment of their democratic rights, were ignored or forgotten.[56] One potent indicator that the war did not in fact override all oppositional sentiment was the number of strikes that took place, despite the fact that strikes had more or less become illegal.[57] Indeed, these continued at a considerable rate, the number in 1941 even exceeding the pre-war figure.[58]

The police, however, recall a more consensual spirit. Indeed, one former pc specifically challenged Calder's thesis, commenting that the British spirit of resistance during the war was no myth:

> I think (Calder) is mistaken. He wasn't alive at the time, and I do know that there was an absolutely invigorating feeling ... I'm absolutely sure of it today that there was common courage. It wasn't a myth, and it spread from the office cleaners whom one met early in the morning on their way to do their cleaning jobs right up to the very top of the government. It was a national feeling.[59]

Rolph went on to comment on the incredibly high morale amongst the police, based on this feeling of communality of purpose. Nevertheless, while parallel memories of high public esteem were flattering to their ego, this did not basically alter the police's view of their job. The normal routine of the beat continued, although the war offered new sources of easy credit for pcs eager to fill their pocket books. Here, the lighting restrictions provided droves of candidates for cautions and summonses, from the myriads caught with bikes or cars showing lights above a one and a half inch aperture, to the irritation of the offenders. The policeman's 'Don't you know there's a war on' would be countered by the comment that 'there's enough trouble in the world withour you causing any more', and remained a potent source of bad feeling between police and public. But a patriotic motive for such actions absolved the police from any sense of unease, while

---

56　See Calder, *The Myth of the Blitz*, p. 90.

57　Under the *Conditions of Employment and National Arbitration Order 1940*, strikes became in effect illegal because of the elaborate provisions which had to be observed before any strike could take place. See Mass Observation (1942) *People in Production: an enquiry into British war production*, p. 246.

58　Ibid., p. 247–8.

59　Interview with C.H. Rolph, City of London police.

in other spheres they were able to carry on with their usual vigilance against drunks and other disturbers of the peace. The pocket book of a Birmingham policeman during the height of the Blitz in 1941 shows that the war had no effect on stopping the police from dealing with stray dogs, drunk and disorderlies, noisy groups in the street, those urinating in public or those riding bikes without lights. [60]

Indeed, the war itself had surprisingly little effect on police routines, which had been so instilled into pcs that they adhered to them come hell or high water. The following account describes the actions of a policeman during the big November bombing raid on Coventry in 1940:

> The sirens went just after six, you could see the flares coming down, it was light as day. My landlady says, you'll never go out in this, surely. I said, I've got to go up there, I got out the old bike ... the firewatchers were out, local firewatchers, and they said 'you're never going up to town, bobby, are you? You'll never make it. Anyhow, I went on, you could hear the bombs coming down ... and all along the way I met different bobbies ... and this bomb fell and I was blown into the foyer of a picture palace. I lay there for a few seconds ... I felt myself, my legs were alright ... I was actually on top of two girls and two fellows, one was dead ... but you couldn't do anything. It was no use saying you would send for an ambulance, there was no ambulance to come. And I pedalled away and eventually got to my station ... We didn't know what to do, because buildings had been bombed around us and there were mountains of rubble, we couldn't get out in the vehicle, you had to climb. So three or four of us, we were all off duty, hadn't shaved, went to Broadgate to see what we could do to help. And pick up what you could. I mean, there was a jewellers on Broadgate flattened, and there was gold and silver all lying about. We picked up what we could and put it in a bag.
>
> *So in fact you tried to do your normal police duties?*
>
> Yes. [61]

There are many similar desciptions in the interviews, of men continuing their police work against all the odds – just as there are accounts of sergeants berating men for turning up unkempt and dirty at the station after they had been out helping during raids. [62] Although discipline may have

---

60  Sergeant Brecon's *Occurrence Book*, 2 March 1941–11 April 1942, B Division, Birmingham City police.

61  Interview with Sergeant Lane, Coventry City police.

62  One plainclothes pc described working all through Sunday and Monday helping people after a bombing incident and being reprimanded by his chief constable

slipped a bit owing to pressure of time and events, it was ultimately still based on the pre-war rules and standards, so that the response in both supervisors and men was like a conditioned reflex, with neither questioning that this was the way it had to be.

Herein lies the resistance to change and the reason why the war did not have the impact on the institution that might have been expected. The war changed some of the tasks, it did not change the outlook of men who had been trained under the pre-war system. Nor were civilians, in the form of reservists or civil defence workers harbingers of change. The gulf between civilians and professionals remained unbridgeable. It was therefore not until after the war that the police service started to alter. It altered from the inside. Former police officers, returning from active service in the forces, often having achieved higher rank than their police supervisors, were in no mood to accept the old style inflexible rules and discipline. Supervisors, who had grown old in the job during the war were slowly replaced by younger men with a different outlook on how to run an efficient police force. The old routinized style of policing came under attack, the more so when a dearth of new recruits brought pressure for increasing motorization, and for hours and conditions of work more in keeping with the rest of society, since men could no longer be found to accept the job on the old terms. It was the post-war boom and manpower shortages that ushered in real change in the police service in the form of more cars and fewer policemen on the beat, rather than the short term wartime impact of bombs, heroic struggle and cameraderie.

But in the eyes of the wartime bobbies, the war was a high point when the right and proper respect for the police went hand in hand with a necessarily disciplined approach to life. They might not have appreciated the strict discipline by which their working lives were governed, they grumbled about it in the interviews and understood that the post-war generation of recruits would no longer accept it, but at the same time they also understood that this internal discipline was the counterpart to their own authority on the streets. Without it, and without the deference and respect that they expected – and largely got – from the public at large, society would go to the dogs, with consequences that are only too evident today to these men. What hurts most is the loss of respect, the questioning of their authority and the open expressions of distrust and dislike the police now routinely expect to attract. The war has therefore come to occupy a symbolic place as a time of moral certainty and social harmony in the narratives of the police of that

---

because he hadn't got an armband indicating that he was a policeman. Interview with Detective Inspector Ellworthy, Warwickshire Constabulary.

generation, all the evidence of strain and ambiguity to the contrary, as they try to salvage their former high sense of self-esteem from the wreckage of a present which derides the routines and values on which they had based their working lives.

# CHAPTER EIGHT

# Policing Crime

## 1) Larceny

In the next two chapters, we turn consider the crimes, misdemeanours and disturbances dealt with by the police over the period, and the manner in which they did so. No judgement will be made about how far the official statistics reflect a 'real' as opposed to a manufactured rate for any particular offence since, as we have seen, the foundations on which the statistics rest are too shaky to be relied on for a picture of the 'objective' truth. Rather than attempting the futile task of trying to disentangle the real from the manufactured, it seems more fruitful to concentrate on police perceptions and responses to trends in the offence rate. This is at least as important an influence on the statistics, if not more important, than the actual number of offences committed.

However, it does not mean that the criminal statistics should be disregarded; rather, that their chief significance lies in the impact they made on the police and the public's perceptions of crime, and in the changes of attitude and policy that came in as a consequence.

The criminal statistics show crime rises of around five per cent per annum from 1915–1930; about seven per cent from 1931–1948; a relatively level period between 1949–1954; and then a rise of ten per cent per annum from 1955 onwards. The First and Second World War appear to have had very little immediate effect on these rates.[1] But the slow pace of change in the crime statistics until after the war, together with their steep upward climb from the mid-1950s was of prime importance in promoting a general view of society as one initially unthreatened by crime, which was then followed by dismay when an annual ten per cent rise – perceived by the media as a 'crime wave' – led to speculation about a new breed of criminal, to a questioning of lenient sentencing practices, and to revelations about corrupt policemen.

---

1    See F.H. McClintock and N.H. Avison (1968) *Crime in England and Wales,* pp. 18–19.

The police view broadly echoed the public one. Overall, crime was perceived by the police as low or practically non-existent until well after the war, when motorization and post-war shortages brought a more organized form of crime and a more violent and ruthless type of criminal into the picture, and fighting crime entered a different phase. Crime in the 1930s, as a feature of day to day policing, has been more or less eradicated from the memories of the prewar bobbies. Nor was there much difference here between rural and urban police. Chief Superintendent Sheen of the Norfolk police claimed that thieving, and crime generally, was uncommon before the war; similarly, Sergeant Dunhill came across very little in his suburban Birmingham division. 'During four and a half years at Bordesley Green, there was virtually nothing ... not even a break-in', he declared.[2] Even in Liverpool, most of the pre-war crime dealt with by CID was pretty small stuff. A detective there recalled that

> although there were a lot of house break-ins, there wasn't a lot of commercial thieves in those days. That's something that has grown up with the yuppie brigade, I think. I never handled any of those big commercial thieves.[3]

Crime was presented as very much under control. In Liverpool, 'one could go for four weeks' nights without a crime', while Inspector Roper of the Birmingham CID noted with pride that 'at one time, before the war, it was said that a known thief would not go through the city centre, he'd go round'.[4] At the same time, the terrible pre-war depression in the worst areas of unemployment brought memories of thieving by unemployed men, women and children. With some shame, former policemen from the Rhondda and the north-western coal fields recall taking people to court for stealing coal off the trucks coming from the collieries:

> The sergeant would say 'it's time we had some coal-stealers'. The coal trucks were lying head to tail all along the riverside to the collieries, and it was a paradise for anybody who wanted to steal coal. I'm not exaggerating when I say that I used to go over to the sidings in the early hours of the morning when dawn was breaking, you looked along the rows of trucks, and there wasn't one person stealing coal, there were hundreds. They were starving, these people, and we used to appear – have to appear – and sadly it was always the old men who couldn't run very fast who got caught.

---

2   Interview with Chief Inspector Sheen, Norfolk County police, and Sergeant Dunhill, Birmingham City police.
3   Interview with Detective Chief Inspector Gough, Liverpool City police.
4   Interviews with Superintendent Clarke, Liverpool City police, and Inspector Roper, Birmingham City police.

Used to take them to court, and fine them a shilling, or something like that, but it just had to be done.[5]

These pre-war memories are all of petty thieving, with very few that related to large scale organized crime and the criminal gangs who live on in public memory – the Sabinis, the Brummagen Boys, Jack Spot and Billy Hill – all men who controlled London's underworld and the race tracks, and whose mantle was to pass on to the Krays and their rivals.[6] However, no one in the sample seems to have had direct dealings with these gangs, nor did they figure in the stories the police related. Only Inspector Cooper mentioned the Sabinis. But while acknowledging their notoreity, he belittled their achievements, which after all rebounded badly on the image of the police as all powerful controllers of the underworld. 'They were centred on Clerkenwell, a little crowd of villains' he said. 'But we hadn't got too many villains, you know'.[7] This is countered in the revisionist view put forward by Jenkins and Potter, which emphasizes the high level of continuity in the history and degree of gangland violence in the metropolis, and shows that the rule of the Krays and the Richardsons was by no means so exceptional as was made out at the time.[8] Certainly, such gangs had been operating long before the 1960s, boosted – amongst other things – by evasions of the police clamp-down on drinking clubs in the late 1920s.[9] Nevertheless they received little acknowledgement in the recollections of London detectives in the sample who might have come across them. There were no triumphant police victories to celebrate here, and much that remains suspect in the relations between gang members and the CID.[10] But, as Robert Murphy has shown, the underworld gangs of the inter-war years were flourishing, despite

---

5    Interview with Inspector Archer, Durham police. A similar story was recounted by Chief Inspector Eyre, Glamorgan County police.

6    See Dick Hobbs (1989 edn) *Doing the Business,* p. 48.

7    Interview with Inspector Cooper, Metropolitan police.

8    Jenkins and Potter deny the 'explosion of violence' that was depicted in the media over the latter's exploits. See Philip Jenkins and Gary Potter (1988) 'Before the Krays: Organized Crime in London 1920–1960', *Criminal Justice History,* vol. 9.

9    The clamp down on drinking clubs and bottle parties which evaded the licensing laws had been initiated by the previous Home Secretary, Joynson Hicks, culminating in a police raid on Mrs Meyrick's Mayfair club in 1928 and exposure of police corruption connected with the club's protection. Most of the men from the West End police division implicated were sacked, but concern over 'bottle parties' continued throughout the 1930s. Here, extortion rackets and police vigilance went hand in hand.

10   See James Morton (1993) *Bent Coppers,* pp. 84–87; Boyle, *Trenchard,* p. 640.

popular suppositions to the contrary. All that had happened with the eradication of the old Victorian rookeries was that a clearer line was now drawn between the dangerous and the labouring classes, so that the underworld in the inter-war years became a smaller, more exclusive society – but still one that kept the gambling, race course betting and drinking clubs under tight control.[11]

Apart from trouble connected with extortion rackets around London's numerous drinking and gaming clubs, there was a flurry of concern in the early 1930s about 'motor bandits', who used cars in a number of smash and grab raids throughout the country.[12] In London, this led to the introduction of 'Q' cars and the formation of the 'Flying Squad',[13] – a development that only came to full fruition in the 1960s, but which was to be of prime importance in changing the scale and nature of the fight against crime. Meanwhile, less financially profligate police authorities such as Reigate recruited a 'Flying Squad' of special constables, consisting of local residents with fast cars who could be enrolled to hunt down the motor bandits.[14] For the rest of the decade, however, there was little apparent concern with crime, which was frequently reported as negligible or decreasing.[15] Retrospective and contemporary views thus coincide in seeing the era of the 1930s as a largely crime free one. The only worry was over juvenile crime rates, which were generally perceived to be rising, and which will be discussed in a separate section below.[16]

---

11  Robert Murphy (1993) *Smash and Grab: Gangsters in the London Underworld*, p. 3.
12  Billy Hill describes the dearth of police cars and absence of wireless equipment and other quick means of police communication that made smash and grab raids popular with 'the boys'. Hill revelled in the publicity which his daylight raids brought, until the formation of the Flying Squad led him to change his tactics. Billy Hill (1955) *Boss of Britain's Underworld*, pp. 41–2; 44–6.
13  The Flying Squad had about twenty cars, each one driven by an expert racing driver and manned by a wireless operator and two detectives. The squad was headed by Chief Inspector Sharpe, who retired in 1937. For an account, see F.D.(Nutty) Sharpe (1938) *Sharpe of the Flying Squad*.
14  *Police Review*, 23 September 1932. The scale of the problem was blown up out of all proportion by the media. In 1931 there had been thirty-one such raids in London, rising to fourteen over a three month period by 1934. *HC Debs, 5s, 264*, 15 April 1931–2; *286*, 19 February 1933–4.
15  *Police Review*, 23 June, 2 July, 7 July 1933; 4 June 1937; 17 June 1938; 28 July 1939; 1 December 1939. The latter report noted the marked decrease in crime in the metropolis since the outbreak of the war.
16  A third of those found guilty of breaking and entering in 1932–3 and in 1934 were aged sixteen or under. *Police Review*, 7 July 1933; 10 July, 1936.

## Crime Rates in Wartime

The accepted view seems to be that crime rates increased, and were bound to do so under wartime conditions. We must therefore consider Mannheim's prediction 'that the present epidemic of war will bring in its wake ... an enormous outbreak of lawlessness ... There is a strong likelihood that crime, and in particular juvenile delinquency, will increase even more than it did during the previous war'.[17] This prediction appears to have been fulfilled in the analysis of the wartime criminal statistics undertaken by the Liverpool social scientist H. Silcock. Although he acknowledged the variable crime recording procedures and the distortions due to this, Silcock believed this applied chiefly to trivial thefts. He thus arrived at a figure of seventy-eight per cent increase in housebreaking and larceny between 1938 and 1947, – a finding that gives ground to the view that the war was indeed a causative factor in the increase in crime.[18] Nevertheless, it must be stressed that most of this increase is no more than that contained in the longer term trend presented by McClintock and Avison, of which the war years simply formed a part.[19] Consequently, selecting out the war, in the expectation that something different and alarming had happened to crime rates during those years, is largely to fall victim to a self-fulfilling prophecy. Certainly, new opportunities presented themselves and new crimes were created as blackout, shortages, bomb damage and call up offered openings for blackmarketeering, looting and freedom from supervision and the normal constraints of everyday life. New regulations also created new offences – although many of these were not routinely dealt with by the police. Much blackmarketeering, for example, was dealt with at the point of sale or illicit manufacture by inspectors from the Ministries of Food, Trade, Supply and Fuel and Power.[20] Here, the numbers prosecuted remained low: in north

---

17  Hermann Mannheim (1941) *War and Crime*, pp. 129, 143. There is a large literature supporting Mannheim's prediction as far as juveniles were concerned. See, for example, G. Godwin (1941) 'War and Juvenile Delinquency', *Contemporary Review*, 160; J.A. Watson (1942) 'The War and the Young Offender', *Fortnightly Review*. Both authors assume that juvenile crime was bound to increase, and that evacuation and lack of family stability would be the cause.

18  H. Silcock (1949) *The Increase in Crimes of Theft, 1938–1947*, Table 1, p. 14.

19  Their own trend analysis of a seven per cent annual rise over the period 1931–48 would give a sixty-three per cent increase in the nine years analysed by Silcock.

20  A Home Office circular urged the police to cooperate with with enforcement officers from the Ministry of Food, but pointed out that the enforcement

London, ninety-four persons were convicted of black market offences between 1941 and 1945, with even lower numbers convicted in the provinces.[21] Pilfering from employers was more of a problem as it moved beyond the range that could be tolerated, with employers themselves now obliged to account closely to the various ministries for the raw materials they obtained.[22] But again the police were only called in on isolated occasions. Incidents concerning theft from military stores were usually dealt with internally, while pilfering from the docks, which was rife both before and during the war, could only be checked by the police outside the dock gates. The police were thus left to patrol the streets and the haunts of criminals on the off-chance of stopping or catching a thief – although in the vicinity of the docks this might be a near certainty. Inspector Cooper recalled the war years in the East End of London, when

> people were thieving so much, it was like picking ripe fruit ... They used to steal tobacco, steal tea, steal wine, anything from the docks, because the docks were half open ... I had the old Section 66, where you could stop, search and detain anybody ... I know people say it's silly, but you work up an instinct. You can sort of stand on the corner with your mate and say, 'I don't like that one' ... and fifty per cent of the time you'd be right.[23]

Elsewhere, the pickings were smaller. Here, the pocket books of Sergeant Brecon and DC Atkin show something of the magnitude of the likely catch. Sergeant Brecon's book runs from March 1941 to April 1942, during which time he made note of seventy-eight incidents, of which five  were concerned with theft – three of money from gas meters and two of petty thefts from work premises.[24] Similarly, DC Atkin's notebook shows the petty nature of crime over a six week period in which he dealt with roughly one case of minor theft a day, chiefly by youths and young children.[25]

---

officers would normally be responsible for prosecuting offenders. *PRO: HO 45 25135/870415* 'Black Market Offences, 1942–50', 18 August 1942.

21  Figures from Edward Smithies (1984) *The Black Economy in Britain since 1914,* pp. 69–71.

22  Edward Smithies (1982) *Crime in Wartime: A Social History of Crime in World War 11*, p. 39.

23  Interview with Inspector Cooper, Metropolitan police.

24  Occurrence Book, 'B' Division (Hay Mills), 2 March 1941–11 April 1942, Birmingham City police.

25  Notebook of DC Walter Allen, 13 October–29 November 1942, Sheffield City police. *M/S, Imperial War Museum.*

Oral testimony corroborates the written evidence: there was no feeling that crime was a problem, or that it rose to any great extent in wartime. On the contrary, Superintendent Batey thought that it had decreased:

> You see, a lot of criminals were fit and capable to go into the forces ... so a considerable proportion of our criminals were in the forces ... There was less crime, yes, certainly.[26]

The supposition that crime levels fell because a large proportion of those normally committing crime were away in the armed forces seems eminently reasonable – despite the results of a small survey conducted by the War Office, which showed that a much higher proportion of civilians than of servicemen were being convicted of larceny.[27] But be that as it may, there was little difference of opinion about levels of crime between town and country policemen. The police were aware that civilian crime was concentrated around areas of high opportunity, whether at military bases in rural areas or at traditional sites such as the docks, and it was here that they continued to find high and rising levels of thieving. Docks, for example, had always been notorious for the pilfering that went on there, while the difficulties of policing at the dock gates are graphically illustrated by the statistic that as many as 346 vehicles and 800 pedestrians might pass through one gate alone during busy periods.[28] In Liverpool, there would be a purge every so often, when two or three extra police would be sent down to search everyone coming through a particular gate. But of course, as Inspector Bates recalled, that would only last five minutes because the word soon got out and the men would go out through another gate. There was a lot of stuff pinched, and there were a lot of people locked up, including a few pcs, according to Superintendent Clarke. He described what might happen:

> What made it worse, of course, was the dockers themselves used to arrange for a sling to come undone with a case of tea, crash down on the docks, the box burst open, and everybody's there with their little bags. Very often with sugar, you were walking in sugar, because of

---

26  Interview with Superintendent Batey, Staffordshire police.
27  *PRO: Mepo 2/7078/1,* 'Incidence of Crime, HM Forces and Civilians', 2 July 1942. Worried about adverse publicity in the press about crime committed by servicemen, the War Office had asked the Metropolitan police for one month's statistics on convictions, separating civilians from servicemen. The results showed that while 43 per cent of civilian convictions were for theft, only 13 per cent of servicemen's convictions came into this category, the vast majority (nearly 70 per cent) being for desertion or AWL.
28  Chief Constable's *Report on the Police Establishment and the State of Crime for the Seven years 1939–45,* Liverpool, April 1946.

the miscreants. The local population, when sugar was in bags on waggons, would get tin tubes and stick it into the sack, sugar used to cascade down into a bag they were carrying. There was a lot of that going on, a lot of petty pilfering ... Looting? Yes, there was looting, obviously ... when people got the opportunity, they used to loot.[29]

The police also were aware that shortages led to pilfering in factories, but since they were not directly involved, they had little to say about it, since none were called in by employers to investigate such thefts. Only Detective Inspector Ellworthy, on a tip-off from a civilian, was able to uncover a huge scale instance of thieving at an RAF station. When it was found that the commissioned ranks were involved, he was stopped from proceeding and the Special Branch took over. But the case came first to the local magistrates court, and he remembered 'we had a court full, lined up with people. Civilians receiving and RAF people stealing everything, parts of cars, tools, food, everything'.[30]

In general, the response to questions about blackmarketeering and looting was negative – there was mostly little to report, apart from some memories of being offered eggs or chickens or what was described by one CID officer as a 'friendly exchange of butter and bacon' with farmers in rural areas – perks that were actually traditional whether in war or in peacetime. Basically, neither offence was taken too seriously, and pcs freely admitted to having been involved themselves. According to Ingleton, the police were no better and no worse than the rest of the population in this regard.[31] Thus, when Inspector Archer was in the CID he was offered some red petrol (for commercial use only) by another pc:

So we drove my car to the police yard and started filling it with red petrol, and next to it was the boss's Humber, so he said 'I'll give the boss a gallon or two, if we get caught, he gets caught too'.[32]

Superintendent Carling maintained that everyone took advantage of the blackmarket (in the sense of buying extra rationed goods) – including the police.[33] As far as looting was concerned, Inspector Outram agreed that it took place and that people could be shot for it. But policemen didn't carry guns, and 'you couldn't go back to the station and get a gun and shoot them,

29  Interviews with Inspector Bates and Superintendent Clarke, Liverpool City police.
30  Interview with Detective Inspector Ellworthy, Warwickshire police.
31  Ingleton, *The Gentlemen at War*, p. 285.
32  Interview with Inspector Archer, Durham County police.
33  Interview with Superintendent Carling, Metropolitan police.

could you?'[34] The looters were often said to be the very people employed to clear up bomb damage, and it was clear that looting in one form or another was extremely widespread.[35] And while most looting was casual and opportunistic, organized gangs were also involved, with 'spotters' used to identify likely sites. Some particularly loathsome stories of looting from dead bodies (and even live bomb victims) have been recounted. One incident that was a bit of a godsend was a direct hit on a bank in London, after which pound notes floated down like manna from heaven. Another was a bomb on a wholesale tobacconists. Within five minutes 'it was like a crowd of sparrows' with people scrabbling for cigarettes.[36] All in all, it seems that both public and police opinion on looting was divided, with one half condemning it outright, and the other maintaining that it was difficult to decide what was looting, and that it was not like ordinary thieving.[37]

Looting was one thing, 'ordinary' crime – where the moral boundaries were more clear-cut – was another. Ultimately, such crime was not regarded as out of control during the war, while looting and blackmarketeering were either believed to be negligible by the majority of pcs or – where they were not – were accepted as the norm. There is a strong sense that neither offence was regarded as criminal by the police, since neither fell easily into accepted categories of crime. Even the Metropolitan Commissioner was unsure about blackmarketeering, regarding it as 'a crime on which it is unsafe to dogmatize ... for the term is very loosely used'.[38] Blackmarketeering as a crime was confined to dealings in articles subject to government price or quantity control, but the police said it was impossible for them to keep abreast of all the changing regulations that applied,[39] while

---

34 Interview with Inspector Outram, Metropolitan police.

35 The account by a mobile canteen driver of being almost forcibly handed hundreds of boxes of face powder by demolition workers at a bombed site is indicative of a general response. See Dorothy Sheridan (ed. 1991) *Wartime Women: an anthology of women's wartime writing for Mass Observation 1937–45*, p. 107.

36 Interviews with Sergeant Blake, Metropolitan police; Sergeant Brecon, Birmingham City police.

37 Mass Observation survey, quoted in Ingelton, *The Gentlemen at War,* p. 269.

38 Annual Report of the Metropolitan Commissioner for the year ending 1944, *PP V*, 1944–45. Sir Philip Game noted that 'there is undoubtedly a large number of individual transactions in the blackmarket ... perhaps we do not realise that if we are prepared to accept without demur a bit more than we are entitled to, we are all to that extent blackmarketeers'.

39 *PRO: Mepo 2/7677*, 'The Police and Food Offences'. 2 July, 5 September 1946. A memo from DI Symes emphasized that if the police were to undertake

the looting of items lying in the open was not perhaps regarded as strictly comparable to thieving from persons or closed premises. Nevertheless, the blackmarket provided huge openings for criminal deals, which members of the old underworld, and others, took full advantage of:

> The growth of the blackmarket diverted a large part of the purchasing power of the country through criminal channels; small-time thieves found it had suddenly become ludicrously easy to acquire hundreds of pounds with very little risk ... the old distinction between criminal and non-criminal has become most conveniently blurred ...[40]

The spiv had arrived, and with him a significant broadening of the criminal social base. During the war, with depleted and over extended resources, not much could be done to contain this phenomena.[41] But soon after, police battle with a much more amorphous and widespread group of criminals was joined.

It is, however, hard to get a sense of what was happening to crime rates 'after the war'– that vague period lasting from the end of hostilities up to retirement – from the recollections of the police. Concern was focussed on the effects of the shortage of new recruits and the coming of motorized policing. The consequent loss of contact with, and therefore information from, the public was one aspect that led to less efficient policing, in the view of many officers, while a better educated public who were more inclined to contest police evidence in court led to a higher acquittal rate.[42] Concern with rising crime was therefore expressed indirectly, whereas concern with their declining authority was of far greater moment to police

---

the task of detecting and prosecuting blackmarket offences, they would have to put aside all other matters, including the detection and prevention of crime.

40  Murphy, *Smash and Grab,* p. 85, quoting Mark Benney, a self-confessed pre-war burglar and author of *Gaol Delivery* (1948).

41  In 1944, 100,000 ration books were stolen from a food office in Romford, worth half a million pounds, which made it the most lucrative haul until the Great Train Robbery in 1963. This was never officially admitted, and the extent of the blackmarket in the war, downplayed. Murphy, Ibid., p. 83.

42  In addition, as the Metropolitan Police Commissioner noted, 'the criminal of today, thanks perhaps to his more thorough education, finds his readiest form of defence in attack: he often accuses the police, without any justification, of irregular procedure and even corruption'. Annual Report, Metropolitan Police Commissioner, *PP XVIII,* 1958–9.

officers.[43] Comparisons regarding crime were generally with present day rates rather than with any 'crime wave' in their own time. As an article in *Police Review* put it, when deriding the media panic about rising crime, 'there appear to be no intermediate stages between normal crime incidence and a "crime wave". A rise of ten per cent in the statistics of indictable offences is enough for a wave; there are no wavelets or ripples.'[44] Most of the officers in the sample were confident that, whether the rise in crime constituted a wave or a ripple, they had crime under control. Indeed, in rural areas, the crime-free daily round appears to have continued undisturbed, as the following random week's sample demonstrates:

> *6 October 1948*: Dog killed by a lorry
> *7 October*: No entry
> *8 October*: Complaint of dog chasing cattle. Two one-pound notes handed in, found in Seaham.
> *9 October*: Pound notes returned to loser.
> Two pubs visited, all quiet and in order.
> *10 October*: Insecure premises, colliery canteen. Woman had a fit in street, police helped by Boy Scout.
> *11 October:* Ration book reported lost, returned direct to loser.
> *12 October*: Dog found and brought to station. Dog killed by van. Ladies shoes found, returned to owner. Confectioner's premises insecure, key holder informed.[45]

This, and similar documents, stand as testimonials to the untroubled tenor and indeed public-spirited rectitude of early post-war daily life in rural disticts. At the same time, if a rural pc reported too many crimes, his superiors would tend to think he was not doing his job. So it was to his advantage to report as few crimes as possible; in this way, low rural rates became a self-fulfilling prophecy. But even in the city, crime remained fairly marginal as far as the uniformed police were concerned.[46]

---

43  Reports on rising indictable crime in the annual Inspectors' and Commissioner's reports from the mid-1950s almost invariably linked this trend to the shortage of recruits.

44  *Police Review*, 4 January 1946.

45  County Durham police, Houghton-le-Spring Division: *Dawdon Station Occurrence Book, 1946–1949*.

46  Sergeant Stevens' *Occurrence Book, 5 July 1948–6 April 1950*, 'C' Division, Birmingham City Police. The note-book of Sergeant Stevens shows that over nearly two years, only twenty out of eighty-five entries referred to theft in one form or another. Stevens was an exceptional officer as far as thief-taking was concerned, and had more commendations for this than any other officer in the sample.

What was stressed was the growth of organized crime towards the end of the period, facilitated by the motorization of criminals.[47] This tended to eradicate differences between urban and rural detective work. Detective Inspector Aylesham, of Durham County police described the crime intelligence unit and the regional crime squad created in 1965 in response to increasing crime by more organized and motorized criminals, whereby he was covering the whole of the eastern part of the county from the Humber up to Berwick by car.[48] Inspector Hay gave a similar account for Birmingham in the early 1960s:

> I was on the forerunner of the Serious Crime Squad for twelve months, which in those days was called the Birmingham Crime Squad. This was a little clan of six detectives and six uniformed pcs who worked in plain clothes as drivers, you had a car with a radio and you had an inspector in charge. And all your job was to catch metal thieves, because metal stealing was prevalent in Birmingham. It had come about as a serious problem, and that's all you did, no routine work, all you did was go out and catch metal thieves ... Crime was getting a bit more organized then. You were getting a few good thieves who were getting little bands around them. It was rising. You had to keep at it, but the crime squad did keep it down at the time, they could keep a bit of a lid on because they never knew where you were ... [49]

Similarly, in Sheffield, the Regional Crime Squad was formed because of travelling criminals, 'since people could do armed robberies in Sheffield and be in London within three hours'. Nevertheless, Detective Superintendent Spender insisted that the police were always in control, and that they only started to lose it in the 1970s and 80s.[50] This, it would seem, was the consensus within the sample. A rising crime rate brought predictable calls for more police from the higher echelons in the service, and pressure on CID for results. But whatever its nature at the time, it was not sufficient to alter the police's view that they were the masters of their

---

47   Clive Emsley makes the point that crime might not in fact have been any more 'organized' than previously, and that it was the spread of the motor car that gave rise to this perception, as the growth of the railway network had done a century beforehand. *Private communication.*

48   Interview with Detectiver Inspector Aylesham, County Durham police.

49   Interview with Inspector Hay, Birmingham City police. The thieving he described was organized thieving from factories, such as one case where the night staff were filling little bags with nickel, and slipping it out to a man waiting to fill the boot of his car. In the course of a week about half a ton would be taken, shipped to London, sold there, and the thieves paid off.

50   Interview with Detective Superintendent Spender, Sheffield City police.

patch, or the cynical attitude, quoted in the previous chapter, that a high turnover of thieves was a good way of raising the detective's clear-up rate. But a high rate of arrests did not necessarily imply a bad relationship with villains. 'It's a fair cop, gov' gives acknowledgement to the quality of gamesmanship involved on both sides, with many police tales of how men they had helped to put behind bars would greet them in the street, shake their hand and buy them drinks. Even in the heightened atmosphere of the South Wales coalfield, with its long history of police/miner acrimony, Chief Inspector Knight denied that there was any bad feeling between police and strikers in the early post-war strikes. 'We knew them, and they knew us' and trouble only started when outside police were brought in.[51] As in the men's preference for foot beat policing before the use of cars broadened the villains' field of operations, it was the personal knowledge and relationships that the police valued, whether with law breakers or law-abiding citizens. Nowadays, it would seem, not even the criminals are as they used to be – men who knew and accepted the rules of the game, who bore no grudges if dealt with fairly, and who respected the police if outwitted by them.

## 2) Juvenile Delinquency

The complexities of police decision-making with regard to adult crime were as nothing when compared with the situation regarding juveniles. Since the time of the 1908 Children Act (or children's charter, as it was popularly known) the principle that juveniles should receive special treatment at all stages of the judicial process meant that juvenile offenders were perceived as a category apart. Indeed, they were not normally described as offenders at all, but as delinquents – a term that became their own.[52] In addition, this group was enlarged in our period by the raising of the age boundary between juvenile and adult from sixteen to seventeen, under the 1933 Children and Young Persons Act. Large numbers of the most criminogenic age groups in the population thus became subject to the latest theories and practices on the causes and remedies for youthful delinquency.

The formative years of humanitarian penal policy-making for young offenders were concentrated in the 1920s when rates of juvenile crime were on a downward path. This had given space to a welfare-oriented attitude on

51  Interview with Chief Inspector Knipe, Glamorganshire police.
52  See Leon Radzinowicz and Roger Hood (1986) *The Emergence of Penal Policy*, pp. 631–2. The 1908 Childrens Bill had wanted to relieve children up to the age of sixteen of all criminal responsibility. While this was not enacted, the liberal spirit behind this proposal largely infused the resulting Act.

the part of policy makers, who accepted Cyril Burt's view that juvenile delinquency was 'nothing but an outstanding example of common childish naughtiness' closely associated with defective family relations and defective discipline,[53] and to the conviction that delinquency was not a self-contained condition but a symptom of social and parental neglect.[54] Faith in the reformative and supportive power of probation and youth work came to outweigh a more punitive approach to the problem. The range of options open to the police and magistrates in dealing with young offenders was wide, and included formal and informal cautions, appearance in juvenile court, probation, detention in a remand home, and in the last resort being sent to foster homes or approved schools. The emphasis throughout was on the effort to provide for an improved family environment. However, by the time the 1933 Act came on the statute book, delinquency rates had started to rise again, and so had the voices demanding a more harshly deterrent system. And although these voices were in the minority, they were able to ensure that birching remained an option, until its abolition in 1948. The Home Office also inclined towards the initiation of a tougher policy towards juveniles, and gave instructions to the Metropolitan Commissioner that ended the period of leniency and emphasis on cautioning in favour of a pro-institutional policy. From 1931 onwards, the MPD became one of the few police departments in the country that did not continue to use a summons procedure for juveniles or to implement a policy of cautioning.[55]

A more sophisticated reaction to the rise in juvenile delinquency than that of the flogging lobby was taken by a number of social scientists.[56] Here, J. H. Bagot's enquiry into juvenile delinquency in Liverpool in 1934 and 1936 is an outstanding example. He ascribed the rise between these dates to changes in police procedure, to a growing reluctance on the part of constables to deal with minor cases on the spot, and to a greater readiness to bring children before court as a result of the 1933 Act. Bagot pointed to the

---

53   C.L. Burt (1925) *The Young Delinquent*, p. viii. Burt exerted a wide influence on both public and academic opinion regarding the sociological influences on crime. See L.S. Hearnshaw (1979), *Cyril Burt, Psychologist*, p. 79.

54   On the background and theories underlying policy making here, see Victor Bailey (1987) *Delinquency and Citizenship*, Chapter 2.

55   Paul Lerman (1984) 'Policing Juveniles in London: shifts in guiding discretion 1893–1968' *British Journal of Criminology*.

56   For a review of this literature in the 1930s, see A. M. Carr-Saunders, H. Mannheim and E.C. Rhodes (1943) *Young Offenders: An Enquiry into Juvenile Delinquency*, Chapter 1. This book was the outcome of a Home Office initiative. See *PRO HO 45 19064/807624*, January and June 1938; *HO 45 19066/807624*, July 1941.

close connection between discretionary police powers to caution or to take juveniles before the court and the delinquency rate: a rise in this rate being positively correlated with a fall in the rate of official cautions.[57] In consequence he did not believe that the rising number of delinquents dealt with in juvenile courts after 1933 necessarily indicated any increase in juvenile delinquency, since he had not observed any recent deterioration in juvenile morals or behaviour.[58]

An early post-war investigation into the nature of juvenile delinquency by Mass Observation lends strong support to Bagot's view that it was not a question of intrinsic differences in behaviour between different sections of the community, but of treatment, which accounted for the rise and fall in the juvenile delinquency figures. The Mass Observation report includes testimony from respectable, unprosecuted individuals who confessed voluntarily to thefts of a wide range of goods from offices, shops, hotels and other public places. An inquiry by Rowntree and Lavers resulted in similar findings.[59] Here, Tom Harrison observed that although Mass Observation was asked specifically to study juvenile delinquency, it soon became clear that such deviant behaviour was an inseparable part of the pattern in many other institutions it had studied.[60] These comments, and those of Bagot, make a strong case for the generally contingent nature of the rise and fall in the criminal statistics.

## Police Remedies for Juvenile Delinquency

The police themselves were confronted with a range of viewpoints and possible courses of action, from the proverbial cuff round the earhole to a court summons, in a situation where their discretion was wider than usual. The choices made largely depended on local traditions and circumstances.

---

57  J. H. Bagot (1941) *Juvenile Delinquency: a comparative study of the position in Liverpool and England and Wales,* pp. 21, 23, 87.

58  See E.C. Rhodes (1939) 'Juvenile Delinquency' *Journal of the Royal Statistical Society.* Bagot's comments were made in the published discussion that followed Rhodes' paper. In his view the rise was largely a matter of treatment and of the expected result of new legislation, as had occurred after the 1847 Larceny Act, in the period 1907–12, and in 1933–38, when the figures rose by nearly 100 per cent.

59  See B. Seebohm Rowntree and G.R. Lavers (1951) *English Life and Leisure,* Chapter 6. 'How Honest is Britain', which shows the widespread petty pilfering and shoplifting that abounded, without it being regarded as dishonest by the perpetrators.

60  H. D. Willcock (1949) *Report on Juvenile Delinquency.*

In Norwich, the police force prided itself on its special police policy towards juveniles. A Lads Club run by the police had been founded there in 1918 by the Chief Constable, John Dain. The idea, and tradition of these clubs as a means of countering juvenile delinquency was by no means new, but Dain was the first to run one under the auspices of the police. Dain helped to reduce the juvenile crime figures through his practice of holding 'Sunday courts' at police headquarters, where offenders were reprimanded and encouraged to join the Lads Club, rather than taken to the juvenile court.[61] The consequent drop in the number of local juvenile delinquents spread the fame of this initiative throughout the country.[62] Right up to the end of the Second World War, the club was being held up to other police authorities for its positive effect in reducing juvenile crime, and in 1938 a royal visit gave the club its official seal of approval.[63] Club work, it was held, brought the boy and the bobby together in fruitful and friendly cooperation, and replaced the boys' former sense of antagonism.[64] A number of other forces took up the challenge.[65]

Testimony from former Norwich policemen underlines the importance assigned to the role of its Lads Club. Sergeant Brighouse, who joined the force as a cadet in 1931, often helped at the club and was sure it had a strong effect on the delinquency figures:

> Juvenile crime was almost negligent of what we call serious crime for the simple reason that my chief, Mr Dain, he wouldn't take youngsters to court for minor offences ... he would have what we called a Sunday court in his office and he would send for these boys, and occasionally girls ... and he would give them a talking to ... Talked to them like perhaps a father would, and the boy would have his parents there. 'If you have any problems you can always come to a policeman and talk about it. And behave yourself in the future.' It was very successful.[66]

Dain came to stake his reputation on the club, and saw to it that it received the support it deserved from inside as well as outside the force. He would

---

61  For an account of the work of the club, see Robert Walker (1990) *Seventy Years Young: A History of the Norwich Lads Club 1918–1988.*

62  The average number of boys charged in the local magistrates court per annum at Norwich since 1922 was reported to be twelve. *Police Review,* 31 March 1939.

63  *Police Review,* 4 November 1938.

64  *Police Review,* 12 June 1931.

65  As the rate for juvenile delinquency continued to rise, Swansea, Manchester, Hull and Croyden followed suit – the first in 1937, and the last in 1947.

66  Interview with Sergeant Brighouse, Norwich City police.

send a pc in uniform round the city businesses to collect subscriptions which, in the view of one Norwich pc, made the businessmen think it was a free pass to park where they liked. The favourite reply of motorists approached by a constable was 'I shan't subscribe to the Lads Club anymore'; while inside the force, the Lads Club was certainly seen as a route to promotion, since most of the sergeants and inspectors had spent time in the club.[67]

Clubs and recreational facilities for juveniles had always received a good press as the best means to counter delinquency.[68] The connection was frequently regarded as self-evident and almost automatically beneficial, as when the Duke of Edinburgh decided to provide a playing field to the London borough with the highest rate of juvenile crime (Finsbury), as part of the Festival of Britain.[69] Nevertheless, where leisure facilities were provided for profit and not with moral improvement in mind, official approval might not be so forthcoming. The LCC, for example, made representation to the Home Office for legislation to ban juveniles under eighteen from access to fun fairs and amusement arcades, on the ground that these encouraged gambling.[70]

In any case, many police authorities thought this work was best left to others and that the police already had too many calls on their time. For those most concerned with the problem, the new development lay not with the extension of police-run clubs, but in police juvenile liaison schemes. Here, Liverpool – a city plagued by high rates of juvenile delinquency since the 1930s – was in the vanguard. Since the war, the chief constable and the watch committee had become increasingly concerned that children were running wild, and that parental control had almost ceased to exist in many districts. A deputation to the Home Office requested the lifting of the freezing order on the police, and pointed out the large proportion of crime due to juveniles, and the inadequate punishments given by the juvenile courts.[71] The local authority decided to appoint a Juvenile Delinquency Committee which recommended setting up a juvenile liaison scheme that

67  Interview with Sergeant Craig, Norwich City police.

68  See, for example, Herbert Morrison's printed Home Office circular on the subject, which concluded that one of the best ways to check delinquency in war as in peace was to provide more and varied recreative facilities. *PRO HO 45 20250/12* June 1941.

69  *PRO Mepo 2/ 9067,* 25 April 1950.

70  *PRO HO 45 25204/903235,* 4 June 1948.

71  *PRO HO 45 25144/8775947*: 'Juvenile delinquency in Liverpool 1943–46', 24 May 1944 and 17 December 1945.

began as an experiment in 1949, and became fully established in 1951.[72] It had evolved out of the recommendations put forward in Bagot's book,[73] but was promoted with particular enthusiasm by Chief Constable Charles Martin. Under this scheme, one full-time police officer was assigned to each of the seven police divisions of the city to deal with juveniles committing minor offences, who admitted the offence, who had not previously come to the notice of the police, and whose parents agreed to cooperate with the police over the help and advice offered. Prevention of further offences was to be achieved through liaison with head teachers, ministers of religion and youth workers, through the introduction of the child to a youth club, and through further home visits by the juvenile liaison officer.[74] The scheme was pronounced a resounding success by the police authorities, who published figures to show the falling rate of juvenile recidivism during its first few years, and who extended it by setting up a Moral Welfare section within the scheme, with six wpcs assigned to help girls who may have been drifting into a life of immorality.[75]

Elsewhere, enthusiasm was tempered by doubts. The Home Office was sufficiently impressed to consider whether the scheme should be applied nationally, but was also concerned about police encroachment on the function of the juvenile courts, and about the lack of specialist training or supervision for juvenile liaison officers. Typically, it therefore confined itself to drafting a circular containing the particulars of the scheme for the information of all chief constables, who could then make up their own minds.[76] Around a dozen followed suit,[77] including Manchester and Birmingham, but opinion on their value became increasingly polarized, with professional associations coming out against, and forces with good experiences of such schemes denying that the work encroached on the rights and duties of the juvenile courts. The Association of Chief Police Officers

---

72  *PRO HO 45 25305*, 'Liverpool Police Juvenile Liaison Scheme' 1952–54.
73  See Simon Stevenson, 'Some social and political tides affecting the development of juvenile justice 1938–64' in T. Gorst, L.Johnman and W.S. Lucas (eds) (1989) *Post-War Britain 1945–64: Themes and Perspectives*.
74  Liverpool City police (1958) *The Police and the Children*.
75  Ibid.
76  *PRO HO 45/25305*, 'Liverpool Juvenile Liaison Scheme, 1952–54'. The Advisory Council on the Treatment of Young Offenders recommended that the scheme was most suitable for built-up industrial areas where petty damage and trespass occurred as a result of children playing there.
77  This was the figure in 1963. By 1969, there were seventeen such schemes in England and Wales, and eight in Scotland. For an assessment of this work, see Evelyn B. Schaffer (1980) *Community Policing*, p. 28–33.

(ACPO) saw them as a natural development of the preventive work that 'village bobbies' had always carried out.[78] However, the Metropolitan Commissioner, Sir Joseph Simpson, as well as the children's court magistrate Sir Basil Henriques,[79] publicly criticized the schemes for usurping the function of the courts.[80] In addition, the warden of the Liverpool University Settlement, John Mays, who in general reported approvingly on the scheme, warned in his book on juvenile delinquency of the inevitable undermining of the work of the probation service. He also queried whether the drop in the numbers of juveniles charged related to a drop in the number of offences committed or instead, to fewer children being prosecuted.[81] The balance between the proper use of police discretion and their proper role as law enforcers remained uneasy, with no one prepared to condemn outright the preventive work of juvenile liaison officers, but no one prepared to insist that they become part of the set up in every force.

**The Police and the Juvenile Courts**

Doubts over the preventive role of the police with regard to juvenile offenders remained at their strongest within the police service. Here, the appendix to Mays' book that recounts a sample of Liverpool police officers' attitudes towards juveniles, is particularly revealing. Although the juvenile liaison scheme is not mentioned by them (in itself noteworthy as showing its marginal role within the force) the consensus of opinion was that the juvenile courts were too cosy and unintimidating, that punishments were not severe enough, and that birching should be brought back.[82] While the attitude of the majority of the police officers was classed as sympathetic to children, most believed that stronger discipline was the answer. They will have sympathized with the view of a London magistrate, when he told a seventeen year old youth that

---

78  *Report of the Committee on Children and Young Persons*, (Ingleby Committee, 1960), Cmnd 1191, p. 50.

79  Chairman of the East London Juvenile Court 1936–55 and President of the London Federation of Boys Clubs.

80  See the Metroplitan Commissioner's evidence to the Ingleby Committee, 1960; *Police Review*, 29 June 1956.

81  John Barron Mays (1964) *Growing Up in the City: a study of juvenile delinquency in an urban neighbourhood*, pp. 142, 145.

82  Mays, *Growing Up in the City*, Appendix B, 'A Study of a Police Division', p. 183.

> Broadly speaking, when a pc tells you to do something, at your age you have jolly well got to do it. It is ridiculous for boys like you to stand on your supposed constitutional rights as if you were grown-up people. It is the duty of the police to see that noisy young men do not make a nuisance of themselves. When they tell you to move, you've jolly well got to move.[83]

Given the nature of the police's chosen occupation, it was almost inevitable that a law enforcement view should predominate over a service view of their work. Juvenile liaison officers (JLOs) consequently experienced a conflict of roles as they sought to maintain a precarious balance between policing and welfare approaches,[84] while a former Liverpool policemen who took part in its juvenile liaison scheme for a period provides an illustration of the confused reaction that might result:

> It was started in Liverpool. Yes, it was a good scheme. But there again, you see, we fell out with the probation service, we fell out with the solicitors and all sorts of people on it, because if somebody commits an offence, its not the police responsibility to judge that individual. What they were doing there was bringing the juvenile delinquents in and finding out all about them ... Obviously, taking children before the magistrates should be avoided, *but* they are little villains, little devils, the recidivism amongst them is terrific. They're all smiles and sweetness and then they'll go out and immediately smash a window, but the probation service didn't want us to take notice.[85]

This quotation highlights the tension between the contemporary 'official' approach to juvenile wrongdoing and the policeman's. The police view that the JLO's purpose in bringing in juvenile delinquents was *to find out all about them* and that they were little devils who needed punishment, contrasts with the official purpose of the JLO, which was to avoid taking them before the juvenile court. In the flux of opinion over desirable action on juvenile delinquency, the police voice within the dominant welfarist one over the period as a whole was consistently on the side of more punitive measures.[86] 'If they've done something wrong, they should be punished'

---

83  *Evening Standard*, 29 October 1955.

84  Maureen Cain (1968) 'Role Conflict among Police Juvenile Liaison Officers' *British Journal of Criminology*. When the role conflict became too great, Cain found that a number of JLOs in the forces she studied left in order to become probation officers.

85  Interview with Superintendent Clarke, Liverpool City police.

86  For example, it was opposition from local police forces that prevented Parliament from raising the age of criminal responsibility to fourteen, when the Children and Young Persons Bill was being debated. See Stevenson, 'Some

was the general police view.[87] Cautioning also had its intimidatory side. In Liverpool, the local chief superintendent held a kind of surgery every Saturday at which juveniles in trouble had to appear.[88] In Sheffield, where there was no liaison scheme, the detective chief inspector

> used to go in from nine o'clock to one o'clock on a Sunday alternate with the other chief inspectors, and that would be the cautioning day, and we just used to put the fear of God into them. I think this was a big success, because very rarely did they come again. If they did, we knew we had got trouble with them for the rest of their lives.[89]

Nevertheless, on a daily basis, juveniles do not seem to have presented the police with much of a problem. The police continued to demand and expect signs of deference from juveniles, to knock their heads together if they didn't get it, or to see them as easy targets in order to raise their own crime figures.[90] The indications are that police behaviour towards juveniles remained unchanged, despite the new initiatives, and they only retrospectively became aware that it might attract criticism. Chief Inspector Eyre, who saw himself as a policeman in the paternalist mode, said that:

> We only had occasional trouble with youths. Mind you, they respected the police, you were a force in your own right, you could always clip them if you wanted to. No complaints – now today, too many complaints. If you clipped somebody's ear, children trespassing or up to no good, clip on the ear with your gloves and they were gone. They respected you for it, the parents did. If you did it today, you'd lose your job.[91]

It was not the police, but the public who first began to change in their response towards the forces of law and order. This applied particularly to the young. Towards the end of the period, social surveys revealed that police behaviour towards teenagers was having an adverse effect on the latter's view of the police, and an increasing proportion began to voice the

---

social and political tides affecting the development of juvenile justice 1938–64'.

87  Interview with PC Hope, Birmingham City police. Hope said he did not approve of juvenile liaison schemes.

88  Interview with Detective Chief Superintendent Driver, Liverpool City police.

89  Interview with Detective Chief Superintendent Spender, Sheffield City police.

90  Interview with PC Price, Warwickshire police.

91  Interview with Chief Inspector Eyre, Glamorgan police. However, PC Moppett remembered an older generation of pcs who put ball bearings into their gloves before admininstering the 'clip round the earhole', which was no longer acceptable by his day. Interview with PC Moppett, Metropolitan police.

opinion that they were being picked on.[92] Others, such as headteachers, also began to resent police intrusion, in the form of JLOs, on the province of school discipline, where formerly they had welcomed it.[93] It begins to look as though the police were the last agency to respond to changing attitudes and the social policy changes in juvenile justice that had been brought in over the period, in line with the other reformist contributions that made up the welfare state.


## 3) Assault

Violence was not regarded as a major social problem in the period. Towards the end, it began to be seen as a problem of police behaviour; but apart from this, it gave rise to no government inquiries, or media investigations or learned articles. When asked to describe the changes they had seen in their lifetime, the police frequently commented on the greater degree of violence today than there had been during their own service years. This perception is quite at odds with the evidence. However, it is not only based on the current escalation in the means of violence, on the impact of a wider use of cars, guns and knives during criminal exploits today[94] (with knives seen as an 'un-British' importation) but also on the fact that much violence –

92   See R.C on the Police, *PP XX 1961–62*, Appendix 1V: R. Morton Williams, 'The Relations between the Police and the Public' in which over half of those aged 18–21 thought there was need for an inquiry into the police, and were generally more critical of them, than were older age-groups. Of more immediate relevance is the large social survey among male teenagers (15–21) carried out for the Home Office in 1963 in order to examine the effectiveness of the influences restraining the young from breaking the law. While both surveys reported a generally positive image of the police, in the latter over a third thought the police always picked on teenagers. *PRO: RG 23/307,* 'Youth and Crime Survey'.

93   Maureen Cain and M. Dearden (1966) 'Initial reactions to a new Juvenile Liaison scheme' *British Journal of Criminology.* The work for this survey was carried out in 1963. It also found that head teachers did not want to act as stool pigeons or create cases for the police.

94   But the use of guns by criminals and by the police has been underacknowledged. For example, fifteen Metropolitan policemen were either wounded or killed by burglars using firearms over an eight year period in the late nineteenth century. See Clive Emsley (1985) '"Thump of Wood on a Swede Turnip": Police Violence in Nineteenth Century England', *Criminal Justice History.* Knife attacks were also commonplace in fights between rival gangs. See Murphy, *Smash and Grab,* Chapter 11.

especially domestic – which would now bring charges of assault was previously totally ignored. Inspector Cooper provides an example:

> We used to get occasional violence, but you never got the sort of thing you get now, with knives being stuck into people. We had a few murders, but that was different, blokes murdering their wives and that. You accepted that.[95]

In addition, greater physical mobility and reduced residential social segregation have spread violence more widely across the social spectrum to areas where its occurrence brings more vocal protest. Finally, today's violence is much more openly and directly targetted at the police, whereas formerly the police were not used to being the targets of unsolicited violence, except by drunks. As Inspector Callow recalled, 'I never had an altercation with anyone who wasn't drunk. I would think in those days most people who were not under the influence of drink wouldn't risk challenging a policeman who looked anything like capable of defending himself'.[96] This latter point was an important part of the policeman's armoury, with the lack of emphasis on physique today seen as part and parcel of the decline in respect for the police. The threat, and reality, of physical force by the police was regarded as a vital ingredient of the qualities needed to make a good copper. The stress laid on physical strength and prowess by chief constables,[97] and by the men themselves, in itself contradicts the assertion that society was previously a less violent one. Much of this violence, which today would enter the statistics as assault on a police constable, was confined to contests in the street. As Sergeant Minch recalled

> One of the interesting things in those days was that one hardly ever charged anybody with assault of the police. If you arrested a drunk, well, if you arrested anybody and there was a fight, well you nearly always wrote it off as part of the job. And it wasn't until solicitors started encouraging their clients to counter-summons the police with assault that we started to charge them with being drunk and disorderly and assaulting a police officer.[98]

In their day, the police also kept out of the way of violent domestic disputes, since they were liable to get caught in the crossfire, and since it was commonplace that wives who wanted to bring charges of assault would

---

95   Interview with Inspector Cooper, Metropolitan police.
96   Interview with Inspector Callow, Hull City police.
97   The chief constable of Colchester, for example (before its amalgamation with Essex in 1947) made a point of recruiting men with boxing skills to the police in this garrison town. Tape recorded interviews, *Colchester Recalled*, Colchester Institute.
98   Interview with Sergeant Minch, Birmingham City police.

change their minds the next day when their husbands were no longer drunk. Battered wives had little redress and little alternative to acceptance of the marital status quo, and the police were rarely thanked, and frequently assaulted themselves, if they intervened. Such cases, while common, were therefore regarded as rubbish work and the police did their best to avoid them. Even in the 1950s, Chief Constable Wiseman described domestic violence as a way of life that police officers were officially advised during training to leave alone.[99] And if they did intervene, their action was likely to remain unrecorded. Sergeant Home was one who took action:

> With battered wives, I used to go and give the husbands a good hiding and tell them 'if you do it again, I'll give you another'. There was no one else to turn to but the police, none of that Town Hall rubbish. Of course, you couldn't do it now.[100]

Another reason intervention in domestic disputes remained unofficial is illustrated by the following example:

> A pc went to a domestic disturbance. A man had been knocking his wife about, so the pc gave him a hiding. The man said, 'I'm going up to the Guildhall about you' The pc said, 'Alright, you know the way'. Of course, the policeman went out and rang up the station and said, 'Look, there's a man coming in to complain about me giving him a hiding.' And the Inspector met him at the door, and took him round the corner and gave him another one.[101]

This major category of assault thus did not figure in the statistics or the public consciousness as a criminal act.

The other main source of violence was by drunks. Saturday night brawls after the pubs closed were traditional and well prepared for by the police, many of whom thoroughly enjoyed the ensuing rough house, and remain proud of it in retrospect. PC Waterford delighted in his nickname 'Rough House Waterford', earned for sorting out the drunks from the Irish Club in Camden Town.[102] In Birmingham, they simply parked a police van near the Irish pub on Saturday night and collared everyone who came out,[103] while PC Seaforth had his own way with drunks:

> The worst thing we had was a shemozzle with drunks on Friday or Saturday. We knew how to handle them, if you couldn't handle a man in them days you was no good as a pc in them days ... I know

99 Interview with Chief Constable Wiseman, Lancashire police.
100 Interview with Sergeant Home, Sheffield City police.
101 Interview with Sergeant Craig, Norwich City police.
102 Interview with PC Waterford, Metropolitan police.
103 Interview with Inspector Cooke, Birmingham City police.

its wrong, but we used to give 'em what they give us, and that was the only language they understood, these blaggards. Men would get drunk, and you had the dance halls going in them days, especially when the Yankees came over here, the black Americans and all. It was always a free for all there, and I used to enjoy it. I enjoyed myself.[104]

In the capital, there was always uproar in the West End on traditional occasions such as the Cup Final or University Boat Race nights. After the boat race, the university students usually wrecked one of the theatres, but the police were strictly briefed not to make arrests, since the universities always paid for the damage. Cup Final revellers, who came from a different strata of society, were not however treated so leniently.[105]

Fights over women and the drunkeness of overseas troops during the war have become proverbial, and policemen from all over the country remembered them all too well. Inspector Eyre confessed that these were the only occasions when he felt a bit frightened, although the military police would also be there to help out. As far as Inspector Astley was concerned, the Canadians were the worst. They were only paid once a fortnight, but pay nights were terrible, since they would all get fighting drunk. Sergeant Haines recalled an occasion when a mob of about 200 Canadians attacked West End Central police station to try and release a number of their compatriots detained there. The situation got so bad that the Commissioner asked for a banning order, questions were asked in Parliament, and the Australians and Canadians were barred from the West End.[106]

But drunks and domestics apart, who were regarded as part of the scenery, everyday life outside the West End was remembered as remarkably peaceful. In retrospect, it is surprising how little credence was given by former policemen to the culture of violence that permeated the force, given their ready admission of its place – and the need for it – in their daily dealings with some sections of the public; while the legal sanction on the use of physical force accorded the police made it difficult, if not impossible, to draw a distinct dividing line between legitimate and illegitimate levels of police violence. Certainly, the police themselves saw no need, either then or in retrospect, for stricter regulations about where the line should be drawn.

104 Interview with PC Seaforth, Neath Borough police.
105 Sergeant Haines M/S, *Ancedotes; Memories of C.J. Haines.*
106 Interview with Inspector Eyre, Glamorganshire police; Inspector Astley, West Sussex police; Sergeant Haines, Metropolitan police. See also the more extensive description of the impact of servicemen on civilian life, in Ingleton, *The Gentlemen at War,* Chapter 9, 'A Rapacious and Licentious Soldiery'.

# CHAPTER NINE

# Policing Public Order

Maintaining public order was a police priority and the chief purpose of the uniform pcs, around which their daily routine was organized.[1] It provided the rationale for the high visibility of the many uniformed officers pounding the beat in cities, towns and villages throughout the country, and gave purpose and meaning to the lives of men who spent their time doing little else. As the eyes and ears of the community, dedicated to upholding the moral order and restoring harmony when it fractured, their remit extended over a much wider field than simply those who broke the law. But the boundaries of their authority remained extremely hazy. Initially imposed on a reluctant or hostile population, by the turn of the twentieth century police surveillance of the whole of daily public life had acquired the impregnability of custom. It took a world war, a post-war shortage of recruits, and a social shift in public attitudes to alter the parameters and priorities of this policing policy. Present day attempts to retrieve the situation and return to this style of policing for the good order it was able to maintain seem doomed to failure in the highly fragmented society of today, since the degree to which it was effective depended to a large extent on a more acquiescent attitude to authority, a more fatalistic acceptance of the existing distribution of power, and a less contested, more unitary and thus more hegemonic value system.[2]

## The Controlling Gaze

How police authority in pursuit of public order was maintained depended largely on the nature of the community and on the particular public order

---

1   As Reiner succinctly emphasizes, most police work is neither social service nor law enforcement, but order maintenance. See Reiner, *The Politics of the Police*, p. 145.

2   See James. Q. Wilson and G.L. Kelling (1982) 'Broken Windows: the police and neighbourhood safety', *Atlantic Monthly*, for an influential account of an American experiment empowering the police to protect communities, rather than individuals, without regard to due process. The description of police behaviour within this experiment tallies precisely with that of the police in the period of the present study.

issue involved. Nevertheless, whatever the type of community, the purpose of all uniformed officers was 'to keep things nice and quiet'.[3] The first point to note is the difference between town and country here. In the towns and cities the policy was to fill the central area with police. 'The whole thing was to saturate the place ... there was a pattern of policemen everywhere' a Liverpool bobby stated. This meant that with so many bobbies out on the beat, 'we knew every move everyone was making'[4]. In rural areas this pattern was not possible, since 'on a detached beat, the policeman couldn't be everywhere at once ... you went where you liked and you worked your beat how you liked, but the thing was for the policeman to be seen.'[5] But whether in town or country, the police were expected to become sensitized to the smallest deviation from normality, so that suspiciousness became part of the police officer's working personality.[6] In other words, they needed to acquire a Foucauldian style 'controlling gaze' that could instinctively spot any irregularities and abnormalities in the pattern of life on their beat.[7] This visual alertness was an important element in the making of a police officer, and indeed several respondents mentioned their own abilities in this field. It was part of the learning process, and where lacking could lead to a reprimand, as Sergeant Haines recalled:

> The chief inspector had a flat above Saville Row, and I remember his wife used to take her dog along to Green Park ... And I remember, I was on the beat there, Piccadilly, Berkeley Square, round the block one Sunday morning. Eventually, I was told the chief inspector wanted to speak to me ... and he said 'You were looking in a shop window at ten o'clock this morning. My wife came along with the dog and she saw you. Don't let this happen again'.[8]

Walking the beat was not the place for day dreams or the pursuit of private interests, and transgression was likely to be spotted by one's superiors. Careful observation soon became second nature, as it was intended it should, to the extent that many police officers referred to their 'instinct'

3   Interview with Sergeant Dunhill, Birmingham City police.

4   Interview with Detective Chief Superintendent Driver, Liverpool City police; Inspector Archer, Durham City police.

5   Interview with Sergeant Brent, Essex police.

6   The phrase is J. Skolnick's. His account of suspiciousness as part of police culture is discussed in his (1966) *Justice Without Trial: Law Enforcement in Democratic Society*, p. 48.

7   Michel Foucault (1977) *Discipline and Punish: The Birth of the Prison*, Pt 3, Chapter 3.

8   Interview with Sergeant Haines, Metropolitan police.

when something or someone was doing wrong. As mentioned in the previous chapter, Inspector Cooper only had to stand at the street corner and think 'I don't like this one', and fifty per cent of the time he was proved right. 'You work up an instinct' he recalled. Inspector Cooke agreed:

> The purpose of the job was to go out and deal with people who were doing something that they shouldn't. You can say you're trained to be observant. Instinct in a way would tell you that they were doing something wrong. A lot of it is instinct. You see something happening and you think, there's something wrong here. And having thought that, you desire to look in to it a bit closer ...[9]

Here, the novice could come a cropper. Sergeant Richards described stopping a man with a sack at five o clock in the morning:

> In those days, the Metropolitan police had Section 66, where you could stop anyone (you were suspicious of). It was only the second week on my own after learning beats, and I was full of powers of arrest etc, and stop and search. There was this big burly chap coming down the towpath, and I stopped him, quoting Section 66. He gave me an old-fashioned look and a rude word. I thought, this is not something I can cope with, what can I arrest him for? He's just not going to let me search him. But that's not what the book says, he's supposed to let me search him. I said, 'I insist on seeing what's in your bag'. 'Right, son'. Empties the sack, it was horse manure he'd been carrying.[10]

A more experienced man would use stop and search to make clear to others his omniscient powers. During the war, for example, Sergeant Martin would deliberately stop young men of service age but out of uniform and ask for their identity card at the busiest roundabout at the Elephant and Castle. This public display served as a warning to others and, he believed, impressed all those looking on.[11]

In the country, close personal knowledge of the inhabitants replaced the impact of numbers in the towns. Informants were not really necessary, because the village policeman

> had the uncanny knack of spending somewhere in the region of 18 hours a day performing his function, so that he seemed to know what was going on ... it was a personal thing, this was your patch, time didn't matter ...[12]

---

9   Interview with Inspector Cooke, Birmingham City police.
10  Interview with Sergeant Richards, Metropolitan police.
11  Interview with Sergeant Martin, Metropolitan police.
12  Interviews with Detective Inspector Aylesham, Durham county police; and PC Hirons, Warwickshire police. Hirons recalled the first time a pc put in an

The village bobby's close knowledge of the local population and his authority over it meant that he could spot anything untoward, such as a stranger's car in the village, or become conscious of such events because people would tell him about it.[13] This sort of relationship took time to establish:

> It took a year before anybody spoke to me in that village, other than to say 'Good Morning', they just ignored you and made out you weren't there. But after a period of time, it could be nine months, I had no need to go to Slimfold ever. If anything was wrong in Slimfold someone would ring up. Now you can't do that in five minutes, you can't rush it. You've got to make yourself liked. Once you've got that, then you know full well that really they would do half your work for you. And the same thing applied to other villages.[14]

Keeping order provided satisfaction. It was Chief Inspector Tate's priority and his way of feeling he was serving the public, as it was Superintendent Hearn's:[15]

> It might sound rather silly these days ... but I used to be out on the beat in this town at night on my own, and I used to feel that I was looking after that town, because you were the only policeman and except for the occasional workman everybody was asleep and thought they were safe, and you used to feel that you were making them safe.

In the cities, the situation was more complex. Here, the consensus was more fragile, the occasions for public disturbance more frequent, and wrongdoers more numerous. The urban uniformed police still maintained as frequently as their rural counterparts that keeping order was their chief purpose, but the means by which they did so were slightly different. In urban areas they needed to gain the compliance and cooperation of the very people whom they regarded as a threat to order, even though their activities might be in no way criminal. This applied mainly to prostitutes, to street bookies who were subject to unenforceable laws, and to costermongers who cluttered up the place. But in fact anyone who hung about the streets – including the proverbial street footballers and street corner boys, as well as those who gained their livelihoods there, was in danger of police surveillance, police

---

overtime sheet, after the war. The sergeant nearly fainted, he had never seen one before.

13  Interview with Inspector Chambers, Essex police.
14  Interview with Inspector Smith, West Sussex police.
15  Interviews with Chief Inspector Tate, City of London police; and Superintendent Hearns, Durham County police.

disapproval and police arrest. The street was the police's domain; and control over the activities that went on there, the police task. 'When you walk on that pavement, *you* are in charge, you don't get out of the way for anyone' the police were told during their training.[16] Hence the resentment against the police, especially from urban working class youths, since the street was their most accessible meeting place; hence the high official approval of lads clubs and the like, since activities taking place off the street reduced the likelihood of arrest. Nevertheless, resentment of the police was most widespread because of interference in the leisure activities of adults.

## Bookies, Toms and Poufs [17]

Here, the prosecution of street betting probably caused more ill feeling between the police and the public than any other legislation with the exception of the traffic laws. The police had moved from a position of enthusiasm for their increased powers against street bookmakers under the Street Betting Act of 1906, to acknowledgement that the Act had become counterproductive. By the early 1930s, the Police Federation was complaining that it was impossible to maintain a law which was not supported by public opinion, with the chief constable of Manchester describing the situation as one where 'no one is with us, every one is against us'.[18] A decade later the Police Federation was still clamouring for the removal of a law that had achieved nothing except turn a large section of otherwise law-abiding people against the police.[19] Its mouthpiece, the *Police Review*, in trying to counter the many charges of police complicity and corruption, was at pains to point out that the law had to be changed not for this reason but because it had fallen into contempt.[20] But despite overwhelming evidence on the detrimental effect of the 1906 Act on

---

16 Interview with PC Moreton, Birmingham City police.

17 Prostitutes were always called toms by the police, who had taken over the terms used for their activities from the prostitutes themselves. See Joan Lock, *Lady Policeman*, p. 12. Homosexuals were referred to by the police as poufs or nancy boys.

18 *1932–33 RC on Lotteries and Betting*, Minutes, q. 708, p. 58.

19 Mark Clapson (1992) *A Bit of a Flutter: Popular gambling and English society, c.1823–1961*, p. 66.

20 *Police Review*, 20 April 1956. This comment was an attempt to vindicate the police from the charges of corruption made in parliament in a debate on betting and lotteries.

police/public relations and on police corruption, it was not repealed until 1960, after which betting was taken off the streets and into legalized betting shops. In the meantime, the police had to make the best of a bad law. As David Dixon cogently points out, police culture has habitually distinguished between corruption over serious crimes and over minor regulatory offences. Thus, in the latter case, corruption was regarded as an acceptable way of negotiating a tolerable everyday relationship with the public. Since eradication was impossible as far as betting was concerned, the priority became its containment, with bookmakers there by permission of the police, containment replacing eradication, and negotiated deals augmenting police power over the use of public space.[21] As many first-hand accounts testify, the outcome was a formalized relationship and ritual, whereby bookmakers' pitches – many of thirty to forty years standing – received a certain amount of police protection in return for cash and the charade of a court appearance, the charging of a runner and the fine paid by the bookmaker.[22] These rituals and rules of the game had to be learnt by police recruits as well as by punters, as Sergeant Minch recounts:

> I remember once when I was a very young policeman, standing on the corner of Barr Street. The sergeant had said to me 'stop these cyclists coming from Lucas's going across'. So I stood there, stopped two or three, stayed there for half an hour, and a bloke came up and said 'What are you doing here?' I said 'what's it to do with you? I'm watching this halt sign.' So he went away. Just after, the sergeant came up. He said 'What are you doing here?' I said 'You told me to watch this halt sign'. And he said, 'Not all the time. Clear off'. I said 'Why?' Because it was a bookies pitch. So you had to work wheels within wheels. The bookies accepted it. If we got to know on a particular day that a fresh runner was there, then we could arrest him. If a bookie changed his regular for a fresh one, he knew he could as good as say, well you've let me off for the last fortnight, take him in for street betting.[23]

But although the police generally operated within a customary set of rules and norms regarding the level of arrests and of bribes taken, there was no doubt over who was in control. The one thing the police would not tolerate

21 David Dixon (1991) *From Prohibition to Regulation: Bookmaking, Anti-Gambling and the Law*, p. 227, 229.
22 *PRO Mepo 2/8553*, 12 October 1949. Letter from an ex-Metropolitan police officer to the chairman of the RC on Betting, in which he comments that during ten years of service he had not met one officer of the rank of subdivisional inspector and above who did not accept favours from bookmakers, and that lower ranks who did not join in were victimized.
23 Interview with Sergeant Minch, Birmingham City police.

was a challenge to their authority over the use of public space, and in such cases they made very clear that offending sections of the public were there on sufferance. This meant that bookmakers were widely used as informers, as part of the quid pro quo. Inspector Cooper gave an example:

> We had this one little bit of trouble and it amounted almost to a murder, so we sent for the local bookmakers. The Detective Inspector sent for these local bookmakers and he said, 'Right, I want the bastard here tomorrow, or I shut down every pitch'. The bloke was in the next day.[24]

The same conditions and relationships with the police also applied to prostitutes in the city centres, before the 1959 Street Offences Act swept them off the streets. As was the case with bookies and other street traders, the resulting symbiotic police/prostitute relationship meant that the prostitutes' business was conducted within a context of bribery and corruption, of informers, and of a ritualized system of police arrest and court fines. But until the laws regarding such ubiquitous and widely pursued forms of behaviour were changed, the effect of the necessarily token systems of public order maintenance in these matters inevitably cast a shadow on the reputation of the police who dealt with them.

Disquiet over police behaviour in the 1920s, especially in the metropolis, had become vocal after a series of inquiries into betting (1923 Select Committee into Betting Duty); prostitution (1927–8 Street Offences Committee); and police corruption (the Sergeant Goddard case); culminating in the 1929 Royal Commission on the police. These inquiries revealed a degree of illegal behaviour that led the Home Secretary to admit that the police had lost public trust, and needed to regain the 'full support and sympathy – as they used to have twenty or even ten years ago – and the affection of the people as a whole'.[25] The outcome was one of those periodic cleansing of the stables that regularly take place in the metropolis, in order to restore the police's public image. The 1930s thus opened with a new commissioner, Lord Trenchard, strongly committed to eradicating police corruption, and to the inauguration of a new 'golden age'. The Street Offences Committee, set up to inquire into the law and practice concerning soliciting in the street, had acknowledged that the police must inevitably be open to bribery in such cases, but had been unable to recommend any solution, apart from the suggestion that convictions should not be secured on the evidence of the police alone. The evidence of witnesses to this committee was never published, but the committee's concern that

24 Interview with Inspector Cooper, Metropolitan police.
25 Quoted Dixon, *From Prohibition to Regulation*, p. 244.

prostitutes should not be convicted on the uncorroborated evidence of the police speaks volumes on the reputation of the police in this field.[26] However, in the absence of any new policy directives, the police continued to deal with prostitution during the 1930s largely as they had throughout the previous decade, with neither prostitutes nor the way they were policed arousing much public comment at this time. It was not until well after the war that the topic once more hit the headlines. Until then, West End prostitutes and those in other large cities centres such as Birmingham were dealt with by rota (always officially denied) by officers operating in pairs:

> These two men, and it's true, they had a roster. A pocket book with all the names of the girls, and they'd go round Piccadilly Circus, Shaftesbury Avenue, Bond Street, anywhere in that area. It was a rather tight area, because the girls only worked where there were a lot of men walking about, not in Mayfair or anywhere like that ... Normally, a male prostitute patrol would go out and take them in in turn, and this was partly because the whole law on the thing was just a mess and it hadn't been changed, and of course the streets were just lined with prostitutes. It was just a kind of a way of not letting it get too out of hand, really.[27]

The prostitutes used to come to court once a fortnight, to be fined 40/– the average number attending the central London court being thirty a day – and as long as they weren't harrassed or victimized, they would readily take their turn to be arrested.[28] It was the 1950s before anyone complained, when the *Daily Graphic* published complaints of importuning by prostitutes and an article entitled 'Clean Up Piccadilly', and the Metropolitan police sought to reassess the action they might need to take. An ingenious economic explanation for the perceived rise in soliciting was provided by the chief superintendent at West End Central. In his estimation soliciting had decreased during the war because

> money was easy and there was no dearth of clients for these women, consequently soliciting openly decreased and this state of affairs continued for some time after the war ended. However, as money became tighter the number of potential clients gradually diminished until at the present time the scarcity of money has brought the

26  Report of the Street Offences Committee, *HMSO Cmd. 3231*, 1928, pp. 26, 28.
27  Interviews with Sergeant Haines and WPC Lake, Metropolitan police. Joan Lock confirms that most West End prostitutes were arrested by a special patrol of about ten officers operating in pairs. Male officers were discouraged from making lone arrests because of the very real risk of allegations by some prostitutes. Joan Lock, *Lady Policeman*, p. 16.
28  Interviews with PC Wavell and Deputy Commander Blatchley, Metropolitan police. A similar system operated in Birmingham.

number of customers to a very low level. In consequence, prostitutes really must solicit, they are becoming more persistent as competition is so keen.[29]

The superintendent went on to provide arrest statistics for soliciting that showed a constant level at around 2500 arrests a year from 1937 to 1949, after which the figure jumped to 5000 in 1951, and 6000 to October 1952.[30] He believed that every prostitute regularly soliciting in the Division (estimated at around 800) had been arrested at one time or another, and that the situation was unalterable under the present law. The divisional commander agreed no more could be done given the resources available, that too much time was already taken up with the prosecution of prostitutes, and that the law needed to be changed.[31] In other words, public pressure to arrest more prostitutes was putting the police into an intolerable position.

The system with regard to prostitution was entirely comparable with the way street betting was dealt with, the punters in both cases regarding the police as the enemy. The police disliked applying a law that set so many against them, at the same time as appreciating (and sometimes misusing[32]) their power over prostitutes, whom they found useful as informants. But the silence throughout nearly the whole period over prostitution and the manner it was dealt with by the police parallels the silence over so many other misdemeanours that received no public acknowledgement at the time, making it difficult to delve beneath the surface of the cosy police presentation of relations with prostitutes who, according to the police, often regarded them as their friends and protectors.

However, this cosy relationship did not extend to the police view of homosexuals. Prostitutes were regarded and treated as persons, even if of an inferior and undesirable type, since they did not present a basic challenge to the policeman's general view of appropriate gender relations. Women's role was to serve the needs of men, whether as wives or as prostitutes. Homosexuals, however, were looked upon as deviants and non-persons, and their sexual preferences and necessarily clandestine life style offended all

---

29 *PRO: Mepo 2/9367*, 'Prostitutes, Homosexuals, Pornography and Rowdyism in the West End', 30 October 1952.

30 By 1955, the figure had risen to 7000, and to 11,000 for the whole MPD. *HC Debs, 5s,* 555, 1955–56, p. 1014.

31 Ibid., 31 Ocotober.

32 See Brogden, on policemen sleeping with prostitutes. *On the Mersey Beat*, pp. 126–7.

the values on which a male police culture was based.[33] As Harry Daley, the homosexual policeman, relates in his autobiography he had to tread very warily in order to achieve a tolerable daily existence with his colleagues.[34] Most police officers claimed never to have come across a homosexual policeman. 'I never knew one' said Sergeant Gleam. He went on to describe how he was taught during his probationary period to deal with 'poufs':

> We were in plain clothes with a uniform man, to show us how to go on. There was this Gents, well this fellow he says, 'Stick around a bit, I'm going in here and if you see anybody run out of here, you kick him as hard as you can. Sure enough, he went in, and one came dashing out, and I kicked his behind all the way up Broad Street. He was one of those silly monkeys you used to get in there. Of course, they're accepted now, these people.[35]

Inspector Gardner was another pc who claimed he had had no knowledge of homosexuals, before he was sent to arrest them:

> Not long after arriving in Barnes I was sent for by the chief superintendent. It appears that a number of poufs who had chosen to frequent the tow path had been mugged by hooligans from Hammersmith. The poufs were reluctant to complain against their aggressors. My job was to remove the cause rather than the effect by arresting the poufs, where the evidence existed ... With a pc in plain clothes I went round the place at night ... There must have been sixty to a hundred men in various places on this site all together in groups and pairs. I have never seen a more revolting sight than the antics of this lot ... They were all guilty, it was a case of which to take ... I think we arrested fifteen to twenty. One of these was fined, the rest were sent to see a psychiatrist. Poor psychiatrist![36]

The police generally regarded homosexuals as the lowest of the low, and even the *Street Offences Committee* offered commiseration for the 'distasteful task' of hunting for them in public lavatories – a process that was known colloquially as 'fox-hunting'. But the use of police *agents provocateur* who toured the cities' public urinals brought in a negligible haul in comparison with the number of prostitutes arrested. In the West End, there were around 100 homosexual arrests annually, with two plain clothes officers 'continually employed on this unpleasant duty'.[37] However,

---

33 Young's anthropological categorization contrasts the masculinity and purity of the police with the impure and polluting qualities of the homosexual. Young, *An Inside Job*, p. 141

34 Harry Daley (1986) *This Small Cloud*.

35 Interview with Sergeant Gleam, Birmingham City police.

36 Inspector Gardner, Metropolitan police, M/S autobiography.

37 *PRO: Mepo 2/9367*, 30 October 1952.

relief was in sight. The decriminalization of homosexual acts between consenting adults that came in after the Wolfenden Report[38] in 1957, together with legislation that took prostitution and betting off the streets, ushered in a new permissive era that eased the task of the police in what had been some of their most disliked, if lucrative, public order duties.

## Marches and Demonstrations

The other chief public order task – also disliked – was the control of public marches and demonstrations. The 1930s was a decade of political unrest and upheaval throughout Western Europe, following economic depression and the rise of organized Fascism and Communism. The bloody street clashes between supporters of opposing ideologies which led, at their most extreme, to civil war in Spain as a precursor to the Second World War, were not entirely absent from Britain. The country did not escape a restrained form of such conflicts, although it would be true to say that the government was never seriously worried by either the Communist or Fascist threat (apart from a short period of governmental jitters over Bolshevism after the First World War) – the comments of individual politicians notwithstanding.[39] Basically, successive governments hoped that by doing nothing too drastic, the problem would go away. Nevertheless, they remained extremely wary of both ideologies, with the communist receiving the lion's share of the authorities attention – and this, indeed, was never relaxed. Furthermore, however limited in scale and degree, the 1930s disturbances and the issues that underlay them aroused so much public debate that the government *was* eventually forced to take legislative action to try and contain them. Similarly, because of the resonance of the issues involved, the lively historical interest in the subject has elicited a large literature, most of which has been focussed on the attitude of the authorities towards the protesters, whether hunger marchers, or Fascists and their opponents. It is widely held that these two disparate groups became linked in the official mind during the search for policies that could as well be used against the one as the other. The charge made is that the 1936 *Public Order Act*, officially brought in to deal with uniformed Fascist gatherings, was more fundamentally directed against the civil liberties of protesters on the left. But the more specific charge, above all against the police, is that they went on to favour

38 *Home Office*: Report of the Committee on Homosexual Offences and Prostitution, September 1957, *Cmnd 247*.
39 John Stevenson and Chris Cook (1979 edn) *The Slump: Society and Politics During the Depression*, p. 265.

the Fascists when dealing with the disturbances of the 1930s. It is on this question that most attention has concentrated and it is here that differences between scholars emerge, from those who support the National Council of Civil Liberties (NCCL) view that the police were both anti-left *and* pro-Fascist to those who see the police as simply pro-police.

Before discussing this question, however, it is necessary to review the official response to demonstrations by left wing and trade union groups that preceded the advent of the Fascists. It is here that the search for ways to curb common law rights to meet and to process were first vigorously pursued in the decade following the end of the war. It is here that the National Unemployed Workers Movement (NUWM), which organized the hunger ma_ches of the 1920s and 30s, first came to the notice of the government as a Communist inspired organization, at a time when official fears of a Bolshevist style insurrection still had some force behind it.[40] The NUWM was therefore placed on Special Branch's list of revolutionary organizations that were to be kept under surveillance; and from this time onwards, never ceased to arouse the authorities' suspicion and hostility.[41] This was carried over to the 1930s and on to the unemployed generally, since after a cut in unemployment benefit in 1931, the latter showed a greater willingness to join the NUWM. The effect on the police was wide-reaching, and involved far more than a few undercover agents. With unemployment rising to new heights and the government in crisis over the issue, the police were encouraged to renew their attention and attacks on unemployed demonstrations, that culminated in clashes with the hunger marchers in Hyde Park in October 1932. Here, 2500 police, many of them specials, confronted the marchers, and violence flared after the specials lost their nerve and attacked the crowd.[42] With the capital crowded with marchers from all over the country and with plans for the presentation of a national petition against unemployment to parliament, the government decided to arrest four leaders of the NUWM in an effort to discredit the organization as a Communist front. This clumsy attempt to silence the marchers, under the charge of 'attempting to cause disaffection among the Metropolitan police' was ultimately counterproductive. Given the dubious

---

40  Barbara Weinberger, 'Police perceptions of labour in the inter-war period: the case of the unemployed and of miners on strike', in F. Snyder and D. Hay (eds.1987) *Labour, Law and Crime: an Historical Perspective*, p. 153.

41  See R. Hayburn (1972) 'The Police and the Hunger Marchers' *International Review of Social History*, which shows that there was at least one informant who had penetrated the highest NUWM circles. There were Special Branch reports on all the hunger marches.

42  Peter Kingsford (1982) *The Hunger Marchers in Britain 1920–1940*, Chap. 6.

legality of the arrests, and the subsequent judgement against the police in the case of *Elias* v. *Pasmore*[43], it was to lead directly to the 1934 *Incitement to Disaffection Act*. This Act, and the events leading up to it, succeeded only in discrediting a government that had so far failed to act against the Fascists, and rallying protesters against the attack on traditional civil liberties.[44] A section of the middle class was drawn in to act as watch-dog in these matters, and for the first time to monitor police behaviour on questions of the policing of public order. The NCCL, set up on the eve of the 1934 hunger march, included a roll call of the liberal left's 'great and good', with E. M. Forster as its president, and Edith Summerskill, Kingsley Martin, Julian Huxley, Clement Attlee, Harold Laski, A.P. Herbert and H. G. Wells among its early members.[45] But it had its origins in the observation of police behaviour first made during the 1932 hunger march demonstrations by the NCCL's founder, Ronald Kidd. Thus it was police behaviour against the left that first rallied this influential section of the middle class, which remained suspicious of the police ever after. The consequence of their critical attitude was to have serious implications for the reputation of the police in the long term, becoming an added strand in the voices of disapproval that gathered pace from the mid-1950s. But at the time, the Home Office seriously misjudged the situation and felt able to dismiss complaints from this quarter as the work of cranks, after Special Branch advised that they were 'palpably holders of left-wing or extremist views ... seeking publicity'.[46] The main effect of such publicity at the time was simply to encourage the police to seek greater powers to deal with threats to public order. Here Lord Trenchard, the new Metropolitan Commissioner, began by imposing what became known as the 'Trenchard ban' to prohibit meetings of the unemployed outside labour exchanges, in order to frustrate the recruiting efforts at these sites by the NUWM. According to the left-wing lawyer and MP, D.N. Pritt, there was absolutely no legal right or justification for this action.[47] Nevertheless, the ban was

---

43 In this case, brought by Sid Elias of the NUWM against the Police Commissioner, the judge ruled that the police had seized and removed documents without legal justification, making clear that the search had been illegal.

44 Anderson claims that the Bill created an aura of distrust that resulted in one of the greatest campaigns against a single piece of legislation in modern British history. See Gerald D. Anderson (1983) *Fascists, Communists and the National Government: civil liberties in Great Britain 1931–1937*, p. 79.

45 Sylvia Scaffardi (1986) *Fire Under the Carpet*, pp. 43–45.

46 *PRO: HO 45 25462/648133/26*, 6 July 1936.

47 *HC Debs, 5s*, 314, 1935–6, 1551.

important, not just in its own right, but because of the case-law judgement
that arose out of it, which endorsed this considerable extension of police
powers. The case of *Duncan* v. *Jones* (1936) concerned the power of the
police to stop meetings on the highway even where no obstruction or
disorder was involved. The charge was that the speaker, Mrs Duncan, had
obstructed the police in the execution of their duty when they tried to stop
her speaking, 'in case she said something, had she been allowed to speak,
which would have led to a breach of the peace'.[48] The police case was
upheld in the High Court, thereby validating the extended powers that the
police had exercised over public meetings ever since the Trenchard ban. In
other words, the police were granted the right to ban any political meeting
in the street, where previously they had only been able to intervene if an
immediate breach of the peace was threatened. But case law does not have
the authority of statute law, and as far as processions were concerned,
Trenchard wanted legislation banning the right to march through central
London. The government were clearly in favour. A Cabinet Committee to
consider the legal position of marches in London was convened
immediately after the 1932 hunger march, and the government prepared a
draft bill that would have enabled the Home Secretary to prevent such
marches if he saw fit. However, the bill foundered on the opposition of the
Attorney-General, who regarded the proposed powers as too extensive.[49] It
is nevertheless significant that what finally emerged as the 1936 Public
Order Act, giving the police enhanced powers to control processions and the
language used at public meetings, was first mooted in connection with the
hunger marchers. The parallels with the way in which the Incitement to
Disaffection Act had its genesis in the failed case against the arrested
hunger march leaders in 1932 is also striking. In Jane Morgan's view, it was
no coincidence that the Public Order Bill was eventually introduced in the
House of Commons on the day after the 1936 national hunger march, since
she believed the Bill was aimed as much at curbing the demonstrations of
the left as of the right; while Ronald Kidd was in no doubt that the Act was
aimed primarily at the labour and left-wing parties, that it originated in
1932 and 1934, and that the Fascist hooliganism merely served to put it on

---

48  Editorial notes from the *New Statesman*, quoted R. Kidd, (1940) *British Liberty in Danger,* p. 23.

49  See John Stevenson, 'The BUF, the Metropolitan Police and Public Order', in K. Lunn and R.C. Thurlow (eds 1980) *British Fascism: essays on the Radical Right in Inter-War Britain.*

the statute book.[50] A rather different emphasis is given by Paul Cohen, who stresses the strenuous efforts of Home Office officials to design an impartial measure that could be applied equally to all sides as the reason for the earlier rejection of the bill,[51] while Richard Thurlow believes that it was the fear that ethnic conflict in the East End would rally protesters to the side of the communists that finally provided the clinching argument for this augmentation of state powers.[52] Ultimately, however, there is little substantive difference between these arguments, since all acknowledge the double-edged purpose of the Public Order Act. If we take into account the long history of governmental attempts to block the efforts of the hunger marchers and their organizers, there remains little doubt that the Fascist demonstrations simply provided the necessary rationale for legislation that could be used against equally well against the left.

The main policing question raised by the events surrounding the Public Order Act was whether it was able to curb the alleged police partiality for the Fascists or whether this partiality was more apparent than real. On the one hand, Skidelsky – and Stevenson and Cook after him – believe that the attitude of the police was not so much pro-Fascist as pro-police, and that the police became increasingly irritated with the demonstrations of the right as well as the left, as well as with the fact that they could so easily be portrayed as protecting the Fascists when they prevented violence at meetings.[53] On the other, as Stevenson and Cook go on to argue, it was clear that the old police suspicion of anything that could be labelled Communist remained, and probably over-rode their dislike of the Fascists. In any event, while there were no recorded incidents of baton charges against the BUF, there were many against their opponents. But the question, in Stevenson's view, cannot be answered fully until the views of those lower down the scale are known, to help confirm whether the attitudes and policies emanating from the higher echelons of the police were reflected by those

50  See Jane Morgan (1987) *Conflict and Order: the Police and Labour Disputes in England and Wales 1900–1939,* Chapter 8; *PRO: HO 45 25463,* Special Branch report of CP meeting addressed by Kidd, 26 July 1937.

51  Paul Cohen (1986) 'The Police, the Home Office and Surveillance of the British Union Fascists', *Intelligence and National Security.*

52  Richard Thurlow, 'Blaming the Blackshirts: Anti-Jewish Disturbances in the 1930s', in Panikos Panayi (ed. 1993) *Racial Violence in Britain, 1840–1950,* p. 115.

53  Robert Skidelsky (1975) *Oswald Mosley,* p. 420; Stevenson and Cook, *The Slump,* p. 420; R. Thurlow (1988) 'British Fascism and State Surveillance 1934–45', *Intelligence and National Security.*

directly involved at street level.[54] Clearly, it would be important to try to establish whether the left's accusations of anti-left, pro-Fascist bias in police attitudes and behaviour was indeed an accurate description of those of the rank and file.

Unfortunately, there is not a great deal that can be added substantively here, since testimony from the present sample is of little more than anecdotal value. Nevertheless, an analysis of the attitudes expressed may take us a little further. Here, the first thing to note is that the hunger marchers, who became such a symbol of the depression in the inter-war years, and whose treatment by the police led to the founding of the NCCL,[55] left little mark on the memories of the pre-war police sample. Jarrow, 'the town that was murdered', is remembered by the police largely as a defaulters station rather than as a town with one of the highest unemployment rates in the country. Inspector Archer was stationed there on his first posting in 1936, the year of the Jarrow hunger march:

> Jarrow! It was noted as a defaulters station, you know. Everybody who had committed a misdemeanour in the county force was sent to Jarrow, because of the harsh surroundings, and the poverty ... *Were you there at the Jarrow hunger march?* Yes, I was there. *Did you police that?* I can't remember now. I do remember a riot at Jarrow, someone had been arrested and they tried to storm the police station. We had a baton charge, the only time I remember a baton charge, and a lot of the older pcs had their targets marked long before the charge took place ...[56]

Although Archer felt sympathy for the plight of the unemployed,[57] he was a policeman first and foremost, and policing was his priority. If the Jarrow poor caused trouble they got trouble back, was his attitude, and the question of taking sides did not arise. Beyond this, there are three other memories of the marchers, all from London. In the first, Inspector Cooper recalled the hunger march in 1934 because it caused him to postpone his wedding. Police leave was cancelled, and the police formed a cordon to stop the marchers from entering London from the north. 'Eventually there were skirmishes, and a lot of these hunger marchers ran away in a panic' was his only, contemptuous, comment. Rather fuller is the account given by Inspector Gardner:

> The Spanish Civil War, Hitler, Mussolini, meant nothing to me. My first real contact with the state of the nation was when I

---

54  John Stevenson, 'The BUF, The Metropolitan Police and Public Order' p. 148.

55  See Ronald Kidd (1940) *British Liberty in Danger,* p. 145.

56  Interview with Inspector Archer, Durham County police.

57  See his comments on coal stealers in Chapter 8.

accompanied the Jarrow marchers when they arrived in London. I was impressed. My colleagues and I at least had a job. Before we started the walk towards inner London with the marchers the police were ordered to take sticks and poles from the banners and break them up. It was so unnecessary, I had never seen a milder crowd of men. As we walked, a conversation struck up between some of the police and the marchers. I was convinced, as I am sure were my colleagues, that there was not and never had been any threat of violence. I think that at last I began to realize what a small world I had lived in and how secure I was compared to these men. But there was no great awakening.[58]

The third memory is Sergeant Martin's, talking about policing the unemployment exchanges. Although he sympathized with the unemployed, because many of them were Geordies as he was, his chief comment was that it was a very attractive duty. Instead of being posted to shift work, there were two men posted to the unemployment exchange from 8.30 to 4.30. His verdict was 'you had a nice lie-in and you had every evening free, and basically you just had to see that there was no disorder'.[59]

The point to note is the personal emphasis in these memories, where public events are remembered for their impact on the individual's private or professional life. Of course this applies to most reminiscences; but beyond this, it also bears out the view cited earlier, that the police were ultimately in favour of no side but their own. Although these points have been made in connection with police policy makers and the priority given to the preservation of public order with the least possible expenditure of time and manpower, the sentiment applies equally at the lower levels. The hunger marchers aroused some police sympathy as fellow members of the working class who were destitute, whereas the police themselves were in work. As Sergeant Tome put it, 'We felt sorry for the hunger marchers, because virtually every policeman had experienced unemployment'.[60] But the constable on the street, as much as his superiors, wanted to be able to maintain order with the least possible calls on his time (especially his unpaid overtime) and the least possible effort on his part. The demand for extra policing during the hunger marches or Fascist disturbances thus became a cause for resentment, and an occasion when the Commissioner was seen as getting his pound of flesh. 'He got an awful lot of policing for nothing', Sergeant Martin noted.[61] Disorder also offended the beat

58 Inspector Gardner, Metropolitan police, M/S autobiography.
59 Interview with Sergeant Martin, Metropolitan police.
60 Interviews with Chief Inspector Tate, City of London police; Sergeant Tome, Metropolitan police.
61 Interview with Sergeant Martin, Metropolitan police.

constable's sense of propriety as much as it worried those higher up the scale; so that by and large, little sense of solidarity with unemployed members of their own social class emerges from these accounts.

Turning now to the police view of the Fascist disturbances, the reporting of Fascist meetings and clashes with anti-Fascists in the police newspaper bears out the totally self-centred orientation of the police, their lack of self-criticism and their imperviousness to criticism from outside. The events which aroused so much debate and criticism of the police outside were hardly mentioned in the police's own paper, the *Police Review*. Of course, the police were supposed to be non-political, yet they were materially involved in policing these events, and one might have expected some comment to be made on what was being said about them. It was not, however, until the notorious baton charge on the anti-Fascist meeting in Thurloe Square in 1936 that the newspaper printed an account of parliamentary criticism of police action at Fascist meetings. Otherwise, the chief mention was of the large number of meetings in the East End the police had attended and the number of policemen involved – this aspect taking precedence to reporting of the clashes themselves.[62]

Respondents showed a similarly low key reaction from which it is difficult to extract any clear view, even though a number were involved in Cable Street and other major Fascist/anti-Fascist incidents. The following three quotations reveal three different standpoints, that probably cover the total range of police attitudes: the first is pro-Fascist, the second is pro-police and the third is inclined against the Fascists. Significantly, however, there is no account which was favourable of the left. Inspector Gardner described the scene during the many Fascist meetings and marches he attended:

> As usual, the police were chucked and spat at and had obscenities hurled at them. The police are supposed to be impartial, but I don't think they really can be, not in a riot situation. It is much easier to like a man who is carrying a Union Jack, who is smart and clean with close-cropped hair, than a man who has shouted an obscene insult at you and spat in your face.

The second quotation comes from PC Waterford:

> I was in the East End at the battle of Cable Street, 1936, and that was a confrontation between the Blackshirts and the Communists. Cable street in particular was choc-a-bloc, so the Commissioner, Sir Philip Game got up on a trolley, a costermonger's trolley, and told them to clear the streets and they didn't. So he read the Riot Act. It

---

62 *Police Review*, 3 April, 17 July, 27 November, 1936. The only other mention of Fascist meetings, confined to enumerating the number of police involved, came in extracts from the Metropolitan Commissioner's annual reports.

was the first time in living memory that the Riot Act had been read. He gave them ten, fifteen minutes to clear the streets, but they didn't. You know his order to us? It was, officers, draw your truncheons and clear the streets. In half an hour the streets were clear.

This version of the pc as hero is directly countered by the memories of East Enders involved in the Cable Street debacle, who recall that it was the police, not the Fascists, who attempted to come into Cable Street, and that it was the police who were beaten up. 'It was the police whose helmets we captured, it was the police whose batons we took away' Phil Piratin, later Communist MP for Mile End, recounted.[63] Views from each side of the barricades thus produce opposing versions of events; but here we are concerned, not so much with events – where recall is often suspect – as with attitudes, where memory is a better guide.

The final account offered here is by Sergeant Tome, who had also been present at the battle of Cable Street:

Our views were, we thought Mosley was a good speaker, but to be honest I thought he was a bit nutty. We used to talk about this in the section house, everyone was convinced of the way Germany was going, and we were all a bit frightened that the same situation would arise over here. So in actual fact, we were all fed up to the back teeth with him.[64]

The police on the streets faced much the same dilemma as the policy makers in the need to be seen to be impartial – a difficult feat when one side deliberately provoked the other, while demanding protection of their own rights to free speech. In this sense, accusations of police preference for the Fascists were unjust. Nevertheless, the instinctive police dislike of the unruly and non law-abiding, coupled with an unquestioning acceptance of their role in support of the status quo, led to an equally instinctive distrust of anything and everything labelled left-wing or Communist. Here, Skolnick offers a persuasive explanation for the police's conservatism as due to the fact that a man engaged in enforcing a set of rules implies that he also becomes implicated in affirming them.[65] But he does not necessarily start out with these values and attitudes. The weight of research does not support the view that police recruits are more authoritarian than civilian control groups. Rather, it would seem, it is their working culture that creates

---

63  'The Battle of Cable Street' Peter Catterall (ed. 1994), *Contemporary Record*.

64  Interviews with Inspector Gardner, PC Waterford and Sergeant Tome, Metropolitan police.

65  Skolnick, *Justice*, p. 59.

a change in values and attitudes.[66] Thus, in so far as the police attitude was consistently against the left but not always against the extreme right, it could be said to have favoured the Fascists. C.H. Rolph, himself a City of London policeman during the 1930s, certainly thought this was the case when talking abut his fellow pcs:

> I rather think that if their sympathies went one way or another it was towards the Fascists, not because they had ever studied Fascism or knew anything at all about it, but because they represented law and order. They marched in a disciplined way, they stepped off on the left foot, did a smart 'eyes right' at the Mansion House, all that sort of thing. And that attracted and held the sympathy, up to a point, of most of the bobbies I knew. On the other hand, the communists did not. I don't suppose they were communists at all, but our people called them that. They didn't attract much sympathy, because they were a rag tail and bob tail kind of rabble, ready for a fight at any moment, ready to throw missiles at the Fascists or the police, although the provocation came from the Fascists. Therefore it was the rebels who got the brunt of such police ill will as there was.[67]

Some policemen sympathized with the British Union of Fascists, while others saw it as a menace to public order, but both had a deep distrust and hostility to the left as a common element. It is in this sense that one can talk of institutionalized bias which, whilst not always in favour of the BUF, was always directed against its opponents.[68] And it is not only in the Home Office papers that one finds countless expressions of a taken for granted anti-leftist stance.[69] The many detailed witness accounts of partisan police behaviour in the NCCL's files give ample ground to the view that the police at all levels, if not pro-Fascist, were certainly anti-leftist.[70] They also often appear to have been anti-semitic, and willing to tolerate racist abuse from Fascist speakers without extending a similar tolerance to the Fascist's opponents. Here, as Richard Temple rightly insists, Sir Philip Game must be held responsibe for the inadequacies of the police response, through his

---

66  See Robert Reiner 'Policing and the Police', in M. Maguire, R. Morgan and R. Reiner (eds 1994) *The Oxford Handbook of Criminology,* p. 732.

67  Interview with Inspector Rolph, City of London police.

68  D.S. Lewis (1987) *Illusions of Grandeur: Mosley, Fascism and British Society 1931–81,* p. 163.

69  See for example *PRO: HO 45 25462/648133/26 and 27,* 6 and 18 July, 1936. The NCCL held their own inquiry into the Thurloe Square incident after the Home Office refused to do so, but a Special Branch report advised that this need not be taken seriously, since it was obvious that the great majority of witnesses were strongly biased.

70  These are most accessible in the NCCL archive at the University of Hull.

failure to confront prejudice and partiality in the ranks and to ensure that the law on racist abuse was stringently enforced. While Section 4 of the Public Order Act strengthened the law against the use of provocative language at public meetings, the statistics for the years following the Act show that although there were over 2000 Fascist meetings in the East End alone up to the end of 1938, in which anti-semitic abuse was the standard polemic, little use was made of this provision in the Act. Game may have been discouraged by the fact that attempts to prosecute anti-semitic speakers were forestalled because the Director of Public Prosecutions did not believe that they could succeed.[71] Nevertheless, only sixteen cautions against Fascist speakers were issued by police officers during this time, whereas fifteen anti-Fascists alone were charged with the use of insulting words and behaviour in the first six months after the Act.[72]

In the debate over the attitude of the two Metropolitan Commissioners involved in the 1930s disturbances, Lord Trenchard has been accused of Fascist sympathies and Sir Philip Game described as a democrat and liberal.[73] But in practical terms, the distinction mattered little. Both were pressing for greater police powers to curb public demonstrations and their own right to decide on which should be banned as a threat to public order; and both placed their arguments within the context of the perceived need to contain the spread of Communist influence. Trenchard began to press for a ban on the Fascist wearing of uniforms as early as 1933, in which his key point was that 'uniforms are provocative and a great stimulus to Communism'.[74] He was also calling for the right to send police in to public meetings and the power to prohibit demonstrations and processions that threatened public order, without waiting for further legislation.[75] His successor, Sir Philip Game, found it no easier to gain authority to ban provocative gatherings, and looked forward to what became the 'battle of Cable Street' in the hope that it would bring things to a head and lead to the

---

71  Thurlow, *'British Fascism and State Surveillance'*.

72  Richard Temple (1995) 'The Metropolitan Police and the British Union of Fascists 1934–1940', *Journal of the Police History Society*. Temple shows how Game refused to supply the Home Office with figures for the numbers cautioned or prosecuted for insulting behaviour since 'he did not want to put the Divisions to the trouble of getting them'.

73  See Andrew Moore (1990) 'Sir Philip Game's "other life": the making of the 1936 Public Order Act in Britain', *Australian Journal of Politics and History*.

74  *PRO: HO 45 25386*, 2 July 1934.

75  Ibid. Trenchard stated that although the root cause of the trouble was the uniformed private army under Mosley, the methods of the Communists were a contributory factor.

banning of processions all over London.[76] He also wanted to deal stringently with anti-semitism because he thought it boosted anti-Fascist alliances with the Communists. Further, his argument for dealing drastically with the Fascists at the time was placed in the context of a possible clash with the Communists in the future. 'I cannot help feeling that the real clash may eventually come not with Fascism but with Communism' he noted in his plea for stronger measures now against the Fascists.[77] His plea was met, to the extent that the Public Order Act was passed the following month, but he never got the power for a blanket ban or one for the length of time he asked for. The Home Office remained cautious in order not to provoke criticism over the curtailment of traditional public rights and freedoms. In the event, he achieved a (renewable) three monthly ban on processions in specified parts of London, starting in June 1937 and continuing in the East End until the BUF was disbanded in 1940. But Game was not the only one to want action against the Fascists in order to stop the Communists. The linking of restrictions on the Fascists in order to facilitate future action against the communists remained a guiding thread of Home Office thought and policy right up to the Second World War, when the Home Secretary queried whether 'early action against the Fascists might not make it easier for the government to take action against the left wing if that developed an anti-war policy'.[78]    Cohen's view is that it was the desire of Home Office officials to be seen to be impartial which delayed the passing of the Public Order Act. This is no doubt correct. But Home Office comments also make clear that the underlying motive was for a measure that would appear absolutely impartial while retaining its effectiveness for use against the left. The price was a measure of restraint that overrode the police chiefs' pressing desire for increased powers to maintain public order in the metropolis, and probably increased the frustration of pcs on the streets when told to remain unmoved as brickbats and insults were hurled at them. Victor Meek, a copper during this period, no doubt summed up the feelings of many, when he wrote that:

> I have often read pious words of regret that have been spoken on behalf of the police when a baton charge has been ordered to prevent further breaches of the peace. My own chief recollection of the few I have taken part in is when, having been pelted with stones, milk bottles and insults for what seemed far too long, the order, 'All right. Get out your sticks and clear the ground' was given, a wicked

---

76  Moore, 'Sir Philip Game'.
77  *PRO: HO 144/20160/169.*
78  *PRO: HO 144 21429*, 28 September 1939.

feeling of joy and rage welled up in me and, judging by the 'Aaah' from my comrades near me, I was not alone in this.[79]

For the average pc, maintaining his or her control of the streets and the wish to punish the unruly remained the prime policing priority, whatever the transgressor's political motives; while the fact that so many came from the left, both before and after the war, was a feature that was simply taken for granted by the police. Certainly, the police stereotype of the anti-Fascist demonstrator is more negative than that of the Fascist. But this does not necessarily make the bobby pro-Fascist. The view from below seems to bear out those who believe that the police were not so much pro-Fascist as pro-police, with their eyes fixed firmly on their own careers. The most that can be said is that the majority were anti-left. They also tended to be conservative and authoritarian, in an ensemble of attitudes that were fostered by the job. Nevertheless, the authority they sought to maintain was their own, and not that of the Fascists. Massed police operations in the context of large-scale demonstrations was not what the police relished or saw as their primary task. Instead, it was the routine maintainance of order on the beat by individual constables that the pc valued and saw as his central role. It was here that he, personally, exercised his authority and received its tributes in the form of respect and obedience. It was here that he found his main job satisfaction.

---

79  Victor Meek (1962) *Cops and Robbers*, pp. 17–18.

# CHAPTER TEN

# Police Scandals

## From Perks to Corruption

Authority, the police's most valued attribute, is based on power, and power corrupts. The police at all levels of the hierarchy had wide power over many aspects of public life, and with this power went the propensity to corruption. Although never openly admitted, the periodic clean up campaigns carried out – above all in the larger urban forces – gives tacit acknowledgement to this fact, even if public statements rarely went beyond the 'rotten apple' thesis.[1] And although there was considerable variation between forces and specialisms, the period under consideration proved no exception, as we have seen from the many examples of illegal police behaviour described in the preceding chapters.

However, the degree to which individual policemen acknowledged or were cognisant of this fact varied greatly. Country and uniform pcs were the least likely to claim knowledge of any corruption; city, CID and plainclothes police the most – while all readily pointed the finger at the Met as a hotbed of illegality. This pattern probably matches the reality quite closely, since opportunities for crooked deals were much better in the cities and amongst plainclothes and CID. The connection is obvious: corruption could only flourish where there were trades and businesses interested buying police protection or complicity, not in areas too poor or in enterprises too lawful to need or be able to afford such services.[2] As discussed in Chapter 9, the police themselves made a distinction between degrees of corruption, and were unlikely to regard things like the publican's traditional offerings as a serious breach of the rules. They were simply established practice that newcomers had to learn about, as much as they had

---

1   See *Police Review,* 24 July 1931, for an early example of this type of comment, typical of the police reaction, after twenty-four Metropolitan policemen were suspended because of corrupt deals with bookmakers. For an account of police corruption throughout this century, see James Morton, *Bent Coppers.*

2   Jerry White connects the alienation of the police from London's working class communities to the system of property relations which gave the police the role of protecting those who had from those who had nothing. Jerry White (1983) 'Police and People in London in the 1930s', *Oral History.*

to learn the route of their beat. The experience of one recruit here must stand for many:

> My first night was with a pc called Lofty who didn't take kindly to this young pc being foisted on him, and as we were walking down Portland Street, he turned and said to me 'Do you drink, boy?'. I said I enjoyed a pint, so he said 'Fall in'. At a restaurant with a large doorman, Lofty says to him 'O.K. Charlie?' 'Yes, Lofty'. Next I knew, I was sitting in the kitchen with my helmet off, clutching a large scotch. Then disaster, I thought, struck. A sergeant entered, and I thought the whole of my fourteen day career was at an end. But the sergeant said 'Hurry up, I want mine' and went and stood at the corner until we came out.[3]

Nevertheless, even if each individual inducement remained little more than a token, taken together they could make a considerable difference to the individual pc's standard of living. Given the opportunity and the desire to capitalize on it, situations where money or favours, however small, were offered in return for a blind eye could well escalate to match the scale and profitability of the businesses run by the people the police were dealing with. It depended on how far the boundaries for 'normal' perks, whether from bookmakers or licensees or others, were maintained. In wealthy areas, where the police operated in the context of a master/servant relationship perks were offered in the form of tips: in the City of London, for instance, aldermen and stockbrokers regarded the police as their 'babies', and at Christmas every man in the force got a pipe and tobacco and presents for his children from the Rothchilds.[4] Elsewhere, in the vast majority of instances the matter no doubt remained within bounds, with a customary level and flow of such perks acknowledged in most police departments. This put strong pressure on individual policemen to conform to these norms, as Inspector Cooper recounted:

> Before I went there, there was observation kept at Lenman Street, and they sacked eleven sergeants. Almost the entire station was cleared out. Well, it was dropsy, I suppose, taking money from bookmakers. We knew a bit about it, we knew the people. It's very hard, if you're working in a little group together and you know that somebody is fiddling, it's very hard to go along and say 'so and so's at it'. You'd rather turn a blind eye.[5]

---

3   Interview with Deputy Commander Blatchley, Metropolitan police.
4   Interview with Chief Inspector Rolph, City of London police.
5   Interview with Inspector Cooper, Metropolitan police.

At constable level, the matter probably rested at a free drink or the odd half crown from the bookmaker.[6] C.H. Rolph believed that corruption was too grand a name for such transactions, since people such as market traders simply could not have functioned at all had they not been allowed, through the payment of a small sum, to park illegally for a time. Such behaviour was ubiquitous and not worth calling corrupt.[7] But as one moved up the police hierarchy, both the power and the stakes became higher, and the payoffs increased accordingly.

A distinction can perhaps be made between the misuse of police funds and manpower by senior police officers, often from county or borough forces, out of personal greed and the desire to cut a dashing figure, and the acceptance of large payoffs for favours received. The deputy chief constable of Glamorganshire was suspended for using funds from the police athletic club for a cruise to Madeira; the chief constable of Newport was forced to resign because he drove a police car on private business and used the services of a pc in duty time as his gardener; and the chief constable of Worcester was imprisoned for eighteen months because of the fraudulent conversion of the Constabulary Club funds.[8] But this sort of dishonesty by an individual who misused his office, differed from that which involved others – of which the following is an example:

> While I was in the City police, they had two tremendous shake-ups at the top level, in the form of enormous sums being paid to police officers by very rich, well known city men to get bail or some kind of preferential treatment; and in the allotment to a police officer of preferential shares that were under investigation.[9]

## Institutional Corruption

Corruption which involved a single police officer may thus be worth distinguishing from the corruption that could infect an entire station or department. It is difficult to estimate how often this was the case, but the

---

6   Harry Daley recounts collecting his half crown from the ledge where the bookmaker had placed it, and complaints from the latter if the constable posted was not 'on the take' and therefore not cooperative. But he also describes making more in tips for 'helping' motorists park at Olympia than his weekly wage. Some beats were thus more lucrative than others. Daley, *This Small Cloud*, pp. 94–5, 107–8.

7   Interview with Chief Inspector Rolph, City of London police.

8   *Police Review*, 6 October 1933; 8 February 1952; 31 October 1958.

9   Interview with Chief Inspector Rolph, City of London police.

likelihood is that once outsiders were involved, corrupt deals necessarily became an institutional rather than a private matter. One single officer – however high up – would have found it difficult to deliver without at least the passive connivance of other officers. Even so, most respondents denied the existence of corruption beyond the traditional levels already mentioned, except on the basis of hearsay. Typical here was the view of Sergeant Brent, who believed that outside the Met, corruption was confined to the small borough forces 'where everybody, councillors and police, were tied up together in a vicious circle'. One flagrant example of the spread of corruption in such a force concerned thirteen officers of the Folkstone borough force, out of a total of seventy-three, who were investigated in 1943 for cases of theft and burglary going back to 1935. After an inquiry, a sergeant and five constables were allowed to resign rather than face dismissal, as the investigators tried to make light of the affair.[10] Once corruption started in such confined circumstances, it proved difficult to eradicate. Here, county chiefs agreed that corruption was easier to deal with in their forces, since if a pc got into trouble, he could be moved to a beat thirty miles away – an option denied to small borough forces.[11] Less frequent was the more direct acknowledgement made by PC Waterford:

> *Was there corruption in your division?* Oh yes ... I can't give you facts, but when I went to Kentish Town, the superintendent of Y Division had only been there a matter of six to eight months, he was superintendent of C Division when Kate Merrick got done. And he was moved out of C Division and transferred to Y Division as part of his punishment and fined four hundred pounds for lack of supervision. And the story at Kentish Town was that he'd only been there twelve months before he'd got his £400 back. [12]

The silence over high level institutional corruption was rarely broken by outside investigators, and even more rarely by those on the inside. The setting up of internal committees of inquiry were simply a pointer to institutional misgivings. Two commissioners at the start and after the end of our period throw some light on Home Office concern at the scope and gravity of corruption within the Metropolitan CID, which these men had been brought in to try and eradicate. Lord Trenchard, who was appointed in

---

10 *Police Review,* 16 January 1943. Ingelton believes that this case encouraged the Home Office to amalgamate all the borough forces in Kent with the county the following year. Ingelton, *The Gentlemen at War,* p. 302.

11 See the investigation in *The Sunday Times* by Trevor Philpot on 'The Police and the Public: Improper Influences', 14 September 1958.

12 Interviews with Sergeant Brent, Essex County police; PC Waterford, Metropolitan police.

1931, dealt with it by trying to unite the uniform branch with CID, and by sending plain clothes officers from one division to watch over police dealings in others. This probably had little effect beyond creating immense suspicion between divisions and of anyone thought to belong to the 'rubber heel squad' – while Trenchard acknowledged that he had only had time to deal with the most flagrant cases of corruption during his tenure.[13] Four decades later, Sir Robert Mark – given a task similar to Trenchard's – stated frankly that the two classes most immune from the criminal law were lawyers and the police.[14] But neither men were able to uncover, nor did they make public, the extent of that immunity. This was left to a former detective sergeant, who waited until 1994 to reveal his own and others' wrongdoing thirty to forty years previously, in the notorious corruption case uncovered by two *Times* reporters in 1969. In order to escape from a posse of senior detectives who had threatened to kill him if he stood trial, Detective Sergeant Symonds spent eight years on the run abroad before giving himself up. His confession is included here because of what it reveals about the CID at the time. Symonds had joined the Metropolitan police in 1956 and was first sent to Bow Street station, which he described as 'an absolute den of corruption' as far as bribes from market porters, homosexuals and others were concerned. But in 1960, when he became an aid to CID

> I found a type of corruption that was entirely new to me, where, in order to become a detective, you have to prove beyond doubt that you're prepared to perjure yourself, and where there's no chance of ever being selected as a detective unless you're prepared to get together, make up evidence, go to court, and carry it off. I must say that the next few years I spent as a detective, I lied practically every day, and so did everybody else. The net result was that a lot of innocent people were sent to prison.[15]

Symond's career is instructive in underlining the extent to which the nature and degree of police corruption is situationally defined. The uniformed branch are not the ones to bring criminal cases to court, so that the degree of their power and influence over the life chances and material well being of defendants is more circumscribed than that of the CID. Hence, the smaller pickings, in what we have seen could nevertheless become an inclusive and lucrative level of small scale bribery. But given the existence of unenforceable laws, its very ubiquity and inevitability gave it a degree of

13  Boyle, *Trenchard,* p. 642.
14  Sir R. Mark (1978) *In the Office of Constable,* p. 97.
15  John Symonds (1994) 'Confessions of a Bent Copper'. Article in *The Times,* 31 March.

cy that corruption in the CID probably lacked. Here, the stakes were
, but so were the risks. Contrary to the general view, CID may
fore have been more rather than less exposed to periodic purges and
rganization than were the uniformed branches, precisely because of its
individualistic mode of operation and the suspicion in which it was held by
the rest of the service.

## Gaining Evidence

The two main ways of getting evidence illegally were violence or
fabrication. Both were routinely used, and openly admitted to by
respondents, who would have seen nothing out of the ordinary in the
behaviour of the Manchester detective who greeted his prisoners with the
enquiry 'Will you talk or be tanned?'[16] Strong arm methods were the norm,
whether for softening up the prisoner, for gaining confessions or for
exacting revenge. Even so, many cases never reached the station, let alone
the courts. For pcs new to an area or beat, it was a question of establishing
one's credentials; while for more seasoned officers the administering of
justice on the streets was simply the beginning and end of the matter. A
Colchester pc who joined in 1938 recalled his first time out on his own,
when he had a confrontation with a gang of young men:

> One of them said 'you are bloody new. I fight all the new ones'
> 'Alright' I said. He said 'I'm Spud Murphy' I let him have it and
> down he went ... 'Next time' I said, 'you'll get a *real* hammering'.

This initiation served its purpose. On a subsequent occasion Spud Murphy
turned up to help the pc:

> I was dealing with three squaddies. Suddenly Murphy was there to
> help. 'We'll share this out' he said ... They fought like men, and if
> you were good enough to beat them, they acknowledged it. But they
> wouldn't see anybody more than one hammering the police.[17]

A more established pc, on the other hand, might offer violence as a sort of
pre-emptive strike. PC Salter recalled one policeman in the 1950s who
would forstall trouble at dances by telling youths 'if you want a fight, I'll
meet you at the back of Stafford swimming baths in half an hour' – and take
his jacket off perhaps, so that he wasn't in uniform. That quietened them
down, he found.[18] Similarly, PC Haigh, when discussing the Sheffield 'rhino

16  Mark, *In the Office of Constable,* p. 52.
17  Interview with Tom Bateman, *Colchester Recalled.*
18  Interview with PC Salter, Staffordshire County police.

whip' police scandal in the early 1960s believed the whole case could have
been avoided

> if they'd hammered the Hartleys out on the street. They wouldn't
> have complained. They'd have expected it because they'd have had
> a chance to fight back ... They shouldn't have done it in the police
> station. It was against all the rules of engagement.[19]

This is a very revealing statement in showing that there were definite norms
regulating the use of violence between the police and their male civilian
counterparts on the streets, and that such norms were an essential
component of the prevailing culture of masculinity prescribing the
behaviour expected between social equals, and involving notions of fair
play acknowledged on both sides of the fence.[20]

However, some pcs were more concerned with getting results. Inspector
Bates recommended going according to the old adage 'If you speak to them,
summons them, if you hit them, lock them up'; while Sergeant Brecon
preferred when bringing in recalcitrant prisoners, to 'belt their earholes a
little bit on the way, as a little bit of chastisement' to soften them up.[21] Once
in the station, and despite the philosophy of the police service that 'if you
hit a prisoner you should do it outside the station'[22] violence could become
an integral part of the means to gain confessions. Sixty out of a hundred
prisoners would confess without a beating, PC Price reckoned, but they
would belt the others, and say that they had got their bruises trying to
escape; while PC Sherman referred to the well known saying that 'the
harder you hit them, the louder they shout guilty'[23]. Sergeant Carver
provides a clear exposé of the rationale used to justify such methods:

> I wouldn't advise anyone to join the police now, because they've no
> authority, no authority over the public. This right to silence for a
> start, it's dreadful, you arrest someone and he sits there like a
> dummy and you can't do anything ... In my day, for instance, the
> sergeant arrested a lad for burglary of £600 worth of jewellery. The
> sergeant said, 'Come on, now, tell your uncle Arthur where you've

19  Interview with PC Haigh, Sheffield City police.
20  Adherence to these rules is exemplified in a description of one pc's tremendous
    fight with a drunk, 'where neither fought dirty. No boots, no knees, no heads,
    and as far as possible, everything above the belt line'. See John Wainright
    (1987) *Wainright's Beat,* pp. 150–1.
21  Interviews with Inspector Bates, Liverpool City police; Sergeant Brecon,
    Birmingham City police.
22  Interview with Sergeant Minch, Birmingham City police.
23  Interviews with PC Price, Warwickshire County police; PC Sherman, Sheffield
    City police.

hidden this jewellery. No reply. So the sergeant hit him, he fell off the back of the chair. What's the matter, son, did the chair slip? Where have you hidden the jewellery? Bang. He told him after that. We went out and recovered £600 worth of jewellery *and* had a convicted thief. Nowadays you can't do that, and that's why criminals get off. You can't treat them like criminals, and they *are* criminals, they're scum, that's what criminals are.[24]

However, not everyone agreed that the use of force was justified, and many said they would never hit a prisoner. Some thought it was a sign of weakness, in that it simply showed the police didn't have enough evidence to bring charges.[25] 'Giving people a thumping was, to me, a weak way of completing a case. There were far better ways of doing it' was one opposing view:

> *Was there fabrication of evidence?* Yes, I would say it went on, but I would stress very strongly that it never went on with an innocent person. If there was any evidence that was stretched a bit – helping them over the fence, we used to call it – he was obviously as guilty as they come.[26]

An officer from another force agreed:

> There's no respect for the police now, and the police are being found out in various things that have discredited the police. Getting convictions regardless of the evidence has always gone on, the police have always manufactured evidence. But in those days there were no computers, in those days they sat and wrote statements, and said 'sign that', and it was a confession, and the fellow wouldn't even know what he'd said. It definitely went on all the time but now, of course, with science its become much more difficult.[27]

Violence and fabrication were the two main illegal means of collecting evidence. Of the two, I would judge violence to have been the more usual, firstly because it was such a widespread feature of the common culture as a way of settling disputes and righting wrongs, and secondly because, as Sergeant Minch put it, 'We were too naive to fabricate evidence'.[28] Many, especially uniformed police, will have fallen into this category.

This leaves a third, and final type of illegal behaviour to be mentioned, that concerns the use of force or fraud to exact revenge or punishment. A

---

24  Interview with Sergeant Carver, Durham County police

25  Interview with Detective Inspector Ellworthy, Warwickshire County police.

26  Interview with Inspector Hay, Birmingham City police.  Inspector Cooper and Sergeant Haines of the Metropolitan and Birmingham police corroborated the 'embellishing' of evidence that went on.

27  Interview with Sergeant Carver, Durham County police

28  Interview with Sergeant Minch, Birmingham City police.

very strong feature of police culture was intolerance of any denigration of police authority, and any besting of the police that could lower the esteem in which they believed they should be held. This would nearly always call forth some retaliatory action. Thus when a man resisted arrest by taking up a carving knife and threatening the police with it, he was overpowered, but on the way to the station Sergeant Gleam said 'this one is for me' and hit him where it wouldn't show. The two pcs with him then did the same, and Gleam commented that 'it was just to put him in his place, he wouldn't do that again'.[29] If a defendent won his case, but the police thought he was guilty, they would try to make sure to get him on another charge. Failing that, they might resort to childish tricks, as when Sergeant Carling and his mate let the cows out of a farmer's field because the farmer had got the better of them in a traffic case. 'Little things like that kept us going' Carling remembered.[30] And any disrespect was quickly dealt with: an inspector asked a lad brought into the station what his name was. 'Pollack' was the reply – upon which the inspector gave the lad an almighty blow and said 'That'll teach you to say bollocks to me'.[31] PC Hope and PC Waterford summed up the attitude that was expected and the means by which it was to be achieved. First of all 'the police force was a *force*, people had got to be in a certain amount of fear'; and then 'nobody created problems in those days because they weren't allowed to. You put your foot on their neck and they were made to obey the law'.[32] Violence and fabrication were all about maintaining the upper hand. This self-evident priority then overcame any doubts about the means used to achieve it.

## Courts and Magistrates

What of police relations with the courts and the magistrates? Most were described as 'good as gold'. Magistrates were perceived to be on the side of the police, they believed what the police told them, and gave no credence to allegations against them. Where some rough and ready methods were used, the magistrates and the judges were prepared to go along with it, because they agreed very much with the principle of putting a lot of criminals behind bars.[33] If a pc was assaulted, the assaulter was always sent to prison;

---

29  Interview with Sergeant Gleam, Birmingham City police.
30  Interview with Sergeant Carling, Staffordshire County police.
31  Hay, *Saga of a Practical Copper.*
32  Interviews with PC Hope, Birmingham City police; PC Waterford, Metropolitan police.
33  Interview with PC Moreton, Birmingham City police.

if the pc was the assaulter, as like as not, the magistrate would say 'you did perfectly right, officer'.[34] Indeed, Superintendent Batey made a virtue of owning up to such matters:

> I remember as a sergeant, this was one of my funny quirks, I used to say, if somebody's hit you, you are entitled to hit him back. And if you think he's going to hit you, you're entitled to hit him, to stop him hitting you. And what's more, go and tell the magistrates that. Well, this was a growing habit, and quite frankly it was a sensible thing to do, because you gained a great advantage with the magistrate.[35]

Similarly, Sergeant Gleam admitted giving a woman a black eye during a fracas with a number of drunks, and the magistrates fined the woman nevertheless. The magistrate was a good fellow, said Gleam. 'They used to look after you, they knew what was going on'.[36] But even where there was no such open admission, the magistrates still gave the police 100 per cent backing. They wouldn't believe people if they made allegations against them, they'd say 'You're telling lies now'.[37] It was chiefly the juvenile courts of which the police were critical, because of their leniency:

> West Juvenile Court, nice people, they just don't understand. They sit in there, and you go to court, and some little character says 'Good morning, Dereck, don't be afraid, we're here to help you.' He'd done fifteen houses, you know, and as soon as he came out he'd say 'silly old sod'.[38]

Juvenile courts apart, the bench of magistrates, made up of local businessmen or other people of influence and standing, had every reason to back the police in what were mostly undefended cases of petty crime, assault and misdemeanour by the poor and disreputable. The police, after all, were their first line of defence in keeping property safe and maintaining peace and quiet in the streets. Nevertheless, attitudes were beginning to change, and tension between the court personnel and the police was rising – even if largely unacknowledged by the officers in our sample.

**Towards the Royal Commission**

In tracing the history of this alteration it is difficult to be clear about who, or what, were the prime movers. Did changes originate from within the

---

34  Interview with Inspector Home, Sheffield City police.
35  Interview with Superintendent Batey, Staffordshire County police.
36  Interview with Sergeant Gleam, Birmingham City police.
37  Interview with Sergeant Carver, Durham County police.
38  Interview with Inspector Cooper, Metropolitan police.

criminal justice system or from outside, was it spearheaded by the media, or
were the media simply a mouthpiece? The history of the broader social
developments on which changing attitudes rested lie outside the scope of
this book; but the effect on the criminal justice system and on the police
was unmistakeable, as the police themselves recognized:

> In the 1950s. 1955, it started with the children at school when they
> got a bit cheeky with the teachers, and the teachers couldn't
> discipline them or slap them, and neither could the policeman, and
> that's when it all started ... This is when the do-gooders came about
> which has proved the root of all evil.[39]

PC Moreton also pinpointed the change as relating to children, and put it
down to Dr Spock:

> At the time of Dr Spock, that would be fiftyish or just afterwards,
> you suddenly found parents saying, 'Well, we ain't allowed to hit
> 'em' ... Probably the first time after the Dr Spock business, I can
> remember collaring a youngster outside a football ground, just took
> him by the scruff of his neck ... the amount of uproar I got from the
> crowd, leave the children alone, type of thing. That was something
> new, completely new, the children suddenly became sacred, they
> must not be touched in any way whatsoever.[40]

Attitudes in court began to change as well, although more slowly, as
prisoners began to stand up for their rights and brought solicitors and
barristers in to defend them – until today it would appear that 'its the police
who are on trial in court now, they're often the prisoner, I think'.[41] There
had indeed been murmurings well before the war from magistrates who
wished to distance themselves from the police and who objected to their
courts being known as 'police courts' 'because it makes people think that
the police and the magistrates are hand in glove'.[42] A decade later the point
was vociferously put in a letter to the *Justice of the Peace:*

> What is the real position of the police in a court of summary
> jurisdiction? ... In petty sessional divisions where the court sits
> perhaps once a week, the local superintendent or inspector usually
> has a seat at the clerks' table and generally appears to run the
> business of the court, even if he does not in fact. In the larger
> divisions and cities and boroughs, one finds uniformed police
> everywhere, acting as court officers, warrant officers, gaolers,

---

39  Interview with PC Foulkes, Warwickshire County police.
40  Interview with PC Moreton, Birmingham City police.
41  Interview with Sergeant Dunhill, Birmingham City police.
42  *Justice of the Peace,* 6 July 1935; 29 April, 1933.

doorkeepers, calling the cases, swearing witnesses and collecting fines.[43]

Official acknowledgement of the wrong impression given by this state of affairs, and indicative of the changing relationship, was the decision then taken, whereby police courts were henceforth to be known as 'magistrates' courts'.[44] It would be too much to say that the courts were becoming generally critical of the police, only that a certain distancing had crept in to the relationship on the part of the magistracy. Thus the pre-war comment in *Justice of the Peace* that 'we have never understood why there is a feeling in some quarters that nobody should be convicted upon the word of a single policeman'[45] would by the end of the war probably have found fewer supporters.

Before the war, it had been the behaviour of the police towards public demonstrators that aroused criticism and led to the founding of the NCCL. However, that criticism had not extended beyond committed left-wing circles, and thus had been derided and largely ignored by police authorities. It was not until the middle of the war that criticism of police behaviour towards individual suspects began to surface. At this point, the Recorder of Liverpool, E.G. Hemmerde, commented on the need to restrain the 'toughs' among the police, after he had had to deal with a number of complaints of police brutality towards prisoners. He also accused the lay magistrates who seemed to think it was their duty to support the police in whatever they said or did.[46] A case of police assault on a young lad, in which £90 was awarded in damages against the detectives, seemed to confirm Hemmerde's concern, and the publicity surrounding these cases led to questions in parliament about the police's manner of dealing with suspected persons.[47] But official criticism died down again, enabling Lord Chief Justice Goddard to dismiss an appeal at Liverpool Assizes from a man who said his confession had been acquired by force.[48] In the 1940s, an isolated voice like Hemmerde's was not sufficient to sway public and judicial opinion into a general questioning of police methods.

The 1950s, however, saw the slow trickle of accusations against the police become something of a flood, culminating at the end of 1959 in the setting

---

43  *Justice of the Peace,* 15 May 1943. A *Departmental Committee on Justices Clerks* was set up in 1938 to look, amongst other things, into this issue. It finally completed its report in 1944.

44  *Justice of the Peace,* 21 October 1944.

45  *Justice of the Peace,* 23 January 1937.

46  *Police Review,* 16 October 1942; 5 February 1943.

47  *Police Review,* 21 May 1943.

48  *Police Review,* 14 April 1950.

up of a Royal Commission. The incidents themselves were nothing untoward; it was the reaction and media publicity that was unprecedented.[49] This reaction was a sign and expression of a new public consciousness that eventually altered for good the existing relations between the police and the public. No longer were the police regarded with such reverence that 'you could walk down the street and they'd go and hide – out of respect'. Now the public were becoming aware of how limited a policeman's rights were, whereas before they used to say 'it must be right if he says so'.[50] Of course, this change did not take place overnight – but there were enough manifestations towards the end of the 1950s and the early 1960s to pinpoint those years as a turning point that have left their mark on the memories of the police of the time. To date, the police had obtained public cooperation, and enjoyed public esteem because they were enforcing standards generally acceptable to the majority.[51] But now, as so many of them commented, not only were the public becoming better educated, more aware of their rights, and losing their fear of and respect for the police. In conjunction with this, attitudes towards authority figures were changing, with a particular emphasis – as we have seen – on the altered attitudes of the young.

This left the police, as a conservative body strongly committed to the old moral order that had valued discipline and hierarchy, at something of a loss. The policeman felt it was up to him to use his discretion to determine the style of policekeeping appropriate in the circumstances; but during the 1950s the policeman's judgement came increasingly into conflict with the general public's view of the nature of acceptable sanctions from those in authority. In particular the beatman's perception that he was working with and within the moral consensus of the community, that was the basis and justification for his work and his self-image, began to falter as socio-economic, cultural and ethnic change gathered pace. Above all, the policeman's traditional easy authority over children and youths' behaviour in the streets now met with an unexpected resistance that baffled him.

> They didn't treat you with the same respect as they used to do. The younger element were being brought up that way, to have no respect for the police .... they didn't take any notice at all. We used to do

---

49 One indication of a new critical outlook were media investigations into the police: a three month investigation by *Reynolds News* at the beginning of 1955 that uncovered 'disturbing tendencies' within the police; and the series of articles in *The Sunday Times* in September 1958, initiated by 'unwelcome public doubts' about the police.

50 Interviews with Sergeant Brecon, Birmingham City police; Sergeant Martin, Metropolitan police.

51 See Banton, *The Policeman in the Community*, p. 3.

special duty at football matches. Used to sit on a canvas stool all
round the ground ... Never any trouble. And then one day, the last
time I went, darts, coins, people had been spitting all down my back
from the crowd ... Around 1960–65, something like that. And I said,
never, no more. And I didn't go anymore.[52]

It was not just the public whose attitude was changing. The courts
themselves no longer sided automatically with the police. At Wrexham
County Court, the judge awarded £25 damages against a policeman whom
he was satisfied had hit a youth, even though the latter was 'a bully and a
hooligan' – where formerly such a description would have been regarded as
sufficient justification for the policeman's behaviour.[53] The notorious
'Thurso boy' incident, which provided one of the incidents directly leading
to the setting up of the Royal Commission is another case in point.

The events were ordinary enough. Six young boys jeered at two pcs when
they entered a café, to which Constable Harper responded 'If there's any
more cheek, I'll mark you for life'. This led to more derision from one of
the lads, John Waters, who was asked to come outside, where he refused to
give his name and swore at the constables. They eventually took him into an
alleyway and Constable Gunn struck the boy a blow. The date was 17
December, 1957. As we have seen, this sort of incident was commonplace.
What made it different was that it led to a tribunal of inquiry, although not
until long after the Procurator Fiscal decided that the two police constables
should *not* be prosecuted. The MP for Caithness and Sutherland, however,
persisted in his calls for an inquiry and, fourteen months later, succeeded in
persuading the government to set one up. The Sorn Tribunal blamed both
constables for their behaviour.[54]

Police behaviour that had been routine was beginning to be challenged by
those at the receiving end, and slowly and reluctantly subjected to public
scrutiny by the authorities. In the Walters case, the Caithness Constabulary
decided to take no disciplinary action against the two police constables.
Similarly, in Birmingham, where a pc was found guilty of assaulting a
youth in the course of questioning, the magistrate imposed a fine of only £3,
complained that the case had attracted notice beyond its real value, and
hoped it would have no effect on the constable's career in the police force.[55]

---

52  Interview with PC Sherman, Sheffield City police.
53  *Police Review*, 3 April 1959.
54  Sorn Tribunal report, *Cmd.718*, 7 April 1959.
55  The comparison with the recent case in Somerset, where PC Guscott was fined
    £100 for 'cuffing' a fourteen year old is instructive. Now, it was the courts' turn
    to come under attack, while the press and the police were inundated with calls
    in support of the pc's action and concern that he was being punished for using

When two men were seriously assaulted in a London police station, the Commissioner found no grounds for disciplinary action, and the Home Secretary refused to allow an independent inquiry.[56] Similarly, the Commissioner of the City of London police denied, during a *Panorama* TV programme on the relations between the police and the public, that prisoners were being beaten up in custody.[57] But press and public concern in these and other cases (such as the Podola affair, in which an informant was questionned for eight hours over the shooting of a detective sergeant, and taken from the police station to hospital suffering from 'concussion'[58]) slowly tipped the balance in favour of a wide-ranging inquiry into the police service. Reiner's judgement that the small-scale character of the incidents leading to the Royal Commission are what make it remarkable is misplaced, in that it ignores the critical role of changing public consciousness and a common refusal to tolerate what until then had been accepted as commonplace.[59] It is also important to stress that this *and* the two previous Royal Commissions on the police had been triggered by incidents concerning complaints over wrongful arrests of members of the middle class.[60] Indeed, nothing brings out more clearly the class based nature on which policing in Britain rested than this fact, whereby what was sauce for the working-class goose was certainly not going to be accepted as sauce for the upper class gander. Even so, the government only reluctantly set up an inquiry, and took the heat out by broadening its terms of reference to include police recruitment, training, organization and discipline; relations with central and local authorities and with parliament; and police/public relations. But it was the slow emergence into public consciousness of the

---

'good, old-fashioned police methods'. This event took place on 13 June, 1994. The wheel has come full circle.

56 The Birmingham and London incidents took place in April 1959. Reported in *Labour Research* (1959) 'Assault by Police', vol. XLVIII no. 8, August.

57 *Police Review,* 18 September 1959.

58 'The Podola Affair', *Spectator*, 24 July 1959.

59 Reiner, 'Policing and Policed', *Oxford Handbook*, p. 711.

60 The first instance concerns the 1906 Royal Commission on the Metropolitan police, set up after the arrest of a respectable middle class woman on charges of soliciting. See S. Petrow (1994) *Policing Morals: the Metropolitan Police and the Home Office 1870–1914*, p. 139; the 1929 RC was set up after charges of police harrassment in the Irene Savidge case, after she and Sir Chiozza Money were arrested in Hyde Park; the 1960 RC arose directly out of the case of *Garrett* v. *Eastmond*, in which a civil servant brought a civil case against a policeman for assault and wrongful arrest in a motoring incident involving the actor, Brian Rix.

'hidden' history of police behaviour during routine inquiries, as well as the
well-publicized case of middle class outrage, that forced, or goaded, the
Home Secretary into conceding the setting up of a Royal Commission in
January 1960. *The Times* was clear that the hand of the government had
been forced over the issue. It noted that:

> Pressure from parliament and from their many critics outside has,
> for the second time in less than a year, made it impossible for
> ministers completely to withhold information. In each case, public
> demand was for knowledge. A tribunal, forced on the government
> by healthy parliamentary action, defeated unwarrantable evasion in
> the Scottish instance. The mishandling of *Garrett* v. *Eastmond* is as
> obvious as was that in the case of the Thurso boy ... What does need
> to be thoroughly gone in to is the undoubted weakening in the old
> instinctive confidence which every law-abiding citizen had in his
> local police force ...[61]

The change, I would submit, was not in the behaviour of the police so much
as in the growing demand for access to information, as *The Times* itself had
noted.

## The Police and Public Response

The police, however, chiefly saw the RC as a means to improve their pay
and conditions of service, and in this they were entirely successful. Sergeant
Martin served as Federation representative giving evidence to the
Commission. He recalled how the Federation co-opted Jim Callaghan MP as
their advisor and spokeman, and how he was able to get the Home Secretary
to agree that police pay would be dealt with first. This indeed is what
happened, and as a result of the interim report in November 1960, police
constables received a forty per cent pay rise.[62] The speed with which this
result was achieved points very strongly to Home Office concern with the
poor recruiting figures, and their wish to attract better educated and
motivated officers as the best way to improve the public image of the
police. As far as the police were concerned, this simply went to show that
the main reason for the RC had been to rectify their falling living standards
and to bring them back to a level commensurate with their social position
and responsibilities. They were able to deny the need for an RC for any
other reason, and the impact of the 'scandals' was thereby brushed aside.

61  *The Times*, 20 November 1959.
62  Interview with Sergeant Martin, Metropolitan police.

> The Royal Commission was introduced because a policeman from Scotland hit a young fellow, and it was blown up out of all proportion to what really happened. In those days, it was quite common for a policeman to slap somebody's face or, as the saying was, thump his ear, but nobody ever objected. But political moves, they blew it up and introduced the Commission to look at the police service. We jumped on it, and said the first thing the RC has got to do is look at police pay and conditions ... As far as we were concerned, that was all we wanted the RC for.[63]

Thus the pay rise is what most pcs remember about the Commission, in accordance with Callaghan's view that 'apart from police pay, I have no doubt that the rest of this Commission will finish up gathering dust on the shelves'.[64]

In this he was not far wrong. Apart from the police pay rises, the RC brought in few changes and came to few clear cut conclusions. It was never debated in parliament and received a lukewarm response in the press. The NCCL, amongst others, criticized the Commission for the inference it drew from the evidence of the existing good relations between the police and the public, while ignoring the negative views of informed experts such as the police, magistrates and lawyers' organizations and from their own social survey. The latter showed that forty-two per cent thought the police sometimes took bribes, thirty-five per cent thought the police sometimes used unfair methods to get information and thirty-two per cent thought the police might distort evidence in court. Since this survey was taken from a random sample where many will have had no direct experience of or contact with the police, the results should have been regarded as damaging rather than encouraging. The police themselves painted a far more pessimistic picture, in which sixty-nine per cent of those sampled thought the public had less respect for them than previously, while a third thought the police themselves had changed for the worse.[65] The tendency to deal in generalities was held to colour the whole approach of the Commission, with the chairman keen on the concept of 'the general public' apart from certain sections of it, so that every time a witness referred to a particular incident, the Commission shied off from hearing about it. But how else, it was asked, could a picture of what in fact happened in bad cases have been built up?[66] Instead of pursuing these cases, the Commission blandly concluded that

---

63  Interview with Sergeant Minch, Birmingham City police.
64  Interview with Sergeant Home, Sheffield City police.
65  NCCL (1962) *Civil Liberty and the Police*. The pamphlet is a commentary on the report of the Royal Commission.
66  Article 'Finest in the World? A criticism of the Royal Commission survey of public opinion', *Times Literary Supplement*, September 1962.

'relations between the police and the public are, in general very good, and there is no reason to suppose that, at all events in recent years, they have ever been otherwise'.[67] But this conclusion was severely criticized:

> the conclusions drawn from (the government social survey) were absurd. Two per cent of the public said they had personal knowledge of serious misconduct by the police within the past ten years ... The compiler of the survey does not think the alleged incidence serious; nor does the Commission see any concern in this finding. But if the figure of two per cent is correct, about 65,000 incidents of serious misconduct by the police take place every year, which is nearly one per police officer per year.[68]

The Commission, together with the government, seemed determined to deny what they were not prepared to try and remedy. The establishment view that it would be dangerous to undermine the police when 'the majority' were still happy with the situation appears to have been its guiding principle.

There was practically no alteration to the complaints procedure and no recommendation for the setting up of an independent complaints tribunal. Complaints continued to be dealt with internally, and *The Times* commented that the public would not be reassured by the minor improvements suggested, which did not meet the need to see that justice was done.[69] But without an independent tribunal, there seemed little prospect of proceeding beyond the situation described by a former Home Secretary, Chuter Ede. In a broadcast discussion between Ede and Colonel Eric St Johnstone (amongst others), the chief constable of Lancashire the difficulty for a private individual to bring a summons against the police was raised:

> *St Johnstone*: Oh, it is quite easy. All he has to do is go to the court clerk, and say, I want a summons against somebody for assault ... and they will issue the summons. Quite easy.
>
> *Chuter Ede:* But after all, you know most of the allegations are that an individual has been beaten up by two or three constables, with possibly a sergeant involved, acting together, and it is quite hopeless to think that one can – could – succeed with such a case where you only have the prisoner's word against two, three or four police officers.[70]

---

67  *Royal Commission on the Police,* Minutes of Evidence, Appendix VI, para 338.
68  *Times Literary Supplement,* 14 September 1962.
69  *The Times*, 1 June 1962.
70  Excerpt from a broadcast discussion in 1959, presented in the evidence from the NCCL to the RC. *Royal Commission on the Police, Minutes of Evidence*, 1962, pp. 735–6.

The RC did little to change this situation. Nevertheless, complaints against the police *were* rising, largely due to the greater recourse to legal representation by defendents. The police took a dim view of this development. To date, complainants 'were shown the door, some of them, pretty quick'.[71] But things changed when you got a complaints tribunal, because 'if you've got a dog, you have to make it work.'[72] Inspector Frome remembered when they brought in a complaints procedure in Sheffield, after the notorious 'rhino whip' case there in 1963:

> There were very few complaints against the police in any shape or form until after we had the rhino whip case in Sheffield, and then they brought that new complaints procedure out and they put thousands of little posters in police stations to give to anybody telling them how to complain against the police. Well, once that happened, you'd got everybody and his grandmother decending on you to complain about the police stopping you for speeding, something like that. Well, if they came to me as an Inspector, I said 'in my opinion you're just trying to get off the hook, and if you want to complain you write to the chief constable, I'm not bothering with you'.[73]

This was the start of what the police regarded as a retrogade development, which in their view was increasingly to tie their hands in their fight against crime, as well as unfairly tilting the general balance within the criminal justice system against the police. The point was made most vociferously by Superintendent Batey:

> You can't treat criminals as you'd expect to treat ordinary people and as you did treat ordinary people. You're dealing with some of the vilest people on earth. And it's no use mollycoddling the rest ... if you keep asking questions, nowadays that's wrong, that's harrassing the bloke. So what's the position? If this goes on, in another few years the majority of CID officers, when they're faced with that situation, they'll just get a pocket book out, they'll write the answer down, they'll raise their titfer and say 'Good night, Mr Jones'. Now that's all very nice, the decencies have been observed, but what have you got? We've got a bloke running away, he's done it, he's laughing at you and he's going to do it again.[74]

It was not the Royal Commission that proved the watershed, it was the period in general, in which the 1960s were perceived as the start of a new era. The police no longer commanded the respect that they saw as their due.

---

71  Interview with Inspector Cooke, Birmingham City police.
72  Interview with Inspector Cooper, Metropolitan police.
73  Interview with Inspector Frome, Sheffield City police.
74  Interview with Superintendent Batey, Staffordshire County police.

There is no sense, however, that they saw themselves to blame – beyond the excesses of some young and poorly qualified pcs – rather that the public now had altered perceptions and expectations of justice and due process. In this, the police believe the public lost more than it gained, since with the erosion of trust and respect they also lost the spirit of dedication and public service that had motivated most police officers.

# Conclusion

This study shows that policing between the 1930s and the 1960s was in no way as unproblematic as is nowadays often assumed. It was a time wracked by depression and high rates of unemployment, by the threat of Fascism and war, by the ravages of the war itself, and by the shortages and deprivations that followed as the country set about reconstruction from a much reduced base. The police were by no means immune from the negative effects of these events and conditions. But the refracted light cast over a period where society is seen and remembered as much less fraught and fragmented, as more stable and homogeneous than the present, has created a rosy glow that provides us with an image of police/public relations that were basically harmonious and acceptable to all, villains included. *Dixon of Dock Green* has become the symbol of this image. Created by Ted Willis for the television series which ran from 1955 to 1976, *Dixon* was an amalgam of Willis' childhood memories of his East End neighbourhood pc, together with his observation of the police inspector who took him, in preparation for the series, on his rounds from Paddington Green station in the 1950s.[1] He was already an anachronism, or distortion, at the time he was created – which probably contributed to his popularity.[2] This was policing as people would have liked it to be, as they liked to remember it, as they hoped it had been. Most police officers in this study felt the same. While they saw it as too cosy a portrayal it was, they felt sure, fairly true to life and – especially in rural areas – might have been an attainable ideal. For the rest, the hard facts of crime and corruption, violence and disorder intruded too sharply to allow the image to go unchallenged. Nevertheless, what is intriguing about the memories on which the oral history accounts are based is the fact that they allow the perceived veracity of the *Dixon* character to exist side by side with their own testimony on police misdeeds, on police arrogance and violence, and on the constraints and boredom, the petty rules and regulations and the struggle for promotion that made up the lives of the police. Of course, the schizoid quality of these memories is not a characteristic that is confined to the police. Memories are always called up

---

1   Interview by author with Lord Willis, November 1991.

2   *The Times* said of *Dixon's* earlier appearance in *The Blue Lamp* that 'this was not the police as they really are but as an indulgent tradition has chosen to think that they are'. *The Times*, 20 January, 1950. Quoted in Clive Emsley, 'The English Bobby: an indulgent tradition' in Roy Porter (ed. 1992) *Myths of the English*, p. 115.

within the context of the present, and it is the constant interplay of comparison between the here and now and the conditions of the past that provides the contradictions and distortions, as well as the tensions in oral testimony. Things were better in the past, often simply because that was when one was young. Even if they were not better, the problems of the past have been solved, or have receded, whereas those of the present remain there to be dealt with. But the police have an especial reason to remember the past as a better place. They grew up in a society that was radically different from the one they inhabit today – a society that was infinitely more favourable to the type of policing that they value, and one in which the attitudes on which their work culture rested played an important part.

These attitudes have much to do with prevailing concepts of masculinity and respectabilty, of the standards of acceptable and expected behaviour for members of the social class from which the police were mostly drawn, out of which the policeman's professional persona was largely constructed.

Coincidentally, there was a close and comfortable meshing of the attributes of masculinity and respectability deemed appropriate in the average pcs class of origin with the qualities considered desirable for the job. This was the single most important factor allowing for the construction of a positive self-image, and for a high valuation of the style of policing current in the period. Moreover, it is the loss of this style in the changed circumstances of the present, where it is no longer regarded as practical or, in many cases, as socially acceptable, that lies behind the regret and nostalgia so often expressed by the interviewees in this study. Their comparisons are with a world where deference and respect were theirs to command, where women, children, sexual deviants, the 'lower orders', and wrongdoers drawn from this class danced to their tune (even if they had sometimes to be helped on their way, and even if it was actually fear and avoidance, rather than respect, that underlay the token gestures offered to the police – such as that illustrated in the behaviour of groups of unemployed, and of barrow boys, described in Chapter 2). In ideal, or idealized terms, the police interpreted such behaviour as a form of respect – which was the response they sought and valued above all others. And because they were so securely embedded in and identified with the dominant, widely accepted value system, and because they believed that they retained the respect of the majority, the police were able to minimize or dismiss the threat that dissident behaviour posed, both to themselves and to the broader society. It was for this reason, too, that the police so readily accepted and indeed regarded with pride, the fact that they were 'non-political'.[3] In a situation where they formed part of the moral majority, there was no need for the intrusion of politics.

It was the task of the police to keep the disreputable moral minority of organized criminals, political and sexual dissidents, or disrespectful youths firmly in their place; and the suggestion that the police might have difficulty in retaining the upper hand in their dealings with these groups was unthinkable. Hence the down-playing of many of the incidents of confrontation described in this book, whether they concerned political demonstrators or organized crime. The police were always the winners, since 'right' was always on their side. Small wonder they deplore the situation facing the police today, while not entirely absolving the police themselves from blame. The police, in their view, need to set an example. Their concept of respectability would not have allowed them to dress and behave in as casual and informal a manner, or to allow a similar sloppiness amongst the general public, as has become customary. Discipline and its maintenance, for oneself and for others, is one attribute of respectability out of step with today's mores, just as social class boundaries have become blurred and less clearly defined. Where the pc in former times would rarely have mistaken the class from which their protagonists were drawn, today's social signals are much weaker, with ethnicity now replacing class as the chief guiding indicator on the police's social map. Similarly, the signals allowing the police to differentiate between good girls and 'slags', between cheeky children and delinquents, between the rough and the respectable, have become all but useless. The former high degree of consensus over the dominant morality and canons of propriety has evaporated.[4] Paternalism, the mainstay of the former bobby in his dealings with most women and children is no longer acceptable. Teachers do not want the police to visit schools to talk to the children, parents do not accept help from the police in the disciplining of their offspring, children are no longer in awe of the police, women have lost their trust, in cases of rape or domestic abuse, where the masculinity of the police becomes another contentious factor. What the police at the time saw as a positive attribute is nowadays rejected. As far as the negative aspects of their concept of masculinity are concerned, these too have come under attack. The police's reliance on physical force to subdue or extract confessions from wrongdoers, or to defend themselves from assault, formed an intrinsic part of this concept, bound by its own rules of what was considered just and fair in the struggles between cops and

---

3 This deeply embedded prejudice against things 'political' recurs again in a later period, in Reiner's survey of chief constables. See R. Reiner (1991) *Chief Constables: Bobbies, Bosses or Bureaucrats?* p. 210.

4 See T. Morris (1989) *Crime and Criminal Justice since 1945,* p. 27.

robbers. And while such 'macho' tactics undoubtedly continue, they are not given the open or tacit official approval they used to receive. All in all, the police of the period have good reason to feel nostalgic today. The values of the class and gender from which they were mostly drawn tied in effortlessly with the manner of policing required by and acceptable to the authorities and general (middle and upper working class) public, in what was a much more stable and clearly defined social order. The only intrusion – a thin end of the wedge that disrupted established relations between the police and the middle class – lay in the policing of motorists. Beyond this, as the social order slowly began to crumble after the war, so did the appropriateness of the style of policing described in this book. The behaviour and expectations of the young, of women, of gays and blacks moved away from the mould and the model into which they had been cast by the police, and to which they had hitherto largely conformed. The police, in the time considered here, may not have been 'the best in the world' but they were certainly exceedingly well adapted, for much of the period and within its own terms, to the policing demands made of them. In addition, at a time when specialist social services were far less developed than they are today, police work intruded into a much wider range of situations, from the bureaucratic to the pastoral, which the police felt duty-bound to take on. However, along with this extension came an extension of the scope of police authority; and it was the sense of authority, and the respect it elicited, that above all gave value and meaning to the self-image and role of the police officer. The period probably brought to a peak the broad coverage and reach of police authority in this country – an authority that is increasingly coming under challenge today. In this respect, the regret of former police officers for the passing of the style of policing current in their time is fully justified.

# Comparative Data From Three Policing Studies

The present police sample is compared in the following tables with data from Maureen Cain's and Robert Reiner's sociological studies on the post-war police. Cain's fieldwork was carried out in 1963, and Reiner's in 1973. Together, the three stuudies allow one to offer comparative data over three to four generations of police. Combining data from several studies presents inevitable problems. In this instance, Cain has separated out those whose fathers were policemen, but has not divided Social Class III into manual/nonmanual categories. The present study has followed suit here. Reiner, on the other hand, assigned fathers' military and agricultural occupations into a 'not applicable' category, for reasons that are not made clear. The present study categorizes armed servicemen as Social Class III (as are policemen), farm workers as Social Class IV and farm labourers, where so described, as Social Class V. Although there is not much statistical sense in comparing these small samples with census figures, the 1971 census data on social class has been included since Reiner uses it to comment on the correspondence of policemen's social class backgrounds with that of the general population.

Table A1: *Social Class Origins: Study sample; Cain (1973); Reiner (1978); and the 1971 census* [1]

| Social Class | I | II | III | PC | IV | V | N.A. | Total |
|---|---|---|---|---|---|---|---|---|
| | % | % | % | % | % | % | % | |
| Study sample (n=77) | 1.2 | 15.5 | 37.6 | 16.8 | 19.4 | 9.0 | - | 99.5 |
| Cain sample (n=119) | - | 22.6 | 58.8 | 8.4 | 8.4 | 1.6 | - | 99.8 |
| Reiner sample (n=168) | 2.4 | 14.9 | 46.1 | 14.0 | 19.1 | 3.6 | 6.5 | 100 |
| 1971 census | 4.91 | 19.8 | 49.0 | 0.6 | 18.6 | 7.7 | - | 100 |

---

1   Cain, *Society and the policeman's role,* Table 35, p. 101; Reiner, *Blue-Coated Worker*, Table 9.1, p. 150.

Comment on the figures in the Table A1 must be tentative, given the variability of the occupational classifications between the studies. In addition, Reiner's sample was drawn from a city force, whereas the others covered both urban and rural forces.[2] Perhaps little more can be added beyond noting that in general the police come from backgrounds that cluster around the centre of the social scale, and are under-represented at the extremes. Nevertheless, a distinguishing feature of the present study is the extent to which recruits were the sons of policemen – a figure that had declined considerably by the time of Cain's survey and only recovered to some extent by the time of Reiner's[3]. It seems that the police were not able to build on an hereditary attraction of the service for succeeding generations unless there were other attracting features such as better wages. Fewer pc's sons in the early post-war period said 'I always wanted to be a policeman' than did so in the pre-war sample. The quite constant percentage of recruits from professional or managerial homes over the three samples is also of interest; but the statistical evidence from three small scale studies does not allow one to do more than suggest that attempts to upgrade the class of recruits over the period was not improved on during the later period of higher educational standards. Since the school-leaving age of recruits in Reiner's study was higher than for the previous generation, this may be a sign that joining the police simply offered an opening for the less academically minded from grammar schools rather than expanding as a preferred job for a wider group from professional/managerial backgrounds. There are few signs that the police service was a direct avenue for upward social mobility, except for the handful who reached the highest supervisory ranks. Indeed, there are signs of downward mobility in the quite large percentage from professional/managerial backgrounds in Cain's sample. Nor does the previous job of recruits indicate much social upgrading. Forty-seven per cent of those in the present study had had white collar jobs prior to joining the police, seventeen per cent had been in skilled manual work and five per cent were police cadets. Joining the police was not generally a way of improving their status, so much as a sideways move indicating a preference for job security, and for an outdoor life away from office or factory work.[4]

---

2   This has some influence on the outcome since, in Cain's study, the social class of the city men was higher than in the county, while twice the percentage in the county than the city were the sons of policemen. Cain, *Society and the policeman's role,* p. 100.

3   Reiner, *Blue-Coated Worker,* p. 150.

4   Reiner notes that while the majority of policemen experienced upward social mobility, in that police work is classified as a non-manual job, most did not use

Table A2[5] shows age of leaving school, taken as a proxy for educational standards in the three studies:

Table A2: *Age of leaving School*

| Age | 14 | 15 | 16 | 17 | 18+ |
|---|---|---|---|---|---|
| Police sample (n=77) | 59.7 | 11.6 | 19.4 | 6.4 | 3.8 |
| Cain sample (n=119) | 39.4 | 37.8 | 15.9 | 4.2 | 2.5 |
| Reiner sample (n= 168) | 19.6 | 14.9 | 45.8 | 11.9 | 7.7 |

The strongest feature of Table A2 is the drop in the percentage of respondents remaining in school from sixteen years onwards in the early post-war cohort. Thus thirty per cent in the present study compared with under a quarter in Cain's study had stayed on at school from age sixteen – a percentage that rose to sixty-five per cent in Reiner's study.

While conclusions based on the previous tables must remain highly tentative, the trends charted in them do tend to suggest that many of the pre-war cohort were better educated than their early post-war counterparts, and that standards did not begin to rise again until after the Royal Commission recommended and achieved a forty per cent pay rise for constables in the early 1960s. Comparison between the three studies is thus primarily of value in pointing to the overall consistency of the data, where variations provide clues to the impact of historically changing circumstances. Over nearly half a century, these surveys confirm that the police continued to be

---

the force as their channel of mobility, since over half had held non-manual jobs before joining the police. Similarly, Cain found that less than two per cent of her city force had a lower occupational status before joining the police. Reiner, *Blue-Coated worker*, p. 150; Cain, *Society and the policeman's role*, p. 102.

5  Interpretation of the figures is difficult because it is not possible to relate school-leaving age to date of entry into the police service in Cain's study. Thus some of Cain's respondents may well have joined the police just before or immediately after the war. Indeed, since fifty per cent had had experience in the armed services apart from national service, this is more than likely. Similarly, Reiner's survey included fourteen men who joined just after the war (although the majority of his sample joined after 1960). The rise in the school-leaving age from fourteen to fifteen in 1947 also weakens comparability between the studies.

drawn from a similar segment of the upper working class, whose educational level showed small signs of improvement.

# Bibliography

**Official Papers**

Hansard, Parliamentary Debates, 5th series.
Annual Reports of HM Inspectors of Constabulary, 1930–1960.
Annual Reports of the Commissioner of the Metropolitan Police, 1930–1960.
Report of the Street Offences Committee, Cmd. 3231, 1928.
Select Committee on Police Force (Amalgamation) PP V 1931–32.
Report of the Departmental Committee on Detective Work and Procedure (Home Office) 1938.
Report of the Committee on Police Conditions of Service, Cmd. 7831, PP 1948–9.
Report of the Committee on Homosexual Offences and Prostitution, Cmd. 247, 1957.
Report of the Sorn Tribunal, Cmd. 718, 1959.
Interim Report of the Royal Commission on the Police, Cmd. 1222, 1960.
Final Report of the Royal Commission on the Police, Cmd. 1728, 1962.
Report of the Committee on Children and Young Persons, Cmd. 1191, 1960.

**Newspapers and Periodicals**

*Evening Standard*
*Justice of the Peace*
*Labour Research*
*New Statesman*
*Police Review*
*Reynolds News*
*Spectator*
*Sunday Times*
*The Times*
*Times Literary Supplement*

**Books And Articles**

Addison, Paul (1975) *The Road to 1945,* Quartet Books, London.

Allen, Mary S. (1925) *The Pioneer Policewoman,* Chatto and Windus, London.

Anderson, Gerald D. (1983) *Fascists, Communists and the National Government: civil liberties in Great Britain 1931–1937,* Columbia University Press, New York.

Bagot, J.H. (1941) *Juvenile Delinquency: a comparative study of the position in Liverpool and England and Wales,* Jonathan Cape, London.

Bailey, Victor (1987) *Delinquency and Citizenship,* Oxford University Press, Oxford.

Banton, Michael (1964) *The Policeman in the Community,* Tavistock, London.

Barnett, Corelli (1986) *The Audit of War,* Macmillan, London.

Benney, Mark (1948) *Gaol Delivery,* Longmans Green, London.

Boyle, Andrew (1962) *Trenchard,* Collins, London.

Brogden, Mike (1991) *On the Mersey Beat: Policing Liverpool between the Wars,* Oxford University Press, Oxford.

Burt, Cyril (1925) *The Young Delinquent,* University of London Press, London.

Cain, Maureen (1968) 'Role Conflict among Juvenile Liaison Officers', *British Journal of Criminology,* vol. 8.

———— (1973) *Society and the Policeman's Role,* Routledge, London.

Cain, Maureen and Dearden, M. (1966) 'Initial Reactions to a new Juvenile Liaison Scheme', *British Journal of Criminology,* vol. 6.

Calder, Angus (1991) *The Myth of the Blitz,* Pimlico, London.

Carrier, John (1988) *The Campaign for the Employment of Women Police Officers,* Avebury/Gower, Aldershot.

Carr-Saunders, A.M., Mannheim, H. and Rhodes, E.C. (1943) *Young Offenders: an Enquiry into Juvenile Delinquency,* Cambridge University Press, Cambridge.

Catterall, Peter (ed.) (1994) 'The Battle of Cable Street', *Contemporary Record,* vol. 8, no. 1.

Clapson, Mark (1992) *A Bit of a Flutter: Popular Gambling and English Society,* Manchester University Press, Manchester.

Cohen, Paul (1986) 'The Police, the Home Office and Surveillance of the British Union of Fascists', *Intelligence and National Security,* vol. 1, no. 3.

Critchley, T.A. (1967) *A History of Police in England and Wales* Constable, London.

Cross, Colin (1961) *The Fascists in Britain*, Barrie and Rockcliff, London.

Daley, Harry (1987) *This Small Cloud*, Weidenfeld and Nicolson, London.

Dixon, David (1991) *From Prohibition to Regulation: Bookmaking, Anti-Gambling and the Law*, Oxford University Press, Oxford.

Emsley, Clive, (1985) '"Thump of Wood on a Swede Turnip": Police Violence in Nineteenth-Century England', *Criminal Justice History*, vol. 4.

————— (1991) *The English Police: a Political and Social History*, Harvester Wheatsheaf, Hemel Hempstead.

————— (1992) 'The English Bobby: an Indulgent Tradition', in Roy Porter (ed.) *Myths of the English*, Polity Press, Cambridge.

————— (1993) '"Mother, what *did* policemen do when there weren't any motors?" The Law, the Police and the regulation of motor traffic in England 1900–1939' *Historical Journal*, vol. 36, no. 2 .

Emsley, Clive and Clapson, Mark (1994) 'Recruiting the English Policeman *c.*1840–1940', *Policing and Society*, vol. 4. no. 3.

Foucault, Michel (1977) *Discipline and Punish*, Penguin Books, Harmondsworth.

Godwin, G. (1941) 'War and Juvenile Delinquency' *Contemporary Review*, vol. 160.

Gorer, Geoffrey (1955) *Exploring English Character*, Cresset Press, London.

Harris, José (1992) 'War and Social History: Britain and the Home Front during the Second World War', *Contemporary European History*, vol. 1, no. 1.

Hayburn, R. (1972) 'The Police and the Hunger Marchers', *International Review of Social History*, vol. 17.

Hearnshaw, L.S. (1979) *Cyril Burt, Psychologist*, Hodder and Stoughton, London.

Heidensohn, Frances (1992) *Women in Control? The Role of Women in Law Enforcement*, Clarendon Press, Oxford.

Hill, Billy (1955) *Boss of Britain's Underworld*, Naldrett Press, London.

Hinsley, F.H. and Simkins, C.A.G. (1990) *British Intelligence in the Second World War: Security and Counter-Intelligence*, vol. 4, HMSO, London.

Hobbs, Dick (1988) *Doing the Business: Entrepreneurship, the Working Class and Detectives in East London*, Oxford University Press, Oxford.

Howgrave-Graham, H.M. (1947) *The Metropolitan Police at War*, HMSO, London.

Ingleton, Roy (1994) *The Gentlemen at War: policing Britain 1939–45*, Cranbourne Publications, Maidstone.

Jenkins, Philip and Potter, Gary (1988) 'Before the Krays: Organized Crime in London 1920–1960', *Criminal Justice History*, vol. 9.

Johnstone, Colonel Eric St (1966) 'Mobility the Answer to Police Shortage', *The Times*, 26 January.

——— (1978) *One Policeman's Story*, Barry Rose, Chichester.

Jones, Sandra (1986) *Policewomen and Equality*, Macmillan, Basingstoke.

Kidd, Ronald (1940) *British Liberty in Danger*, Lawrence and Wishart, London.

Kingsford, Peter (1982) *The Hunger Marchers in Britain 1920–1940*, Lawrence and Wishart, London.

Lerman, Paul (1984) 'Policing Juveniles in London: Shifts in Guiding Discretion 1893–1968', *British Journal of Criminology*, vol. 24.

Levine, Philippa (1994) '"Walking the Streets in a Way No Decent Woman Should": Women Police in World War I, *Journal of Modern History*, vol. 66, no. 1.

Lewis, D.S. (1987) *Illusions of Grandeur: Mosley, Fascism and British Society*, Manchester University Press, Manchester.

Light, Alison (1991) *Forever England: Femininity, Literature and Conservatism between the Wars*, Routledge, London.

Liverpool City Police (1958) *The Police and the Children*, Liverpool Police (pamphlet), Liverpool.

Lock, Joan (1968) *Lady Policeman*, Robert Hale, London.

——— (1979) *The British Policewoman: Her Story*, Robert Hale, London.

Mark, Sir Robert (1978) *In the Office of Constable*, Collins, London.

Mannheim, Hermann (1941) *War and Crime*, Watts, London.

Martin, S.E. (1992) 'POLICEwomen and WOMENpolice: Occupational Role Dilemmas and Choices of Female Offenders', *Journal of Police Science and Administration*, vol. 2, no. 3.

Martin J.P. and Wilson G. (1969) *The Police: a Study in Manpower*, Heineman Educational, London.

Marwick, Arthur (1974) *War and Social Change in the Twentieth Century*, Macmillan, London.

Mass Observation (1942) *People in Production: an Enquiry into British War Production*, Penguin, Harmondsworth.

Mays, John Barron (1964) *Growing Up in the City: a Study of Juvenile Delinquency in an Urban Neighbourhood*, Liverpool University Press, Liverpool.

McClintock, F.H. and Avison, N.H. (1968) *Crime in England and Wales*, Heinemann, London.

McClure, James (1980) *Spike Island: Portrait of a Police Division*, Macmillan, London.

Meek, Victor (1962) *Cops and Robbers,* Gerald Duckworth and Co., London.

Moore, Andrew (1990) 'Sir Philip Game's "Other Life": the Making of the 1936 Public Order Act in Britain', *Australian Journal of Politics and History,* vol. 36, no. 1.

Morgan, Jane (1987) *Conflict and Order: the Police and Labour Disputes in England and Wales 1900–1939,* Clarendon Press, Oxford.

Morris, T. (1989) *Crime and Criminal Justice since 1945,* Blackwell, Oxford.

Morton, James (1993) *Bent Coppers,* Little, Brown and Company, London.

Murphy, Robert (1993) *Smash and Grab: Gangsters in the London Underworld,* Faber and Faber, London.

NCCL (1962) *Civil Liberty and the Police,* London.

O'Brien, T.H. (1955) *Civil Defence,* HMSO, London.

Petrow, Stefan (1994) *Policing Morals: the Metropolitan Police and the Home Office 1870–1914,* Clarendon Press, Oxford.

Philpot, Trevor (1958) 'The Police and the Public: Improper Influences', *The Sunday Times,* 14 September.

Plowden, W. (1971) *The Motor Car and Politics, 1896–1970,* Bodley Head, London.

Radzinowicz, Leon and Hood, Roger (1986) *The Emergence of Penal Policy in Victorian and Edwardian England,* Clarendon Press, Oxford.

Reiner, Robert (1978a) *The Blue-Coated Worker: a Sociological Study of Police Unionism,* Cambridge University Press, Cambridge.

——— (1978b) 'The Police in the Class Structure' *British Journal of Law and Society,* vol. 5, no. 2.

——— (1985) *The Politics of the Police,* Harvester Press, Brighton.

——— (1991) *Chief Constables: Bobbies, Bosses, or Bureaucrats?,* Oxford University Press, Oxford.

——— (1994) 'Policing and the Police', in Maguire, R., Morgan, R., and Reiner, R. (eds) *The Oxford Handbook of Criminology,* Oxford University Press, Oxford.

Radford, Jill (1989) 'Women and Policing: Contradictions Old and New', in Hanmer, J., Radford, J., and Stanko, E.A. (eds) *Women, Policing and Male Violence,* Routledge, London.

Rhodes, E.C. (1939) 'Juvenile Delinquency', *Journal of the Royal Statistical Society,* vol. 102.

Rolph, C.H. (1987) *Further Particulars,* Oxford University Press, Oxford.

Rowntree, B. Seebohm and Lavers, G.R. (1951) *English Life and Leisure,* Longmans Green, London.

Russell C.E.B and Campagnac E.T., (1900) 'The Organisation of Costermongers and Street Vendors in Manchester', *Economic Review*, vol. 10.

Scaffardi, Sylvia (1986) *Fire Under the Carpet*, Lawrence and Wishart, London.

Scott, Sir Harold (1959) *Your Obedient Servant*, André Deutsch, London.

Smith, Harold. L. (ed.) (1986) *War and Social Change*, Manchester University Press, Manchester.

Sharpe, F.D. (Nutty) (1938) *Sharpe of the Flying Squad*, John Long, London.

Sheridan, Dorothy (ed.) (1991) *Wartime Women: a Mass Observation Anthology*, Mandarin Paperbacks edn, London.

Shpayer-Makov, Haia (1991) 'Career Prospects in the London Metropolitan Police in the Early Twentieth Century', *Journal of Historical Sociology*, vol. 4, no. 4.

Silcock, H. (1949) *The Increase in Crimes of Theft 1938–1947*, Liverpool *University Press*, Liverpool..

Simpson, A.W. Brian (1992) *In the Highest Degree Odious: Detention without Trial in Wartime Britain*, Oxford University Press, Oxford.

Skidelsky, Robert (1975) *Oswald Mosley*, Holt, Rinehart and Winston, New York.

Skolnick, J. (1966) *Justice Without Trial: Law Enforcement in Democratic Society*, Wiley, New York.

Smithies, Edward (1982) *Crime in Wartime: a Social History of Crime in World War II*, Allen and Unwin, London.

Stammers, Neil (1983) *Civil Liberties in Britain during the Second World War*, Croom Helm, London.

Steedman, Carolyn (1984) *Policing the Victorian Community: the Formation of English Provincial Police Forces 1856–80*, Routledge, London.

Stevenson, John (1980) 'The BUF, the Metropolitan Police and Public Order' in Lunn, K. and Thurlow, R.C. (eds) *British Fascism: Essays on the Radical Right in Inter-war Britain*, Croom Helm, London.

Stevenson, John and Cook, Chris (1979) *The Slump: Society and Politics during the Depression*, Quartet Books, London.

Stevenson, Simon (1989) 'Some Social and Political Tides affecting the Development of Juvenile Justice 1938–64', in Gorst, T., Johnman, L., and Lucas W.S. (eds) *Post-War Britain 1945–64: Themes and Perspectives*, Pinter, London.

Summerfield, Penny (1984) *Women Workers in the Second World War*, Routledge, London.

Symonds, John (1994) 'Confessions of a Bent Copper', *The Times*, 31 March.

Tancred, Edith (n.d.) *Women Police 1914–1950*, National Council of Women of Great Britain, London.

Temple, Richard (1995) 'The Metropolitan Police and the British Union of Fascists 1934–1940', *Journal of the Police History Society,* no. 10.

Thompson, Paul (1975) *The Edwardians: the Remaking of British Society*, Weidenfeld and Nicolson, London.

Thurlow, Richard (1993) 'Blaming the Blackshirts: Anti-Jewish Disturbances in the 1930s', in Panayi, Panikos (ed.) *Racial Violence in Britain 1840–1950*, Leicester University Press, Leicester.

Titmuss, R.M. (1950) *Problems of Social Policy*, HMSO, London.

Wainright, John (1987) *Wainright's Beat*, Macmillan, London.

Walker, Robert (1990) *A History of the Norwich Lads' Club,* Norwich Lads' Club, Norwich.

Watson, J.A. (1942) 'The War and the Young Offender' *Fortnightly Review*, vol. 151.

Weinberger, Barbara (1987) 'Police Perceptions of Labour in the Inter-war Period: the Case of the Unemployed and of Miners on Strike' in Snyder, F. and Hay, D. (eds) *Labour, Law and Crime: an Historical Perspective*, Tavistock, London.

———— (1991) *Keeping the Peace? Policing Strikes in Britain 1906–26*, Berg, Oxford.

White, Jerry (1983) 'Police and People in London in the 1930s', *Oral History*, vol. 11, no. 2.

Willcock, H.D. (1949) *Report on Juvenile Delinquency*, Falcon Press, London.

Williamson, Philip (1992) *National Crisis and National Government: British Politics, the Economy and Empire, 1926–1932,* Cambridge University Press, Cambridge.

Wilson, James Q. and Kelling, G.L. (1982) 'Broken Windows: the Police and Neighbourhood Safety', *Atlantic Monthly*, March.

Woodeson, Alison (1993) 'The First Women Police: a Force for Equality or Infringement?', *Women's History Review*, vol. 2, no. 2.

Wyles, Lilian (1952) *A Woman at Scotland Yard*, Faber and Faber, London.

Young, Malcolm (1984) 'Police Wives: a Reflection of Police Concepts of Order and Control', in Callan, H., and Ardener, S. (eds) *The Incorporated Wife*, Croom Helm, London.

———— (1991) *An Inside Job: Policing and Police Culture in Britain*, Clarendon Press, Oxford.

## Theses and Unpublished Manuscripts

Amidon, Lynne (1986) 'Ladies in Blue: Feminism and Policing in the late 19th and early 20th centuries', PhD thesis, State University of New York, Binghampton.

Anon (1940) 'Day Diary of a Wartime Policeman', Mass Observation Archive, University of Sussex.

Dixon, Sir A.L. (1963) 'The Emergency Work of the Police Forces in the Second World War', unpublished M/S, Bramshill Police College Library, Bramshill.

———— (1966) 'The Home Office and the Police between the Two World Wars, Unpublished M/S, Bramshill Police College Library, Bramshill.

Haines, Sergeant (n.d.) 'Anecdotes; Memories of C.J. Haines', MS autobiography.

Hay, Inspector F. (n.d.) 'The Saga of a Practical Copper' MS autobiography.

Klein, JoanneMarie (1991) 'A Hot Meal at any Hour: Police Marriage in Manchester, Birmingham and Liverpool 1900–1939', unpublished paper, March 1991, delivered to the Southwestern Historical Association Conference, San Antonio, Texas.

———— (1992) 'Invisible Working-Class Men: Police Constables in Manchester, Birmingham and Liverpool 1900–1939', PhD thesis, Rice University, Houston.

Peto, Dorothy (1970) 'The Memoirs of Miss Dorothy Olivia Georgiana Peto', M/S , Birmingham Police Museum.

# Index

Game, Sir Philip, 143, 178, 180–81
Geddes Axe, 16, 91
Goddard, Lord Chief Justice, 17, 167,
    196

Heidensohn, Frances, 89
Hemmerde, E.G., 196
Hendon Police College, 18
Henriques, Sir Basil, 153
Hill, Billy, 137–8
Hobbs, Dick, 81–2, 137
Home Office
    amalgamation, support for, 38
    cadet schemes, 25
    Committee on Detective Work,
        75–6
    encouragement wpcs, 98
    experimental motor patrols, 69
    links with chief constables, 11
    mechanization, 45
    Metropolitan CID inquiry, 75–6
    Metropolitan police corruption, 186
    police college, 18
    Police War Instructions, 115
    policy juveniles, 148, 152
    pre-war demonstrations, 173, 182
    recognition sex equality, 93
    recommendation economies, 19
    reconstruction committee, 41
    review of beat system, 35
    wartime regulations, 127

Jarrow, 31–2, 176–7
juvenile delinquency
    juvenile liaison schemes, 151, 153
    Lads Clubs, 150–51
    police procedures, 148–9
    police response, 153–6
    use of term, 147

Kemble, Commander, 52, 56
Kidd, Ronald, 173, 176
Klein, JoanneMarie, 12, 108

Light, Alison, 101
Liverpool, 1, 4, 8–9, 12, 37, 44, 51,

56, 68, 78, 85, 105, 136, 139,
    141–2, 148–9, 151–5, 162, 191,
    196
Lock, Joan, 90–91, 94, 165, 168

MacDonald, Ramsey, 7
Mark, Sir Robert, 25, 101, 189
Martin, Charles C., 56
May Committee, 7
Metropolitan
    promotion rates, 48
    recruits, supply of, 14
Metropolitan police
    and the unemployed, 173
    cadet scheme, 24
    corruption, 185, 188–9
    ex-servicemen, 20
    motorization, 40
    new beat system, 35
    officer class, 17–18, 55
    pleas for greater powers, 181–2
    policy juveniles, 148
    promotion rates, 48
    recruits, supply of, 15, 19–20, 23
    reform proposals, 17
    response to wpcs, 91–2
    short service scheme, 18–19
Morgan, Jane, 174–5
Moriarty, C.C.H., 28, 57
Morrison, Herbert, 64, 125, 151
Mosley, Oswald, 175
Murphy, Robert, 137–8

NCCL, 172–3, 176, 180, 196,
    201–2
NCW, 92
NUWM, 172–3

Oaksey Committee, 23, 41–2, 93
oral history
    nature of memory, 179, 205–6
    testimony, 9, 17, 141, 176
    use of, 2–4

Piratin, Phil, 179
Podola affair, 199